HANNAH MARTIN: ICONOCLAST

HANNAH MARTIN: ICONOCLAST
A JEWELLERY REBELLION

TINA ISAAC-GOIZÉ

FOREWORD
VIVIENNE BECKER

DESIGN
LOUISE BRODY

PROJECT CONCEPTION
HÉLÈNE LE BLANC

ACC ART BOOKS

❝ For me, true creativity is about

changing the way people look at things. ❞

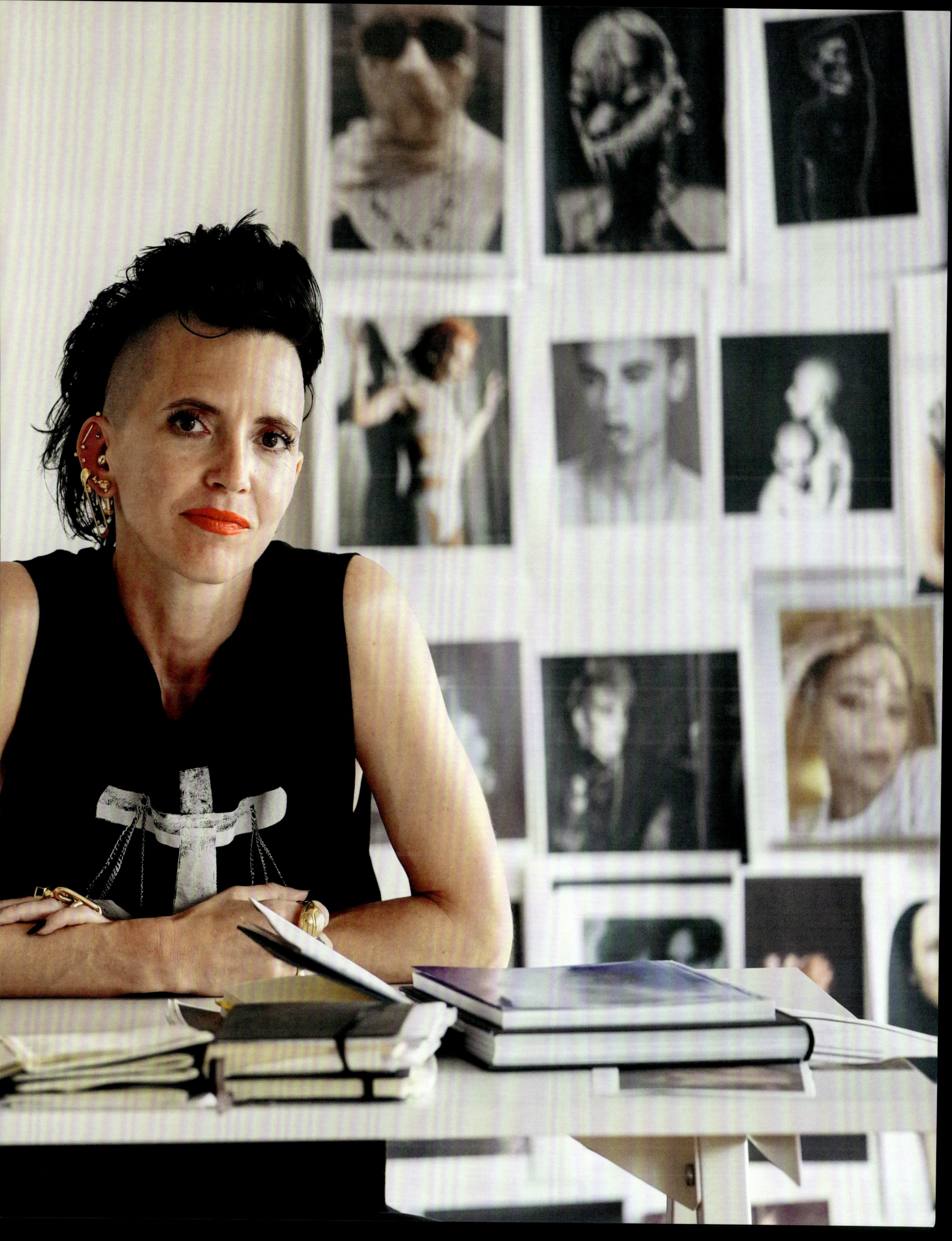

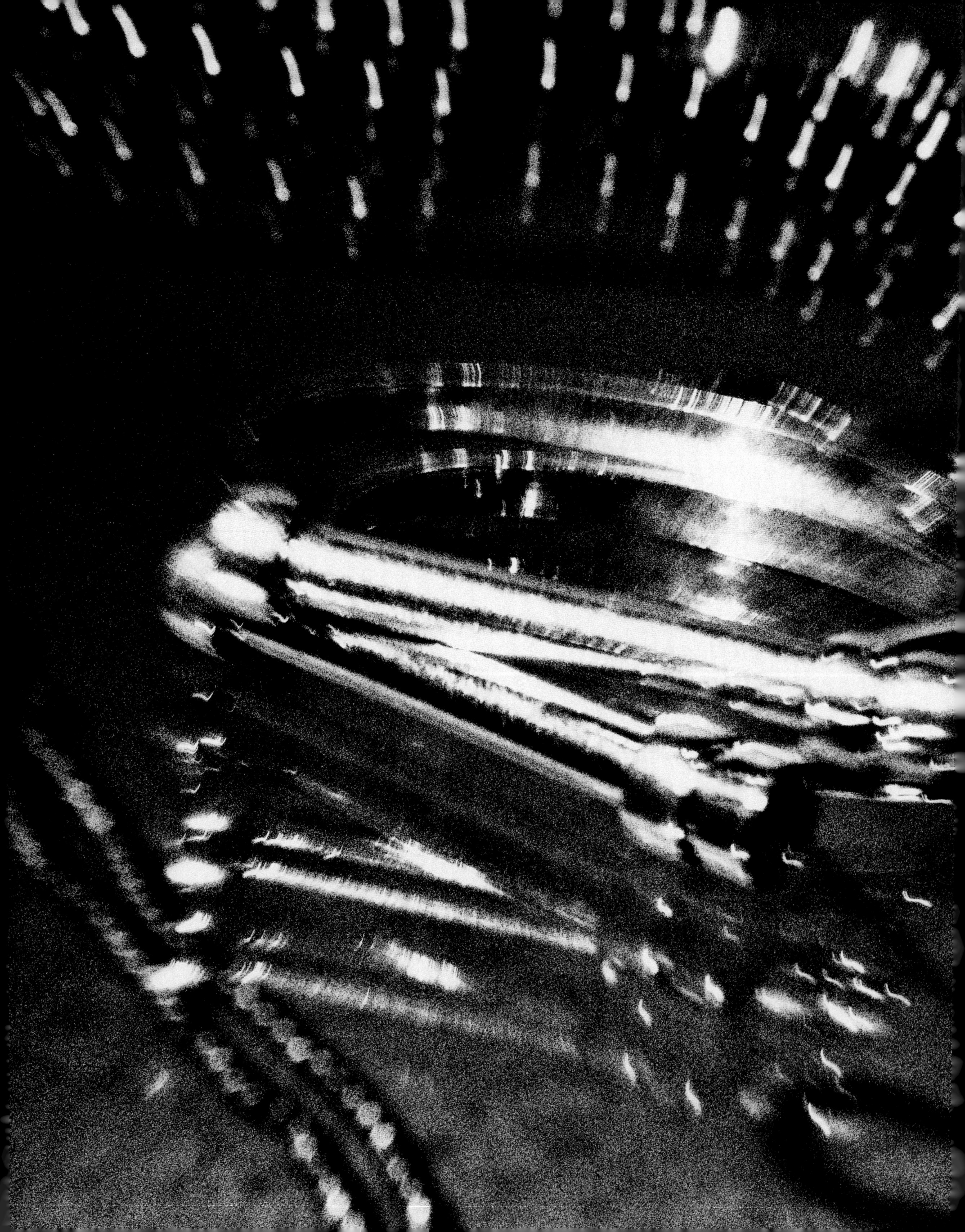

CONTENTS

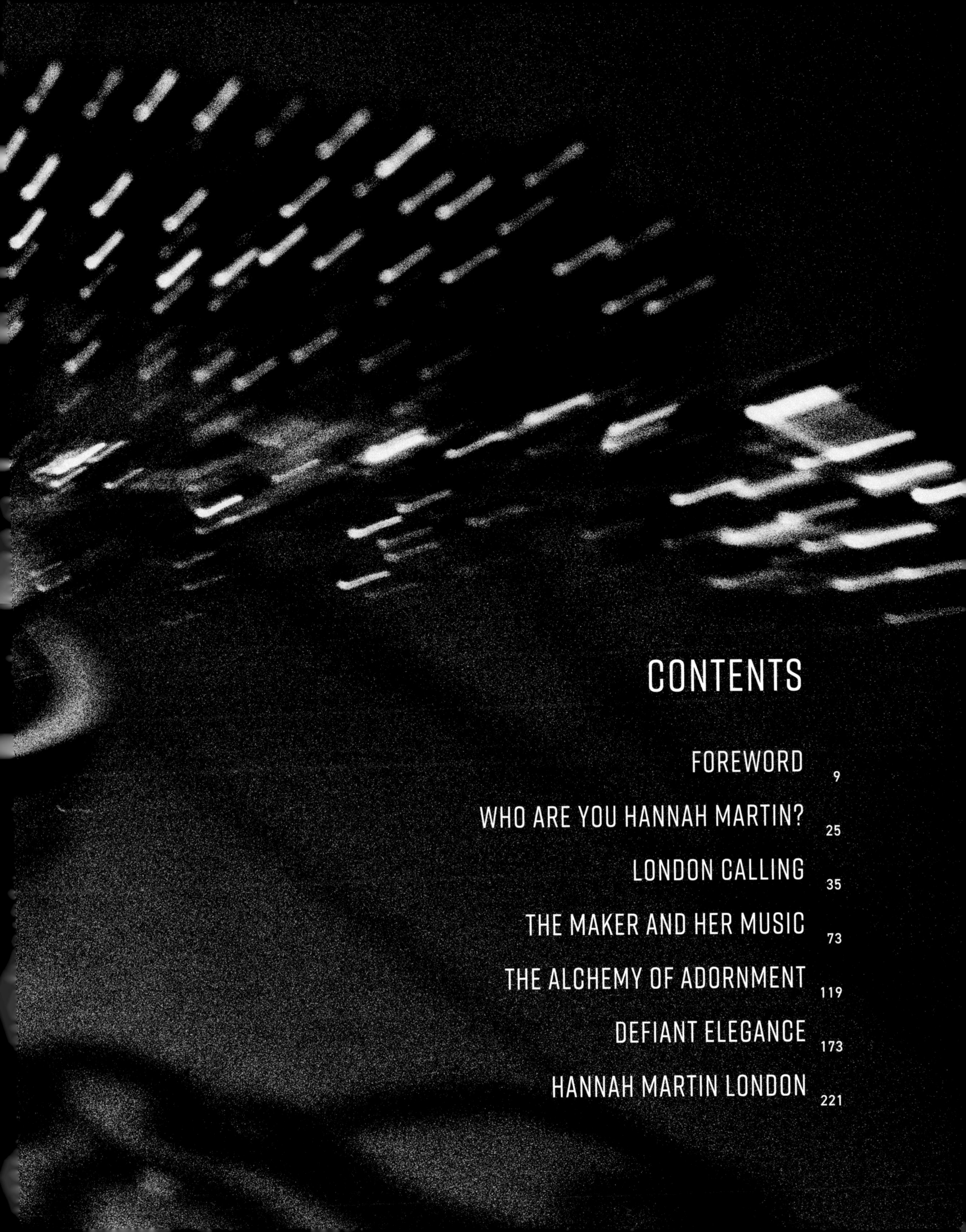

FOREWORD 9

WHO ARE YOU HANNAH MARTIN? 25

LONDON CALLING 35

THE MAKER AND HER MUSIC 73

THE ALCHEMY OF ADORNMENT 119

DEFIANT ELEGANCE 173

HANNAH MARTIN LONDON 221

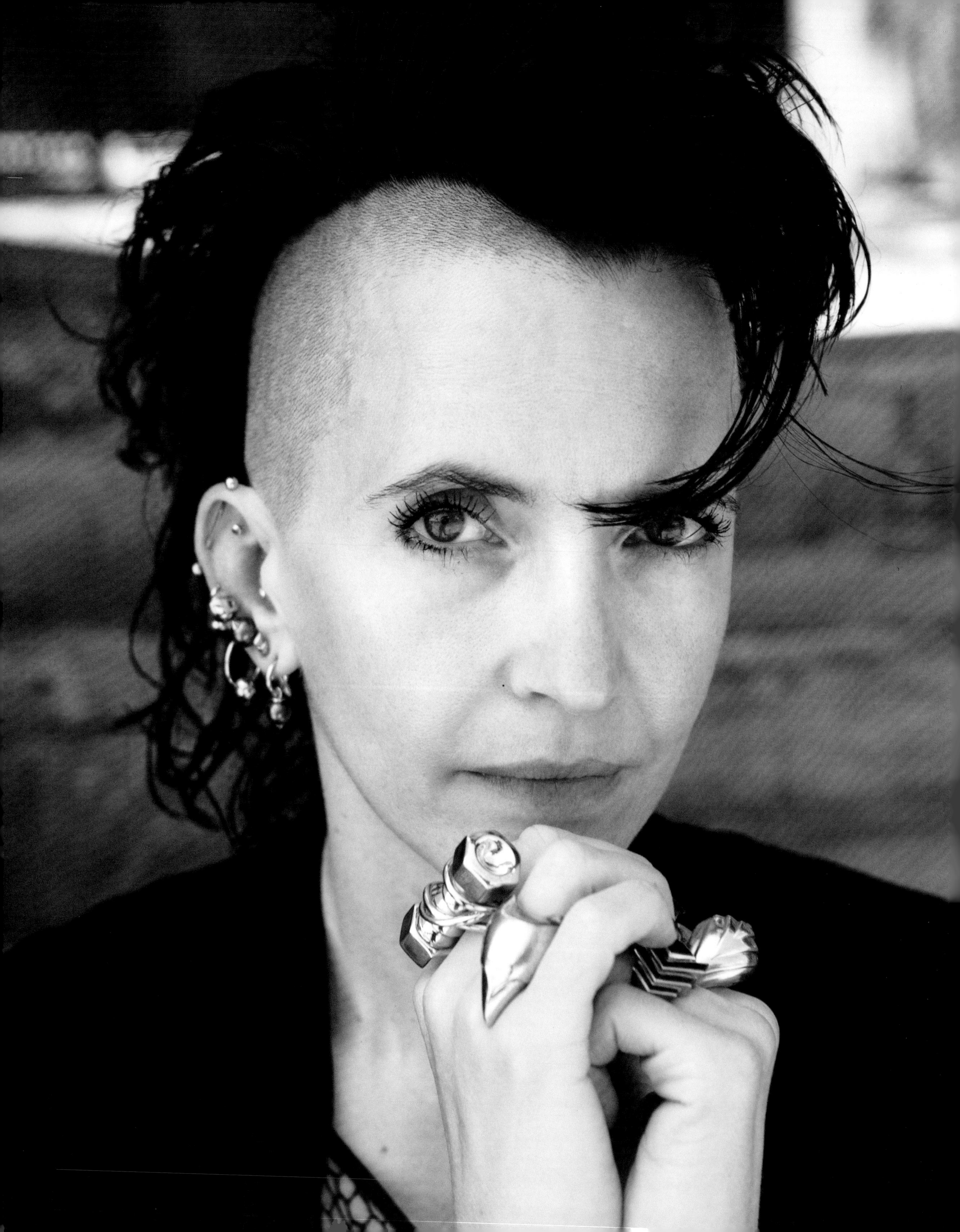

FOREWORD

Over two decades ago, I first met Hannah Martin at Central Saint Martins' jewellery degree show, when she talked me through her final collection. I remember her infectious enthusiasm and exuberance and the professionalism of her approach, the depth of thought and research that had shaped her chosen theme – It's Only Rock 'n' Roll. I remember thinking that this was a series of sophisticated, well-made jewels, and being struck by their contemporary relevance. Hannah Martin's first creations were jewels with a subversive rock 'n' roll edge that still managed to exude elegance. Here were jewels with something to say; something provocative, challenging, even shocking. Hannah explained how her degree show collection had grown out of the theme of her final dissertation, 'The Peacock and the Ladyboy', exploring jewellery for men and with it broader questions around gender identity. She wanted to challenge gender norms in jewellery, to blend feminine and masculine, to blur boundaries and delve deep into the ways in which jewellery expresses our identity. Looking back, Hannah Martin clearly anticipated today's focus on gender fluidity by some two decades, and pioneered men's jewellery and concepts of androgyny.

Having been involved in trend forecasting for the jewellery industry, I understood Hannah's concept as excitingly directional, socially and culturally. While as a jewellery historian, I knew that jewels that captured the spirit of their moment in time were the jewels that, however avant-garde at the time of their making, would very likely become classics of the future. It just takes a designer who understands the world around them, who challenges that world, who dares to take jewellery out of its ivory tower and most importantly a designer with the talent and imagination – and courage – to distil such controversial concepts into seductively, appealingly wearable jewellery.

Intrigued, I found out that Hannah had won the coveted Cartier Award, which led her into the hallowed workshops of the great Parisian heritage Maisons. She trained at the bench alongside experienced and highly skilled goldsmiths and jewellers. Much later, in one of several interviews, she explained how this experience had intensified her love of craftsmanship, engendered an appreciation of refinement of detail and fuelled her sense of wonder at handling, sculpting and manipulating precious materials, especially gold. At the same time, however, as she came face to face with strict conventions surrounding the art of the jewel, with time-honoured skills and disciplines, the experience in Paris also strengthened her resolve to challenge these conventions and age-old, unchanging traditions. This balance of reverence and rebellion comes naturally to Hannah Martin; I see it as a crucial component of her creative identity. Instinctively she brings harmony to contrasts and contradictions, building captivating tension through polarities: raw and refined, subversion and sophistication, toughness and sensuality, the warmly familiar – as in her use of gold and traditional skills – and the provocatively unexpected, as in her punk or fetish references. There's a particular thrill in seeing a Hannah Martin client, mature, ultra-chic, cultivated and designer-dressed, sporting a malachite ring pierced through with a safety pin, or a razor-shaped pendant; co-conspirators subtly but surely joining the insurrection.

Through the years, I have watched as Hannah has blossomed into a renowned and successful designer-jeweller. I've seen how she has honed her protean talent, developing and enriching her intense, thought-provoking, rebellious ideas, and constructing the character-filled narratives and cinematic scenarios she so loves to form the backdrop to each new collection. I admire how Hannah has always remained true to herself, to the original driving forces of her creativity. How she has drawn on her own passions and predilections, sometimes idiosyncratic,

It's Only Rock 'n' Roll, 2005. Safety Pin with Pearls, created as part of her Central Saint Martins graduate collection.

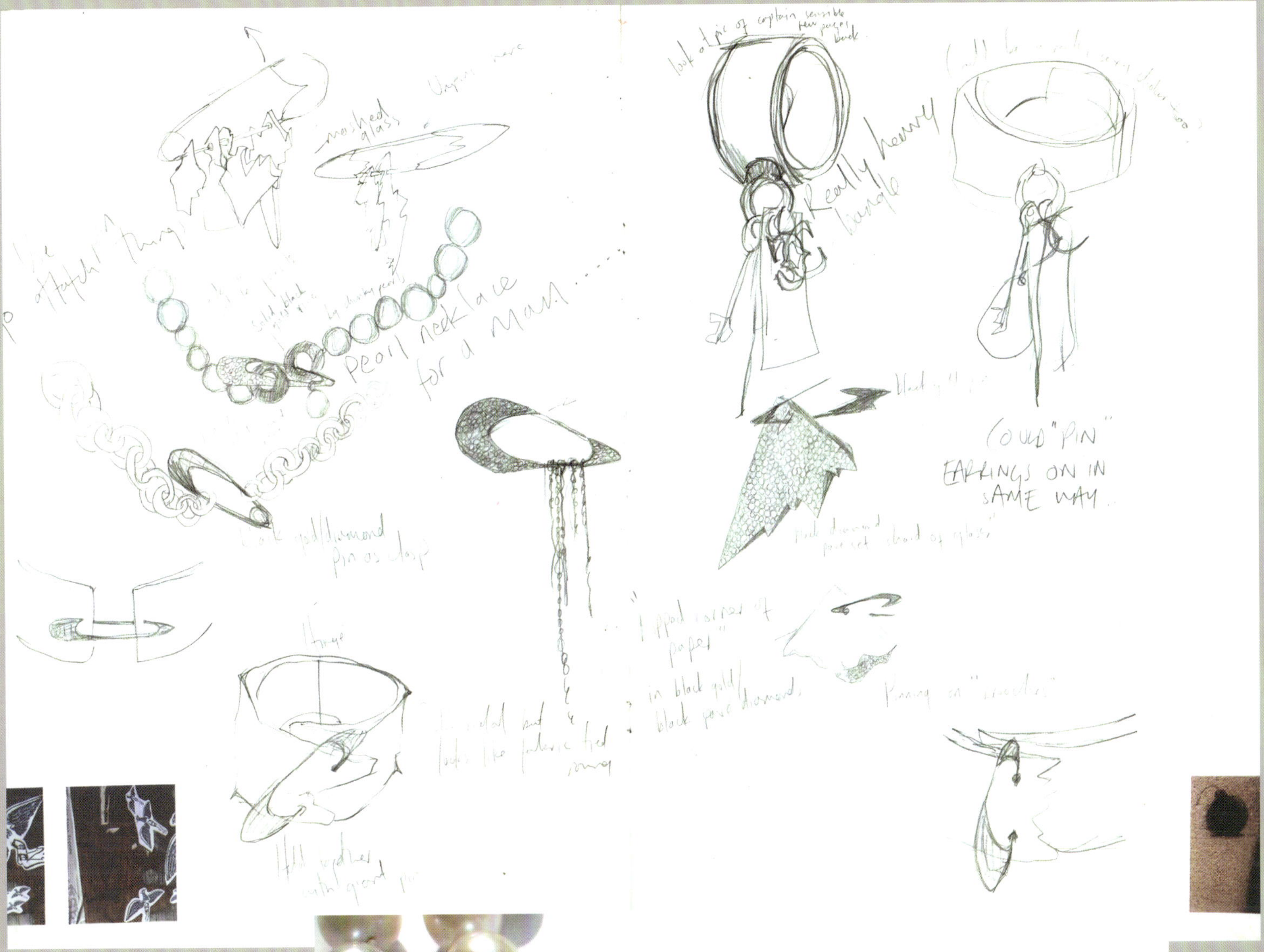
mashed glass
pearl necklace for a MAN......
Really heavy bangle
COULD "PIN" EARRINGS ON IN SAME WAY.

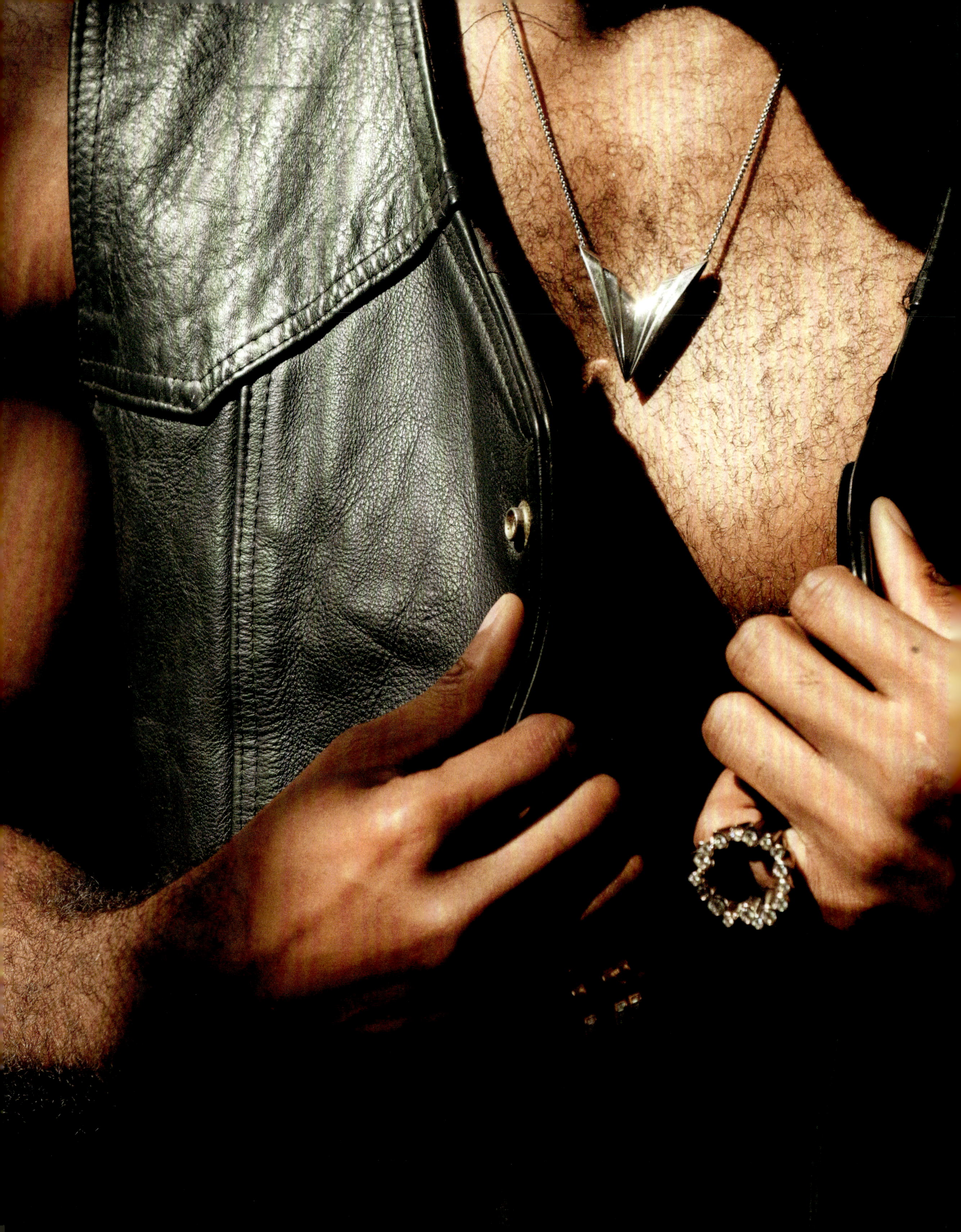

often connected to music, to loves and losses, joy and fear, struggles and triumphs, so that each new collection is an organic evolution, a deeply personal expression of her world view, as it too evolves and matures. Personal and artistic integrity lies at the heart of her work. Hannah has never compromised on her vision or her values, she has never 'sold out' to commercialism or succumbed to the lure of corporate culture, and its undoubted financial rewards. Perhaps most impressively, Hannah Martin has remained ferociously independent, and steadfastly individualistic, in an industry dominated by dynastic brands and powerful conglomerates with massive marketing might, in a global market that stacks the odds against the individual, self-funded, self-reliant designer jeweller.

With each new collection, Hannah's voice grows stronger, the narrative more nuanced, and the jewels themselves more original, ingeniously innovative, audacious and in many ways more refined. When she established her business in 2005, Hannah dug deeper into the theme of her degree show series, wondering why there was so little jewellery for men, and wondering why there should be such demarcation between jewellery for men and women. The collection, which remains a best seller today, evolved the rock 'n' roll theme and at the same time told the story of 'Jewels for men that girlfriends would want to steal'. With this, once again, Hannah was way ahead of her time, anticipating the 'boyfriend' trend, as in jeans and watches.

I was especially interested in the subtle echoes of history that reverberated through the modernity of the collection. In Europe, before the late Renaissance, it was men who wore most jewellery – the peacocks. Jewels and gems were the prerogative of kings, princes and potentates, while in India the Mughal Emperors and later the Maharajahs wore lavishly layered gems,

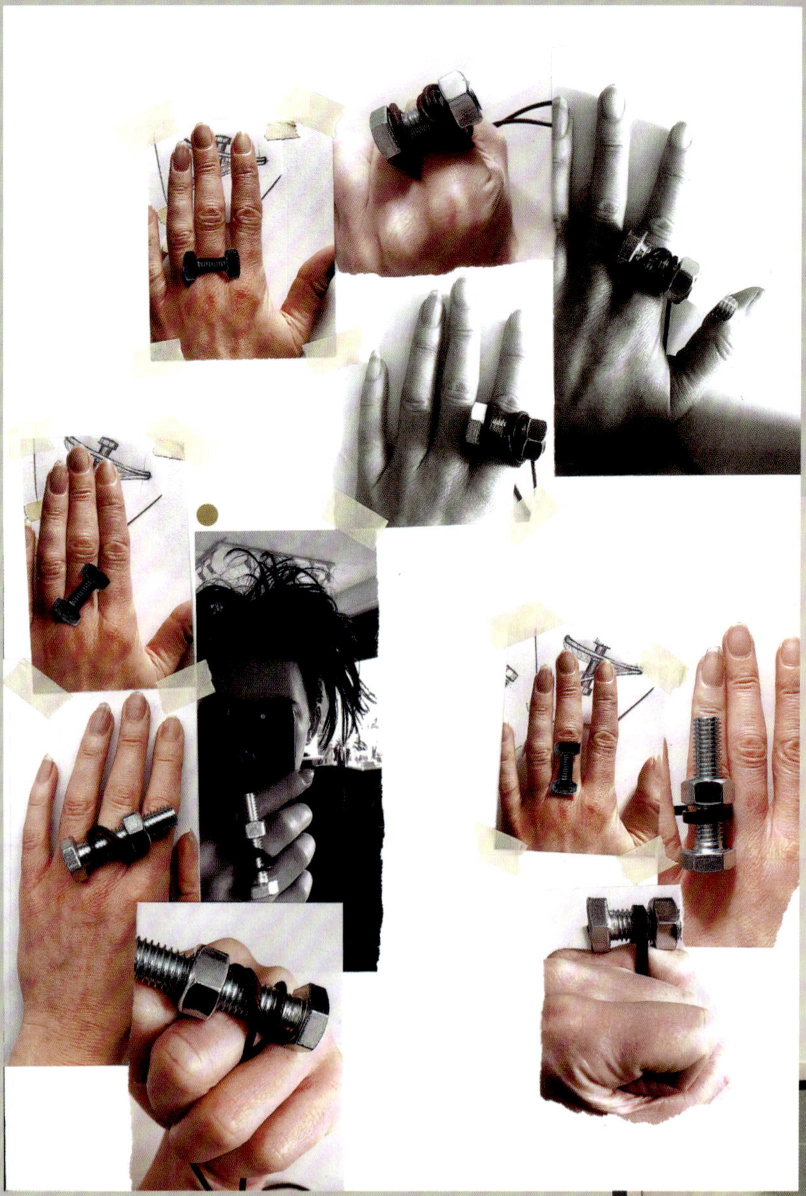
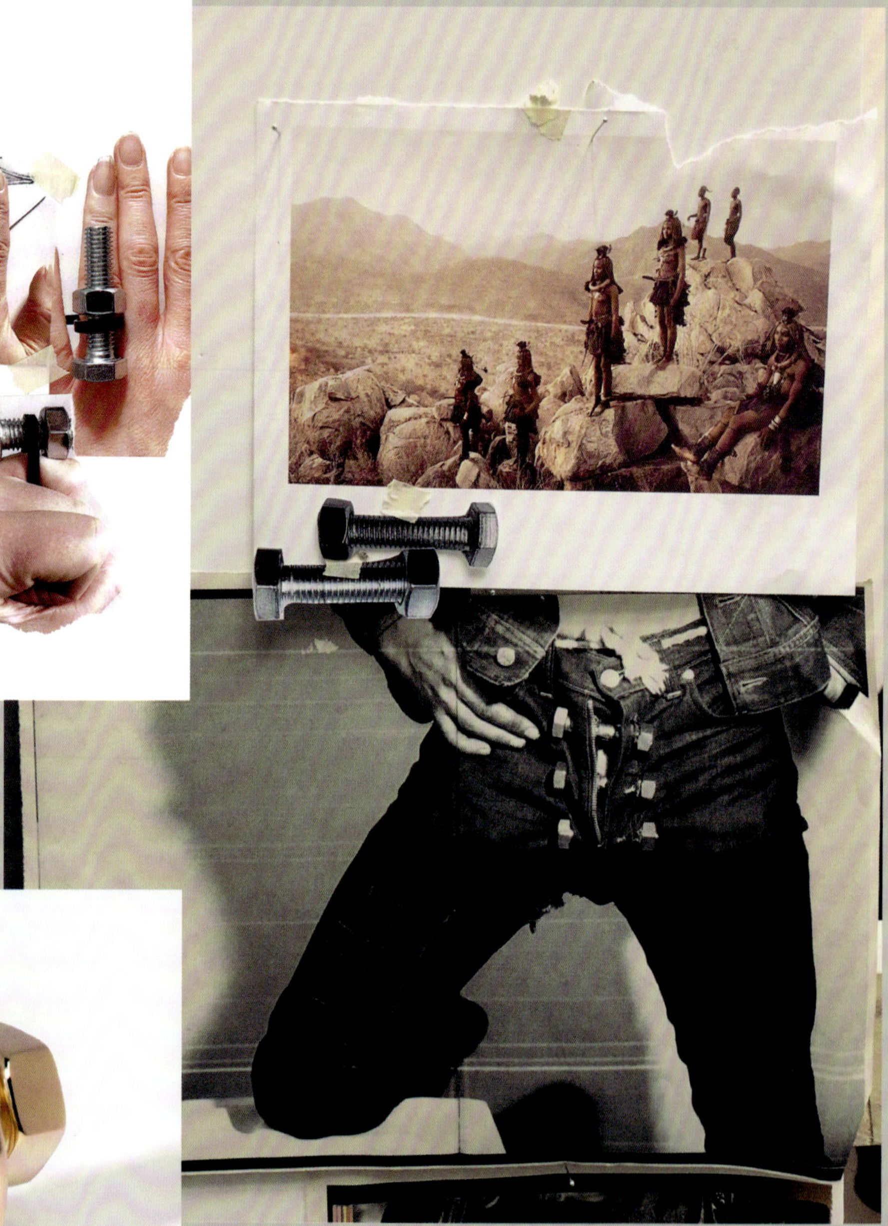
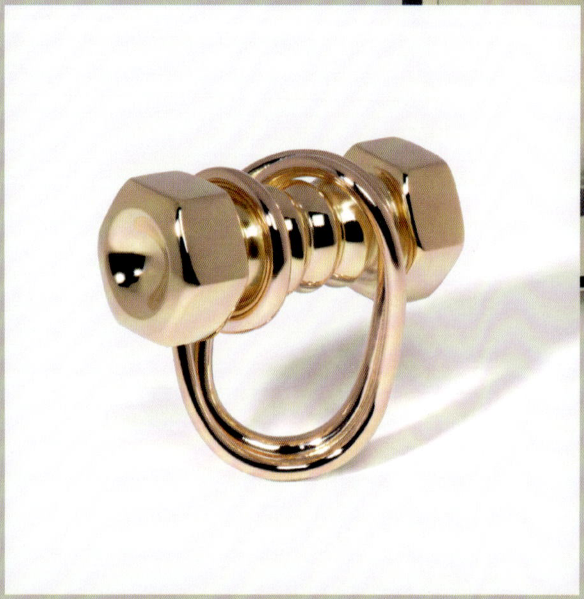

A New Act Of Rebellion, 2020.
Rebel Hero Bolt Ring, 18ct gold.

pearls and flamboyant jewels with immense natural style, that nevertheless asserted authority and inspired allegiance, crucially identifying them as rulers and leaders. In both cultures, and across the world, jewels were symbols of power and authority, their miraculous light and beauty aligned with the divine right to rule. It seems to me that Hannah has channelled that power in her jewels, dismantling its royal and elitist associations, redirecting the energy inherent to the jewel, particularly to gold and gemstones, towards a democratic form of self-expression; a way of reaching out and engaging with the world. At the same time, re-interpreting the early talismanic, protective role of the jewel as gleaming modern-day armour for the urban warrior. There is certainly a strong flavour of armour, weaponry and a leitmotif of protection running throughout Hannah Martin collections – for example in her Possession Bangle, with its sharp shiny planes, killer angles and edges, and its tantalising glimpse of flesh, fragility and vulnerability beneath. The Orbit ring, architectural and curvaceous, is like an armadillo shell, while the huge Rebel Hero Bolt Ring is undoubtedly a knuckleduster, a fierce warning not to get too close. This sense of protection is a counterpoint to the element of danger, of living on the edge, that is a defining feature of Hannah Martin jewellery. Just as gold, with its undimming light, warmth and optimism, is the counterpoint to the dark shadows of the underworld, of gangster-land – one of Hannah's enduring inspirations.

Gold plays a central role in Hannah's work, always the main event rather than a supporting act, smooth, polished and gleaming, building bold, monumental structures. She luxuriates in gold: its heroism, sumptuous sheen, its richness and sculptural malleability, and surely too she loves gold for its reassuring weight in wear, for its tactility, like silk on the skin, and the way in which it acquires a patina, so personal to the wearer. Hannah uses gold in abundance,

foreword < 15

16 > foreword

generously and unstintingly, so evocative of treasure, of the life force of the sun and the elixir of life. Gold, lusted after for millennia, imbued with magical properties, is also connected to one of Hannah's preoccupations; the idea of possession: gold as the quintessential treasured possession but also, in the form of a jewel, worn by a woman, the sign of male ownership, of one person belonging in some way to another, or to an affiliation, society, family heritage or even signifying attachment to a memory. She ponders the contradictions within the jewel's role, between this element of possession, belonging, commitment and freedom of self-expression. This strikes a particular chord today, in our era of female empowerment. Freedom is clearly important to Hannah; her gold Shackle Bangle, now a Hannah Martin signature, originally in the Aguila Dorada collection, referencing sunken treasure, is, she says, not about capture or imprisonment but about a bid for freedom.

The Shackle Bangle, recognised as a contemporary classic, points to Hannah's recurring use of hard-edged, mechanistic, masculine and industrial motifs, like the bolt, screw or safety pin, all intimately connected to the punk movement, one of Hannah Martin's original and enduring inspirations. In 2020, she launched the New Act of Rebellion, a supremely confident, uncompromisingly bold screaming outburst of a collection, huge in scale, power and presence, and forceful in its re-imagining of quintessential punk emblems and attributes, notably the chain and the safety pin. Explaining the narrative she had dreamt up as the background to the collection, Hannah said she envisaged an empty, destroyed, post-party room, still vibrating with energy. The chain was central to the collection, inspired, Hannah says, by heavy, industrial steel chains of the kind found with massive padlocks on gates, the perfect expression of heavy metal. Although, as with the shackle, Hannah saw the chain not as a restraint but as a symbol of strength, power and ultimately freedom.

Aguila Dorada, 2007.
Single Shackle Bangle,
18ct gold.

broken shackles

maybe do some forging?

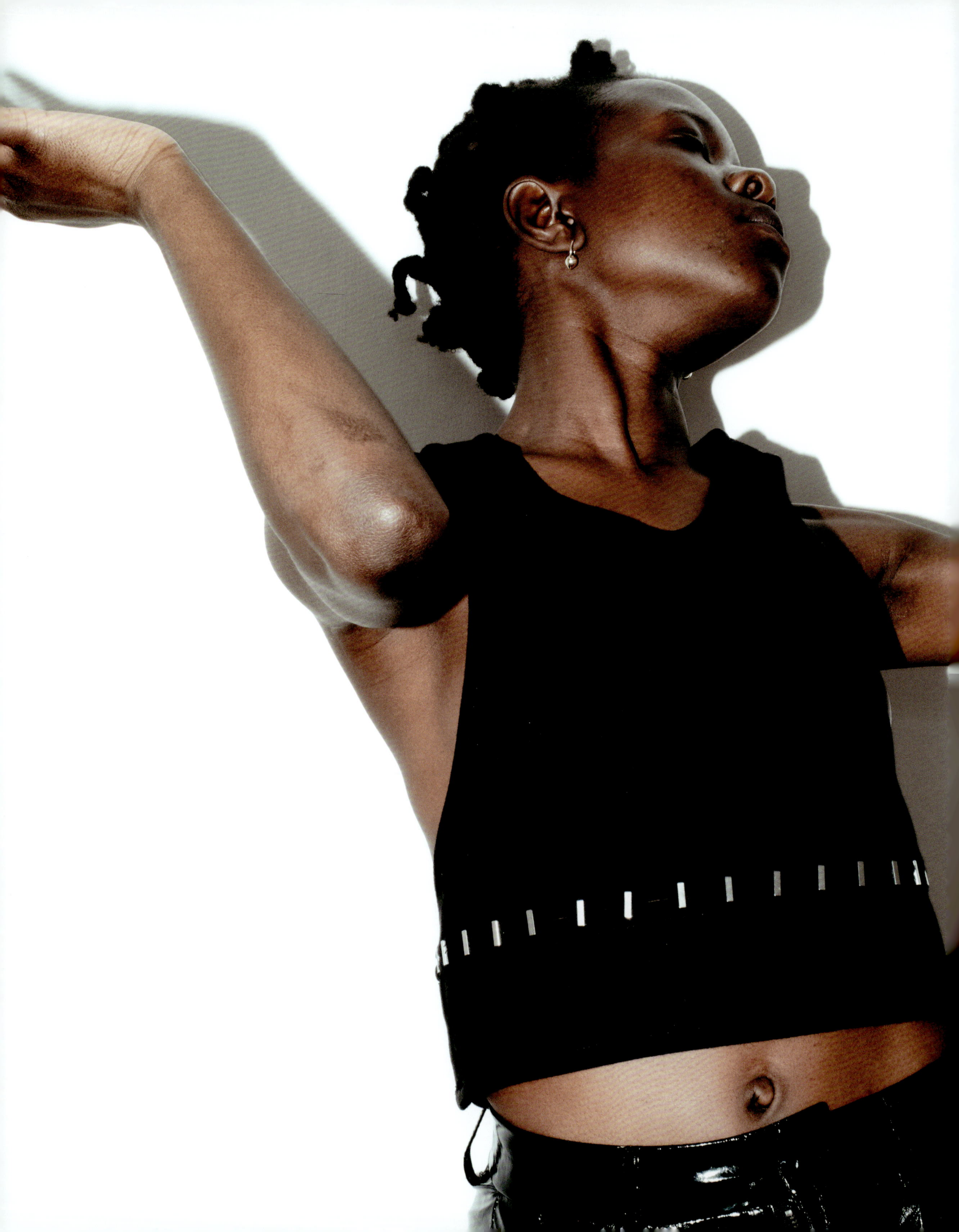

The themes that emerge for each collection, singular, clearly-defined and directional as they are, belie the wealth of inspirations, influences and references explored by Hannah, in depth, during the long gestation process, in which she shuts herself away to think, dream, sketch and imagine. For each collection, even as she remains faithful to her original vision, she dips into a rich and varied treasure chest of ideas and inspirations, from art, pop culture, photography, music, literature, history, from counterculture, fetishism, underworld gangsters, both suave and dangerous, a world of characters that holds a fascination for her. It seems to me that with each exploration, Hannah awakens another layer of creativity and self-realisation.

Hannah's 2024 collection, The Perfect Drug, represents a dramatic reawakening, in which she laid her soul bare, showing that she is never afraid to face her feelings, or her personal trials and tribulations, and share them through her work. Her 10th collection, The Perfect Drug was a prelude to her 20th anniversary milestone, celebrated so perfectly and honestly in this book.

Technically complex, for the first time incorporating both silver and gold, and highlighted by hand-made silky gold mesh, the collection encapsulates Hannah Martin's potent mix of elegance and irreverence, and showcases her fearlessness in tackling risky, even discomforting themes. She lures us with effortless design, refined details, superb craftsmanship and perfect proportions, with irresistibly tactile jewels that morph partway into fashion and fabric, beckoning us into what she calls 'unsafe' territory, pushing us out of our comfort zone, taking her signature edginess even closer to the edge and, as ever seductive and alluring, taking us with her along the path to self-discovery and new possibilities.

foreword

The idea came out of heartbreak, out of the embers of a broken love affair, as Hannah emerged from the numbness of emotional pain to feel joy again, even beyond joy, the intoxicating euphoria of coming back to life. The risqué theme of The Perfect Drug is a blend of inspirations, from fetishism and erotica, through the sculptural sensuality of Brancusi and Noguchi, to the serene beauty of Man Ray's nudes and naturally the pugilistic provocation of Vivienne Westwood's punk. While thrillingly new, it is a collection that, after 20 years, comes full circle, showcasing Hannah Martin as a skilful goldsmith, a brilliant technical innovator, a courageous self-made individualist, who, like 20th-century avant-garde designers and artist-jewellers before her, has always dared to break the rules she learnt so well, to crash conventions and push the limits. Even more, Hannah's work is important in the role it plays in charting the course of changing ideals of femininity as jewellery so often does. Yet, while the historian in me tries to place Hannah Martin in the context of jewellery history, I realise that she has forged her own untrodden path through that long story, carving out an entirely new place for herself and for jewellery that is both precious and refined yet intimately connected to social and cultural movements, to activism and ideas. Just as this book, so unexpected and different from the norm, is a fitting celebration of Hannah Martin's unique contribution to contemporary jewellery, to our understanding of a fast-changing world, a revelation of one woman's indefatigable determination to change perceptions of what a jewel should or could be. To create the ultimate act of rebellion, jewels that connect us to intense feelings, love and loss, joy and fear, that both delight and shock the senses and stir emotions, provoking a powerful physical, visceral response, jewels that beat with the pulse of life, with one woman's vision and her moment in time.

VIVIENNE BECKER

The Perfect Drug, 2024.

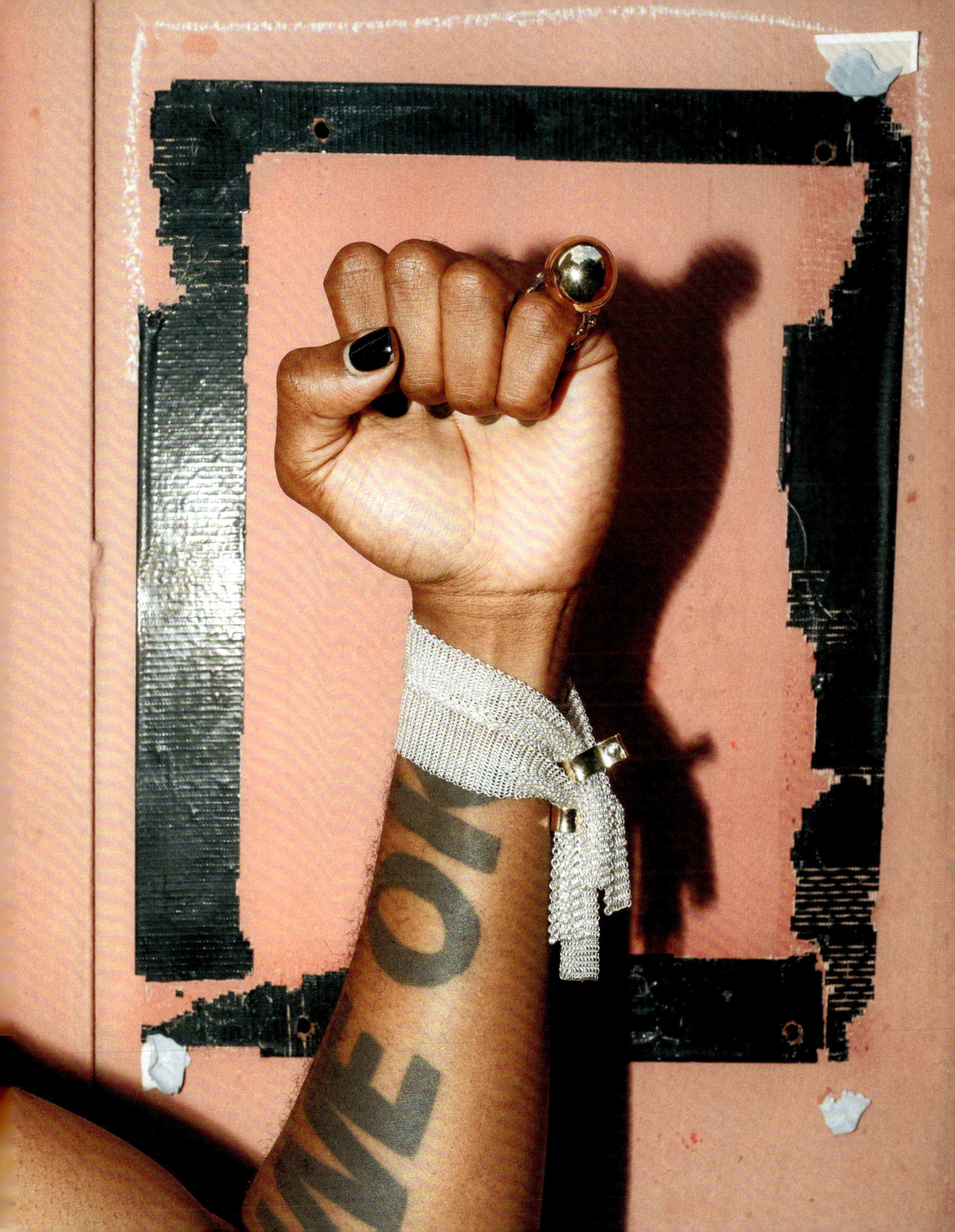

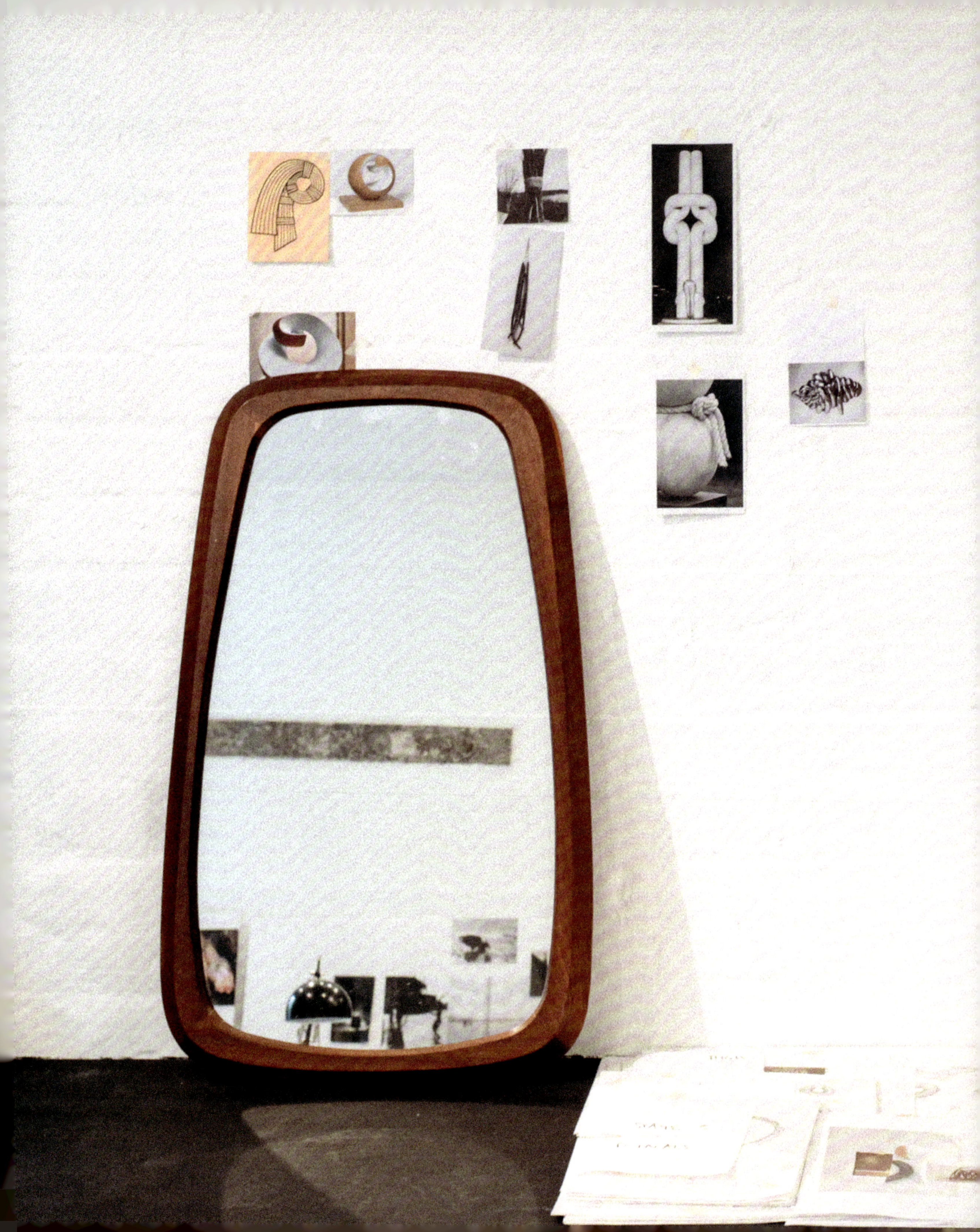

❝ Making something beautiful is not enough; you need to be different and meaningful. ❞

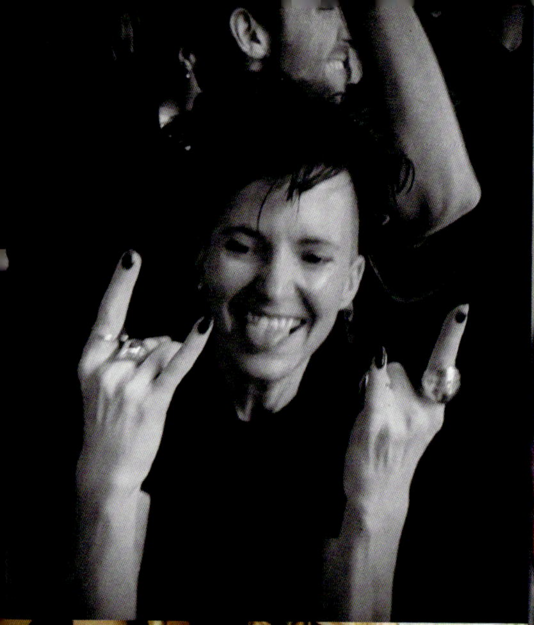
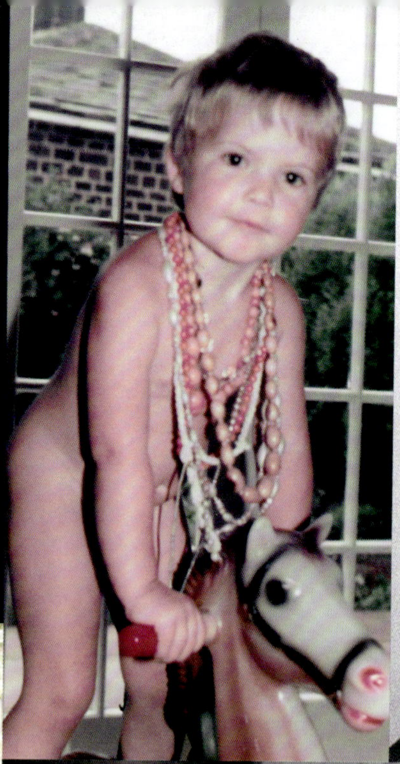
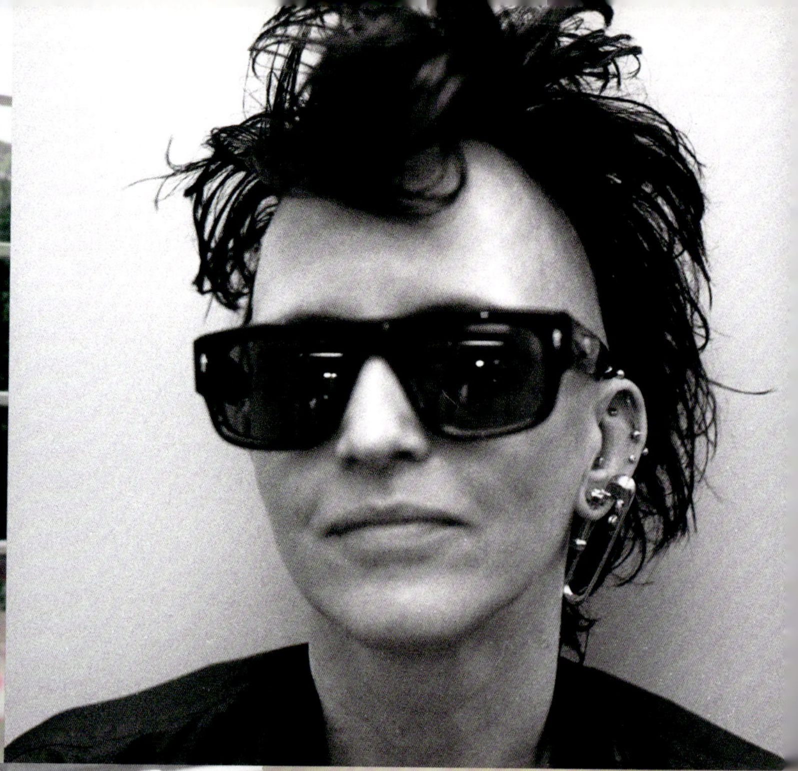
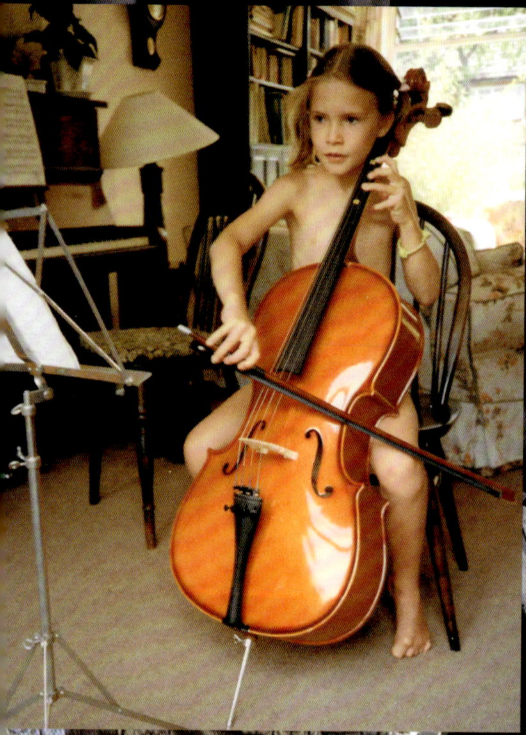
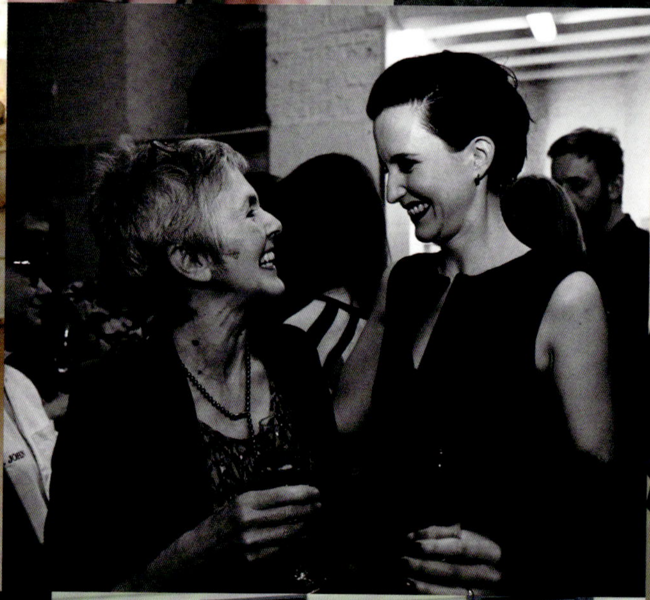
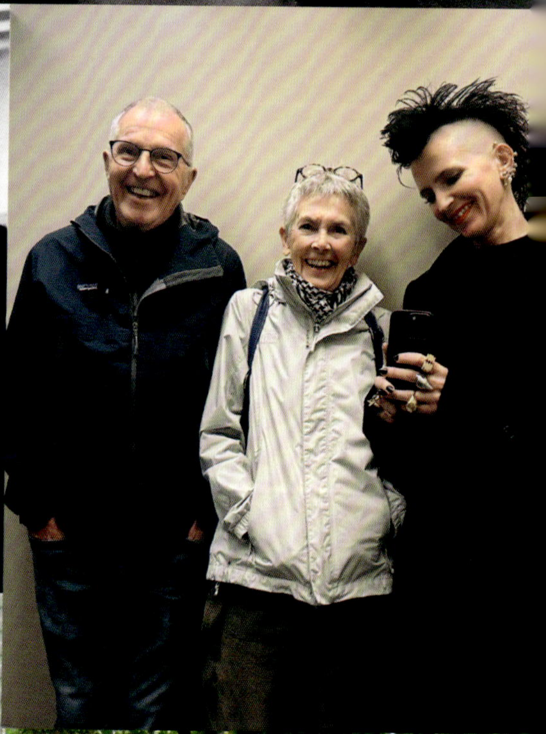
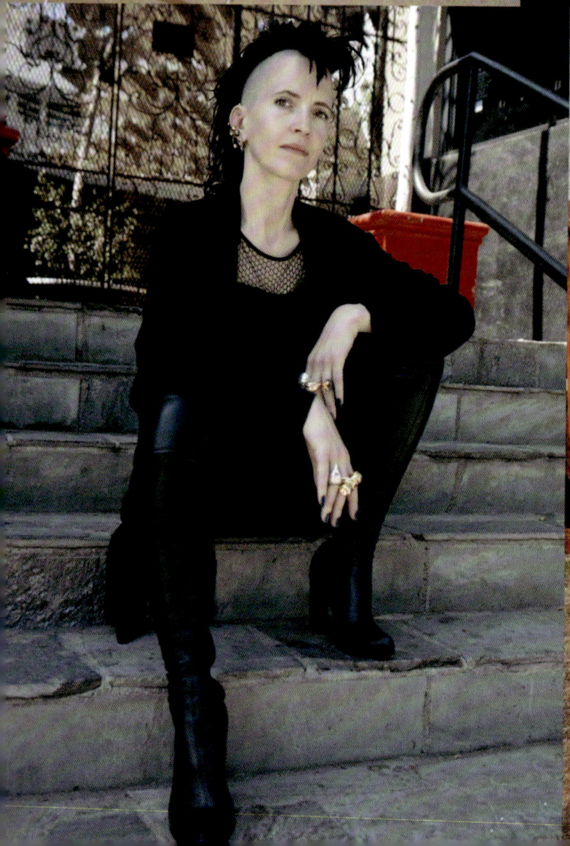
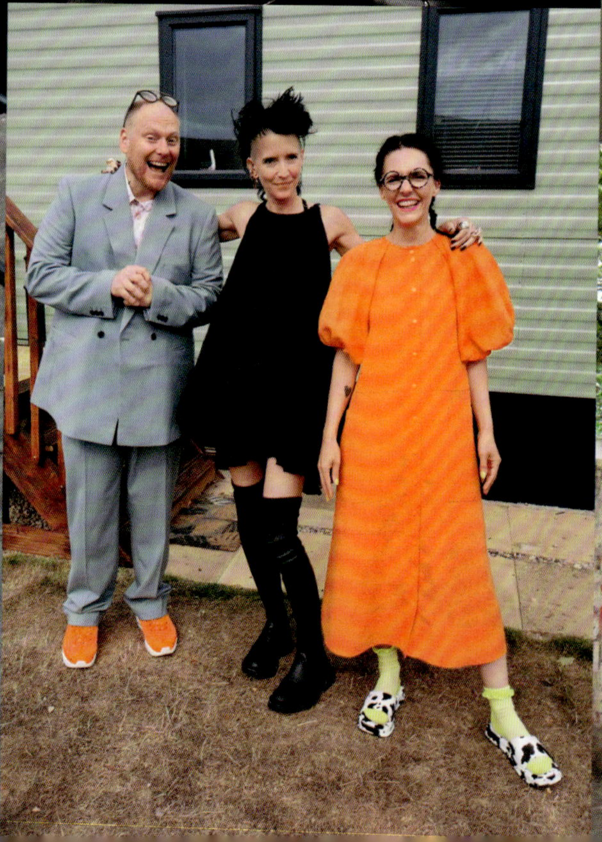
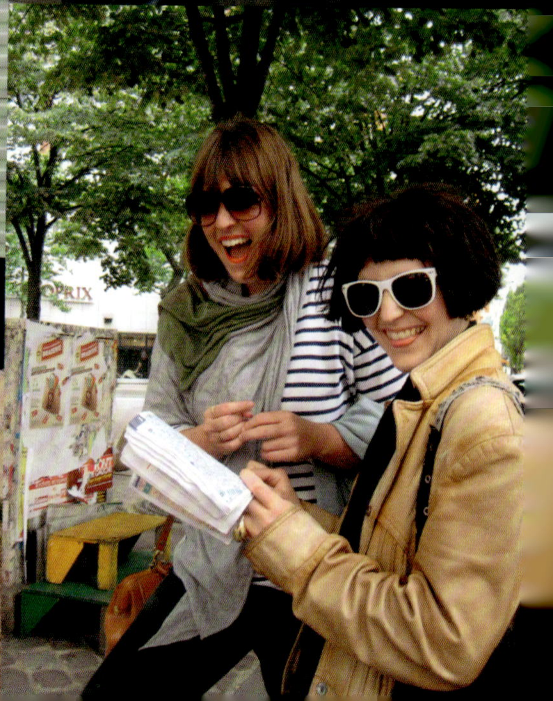

WHO ARE YOU
HANNAH MARTIN?

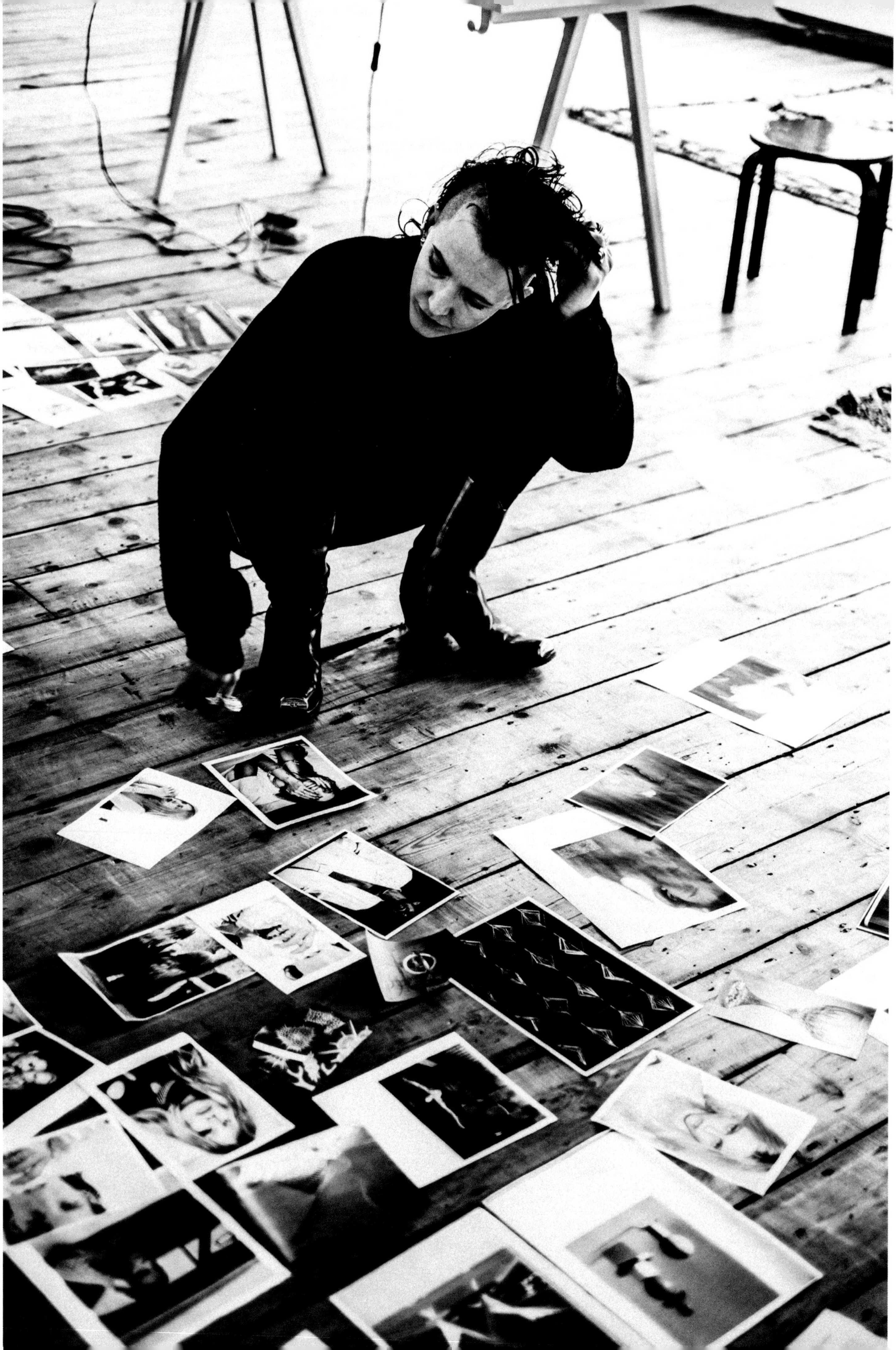

Q: Did you always know you wanted to be a jeweller?

A: No. I fell into it. It's such an odd place for me to have ended up.

Q: You originally wanted to be a sculptor. What drew you to jewellery?

A: Jewellery is sexy. Jewellery-making is also sexy.

Q: What turns you on about jewellery?

A: It's a real, specific high. It's about the process but also the sensuality of the materials. Even after 20 years I'm still in awe of the materials and the act of transforming them.

Q: What is your greatest indulgence?

A: When I put my phone on 'absolutely-fuck-off mode' and immerse myself in my process. It's my favourite thing in the world.

28 > who are you hannah martin?

Q: How does it feel to have your designs copied, and so blatantly?

A: It's like being stabbed through the heart, every time. But, I would rather be copied than to copy. As a creative, it's actually quite tragic to be the latter.

Q: Who are your favourite fashion designers?

A: Azzedine Alaïa, Alexander McQueen and Rick Owens, all true creators. Like McQueen, I'm conscious of not being part of the club. And that's fine with me.

Q: Who is your hero?

A: My sister.

Q: If you weren't a jeweller, what would you be?

A: A sculptor. Or, a bass player.

Q: Do you get attached to what you create?

A: No. Once we've brought something to life, I'm OK with it. It's out there and I'm on to the next thing.

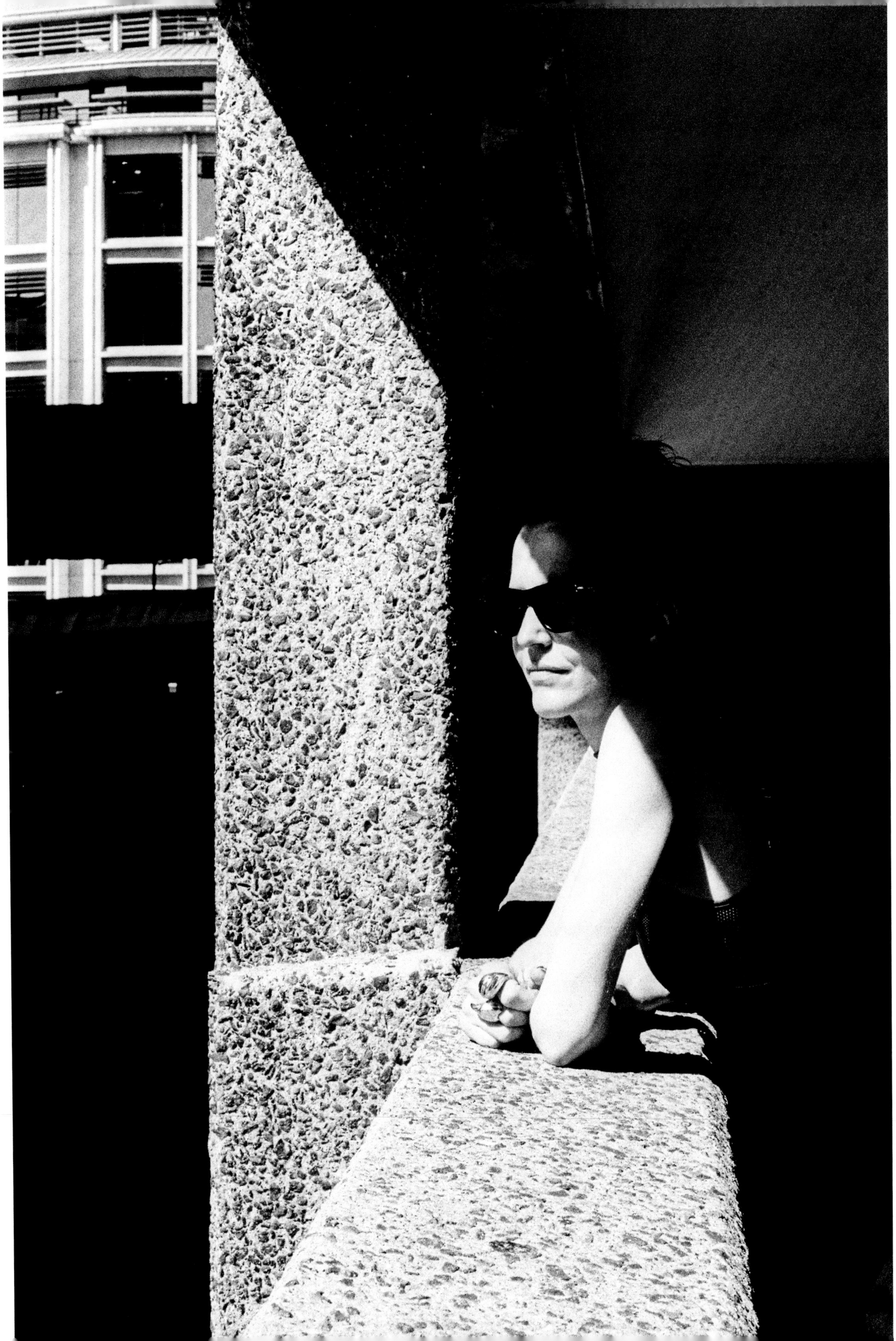

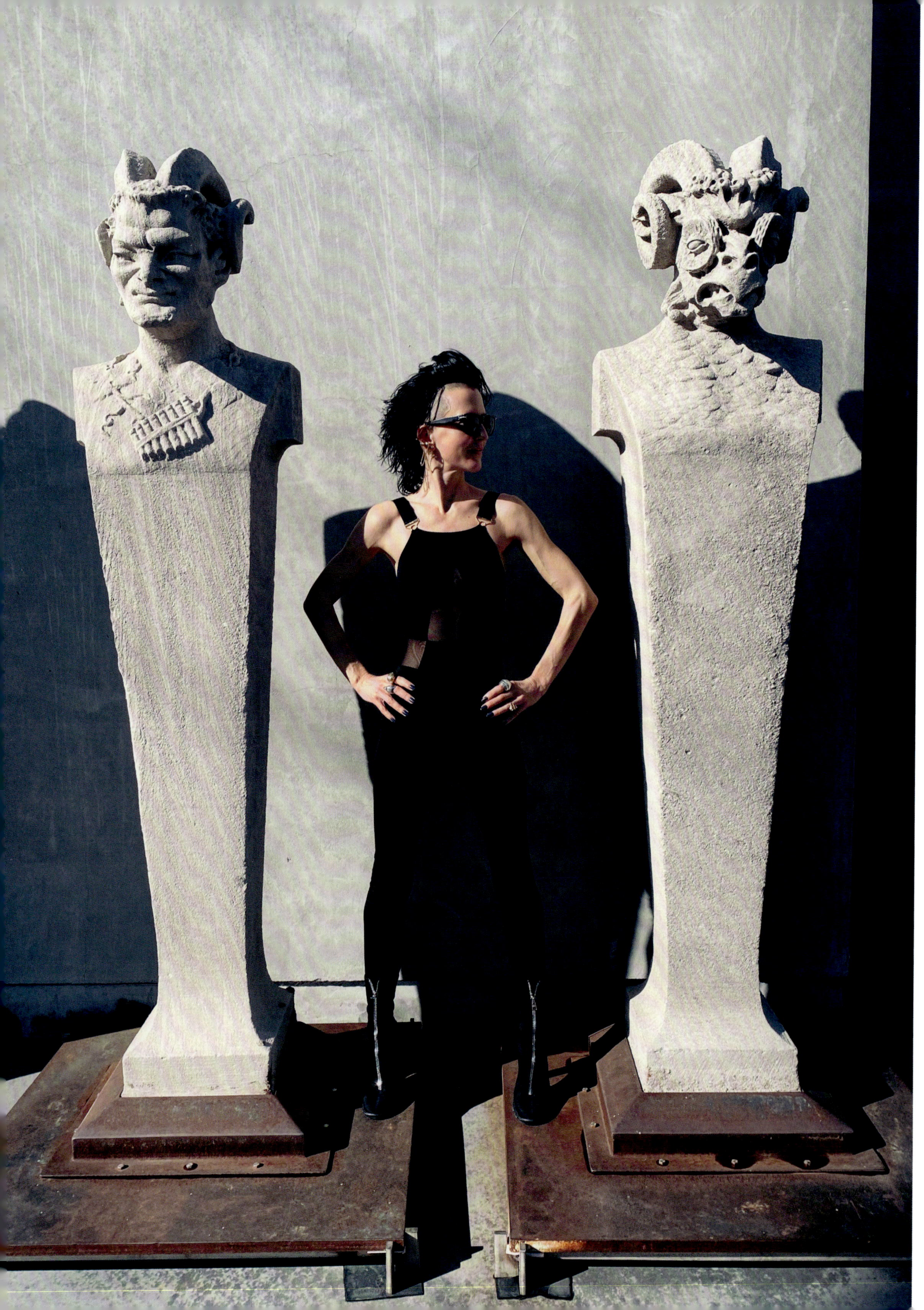

Q: What's that *thing* that gives you a voice?

A: Luxury is not in my blood, so I still feel like I can fuck with it.

Q: Tell us something about yourself that no one would ever suspect.

A: I may be outspoken and my style is quite full-on, but I am actually quite shy.

Q: What, if anything, do you have to say about making a name in such a competitive industry?

A: Success does not fill any hole.

Q: You are entirely independent. What's your backup plan?

A: Me, myself and I. And my playlists.

Q: What does it take to make a collection?

A: Some inspiration and a shit tonne of money.

The Peacock and The Ladyboy

> NORMALLY BEFORE A BATTLE THE MEN WOULD MAKE THEMSELVES UP TO LOOK AS BEAUTIFUL AND AMAZING AS POSSIBLE. THEN THEY'D GO OUT AND HACK EACH OTHER TO PIECES. THAT'S NOT MY BAG, OF COURSE. BUT BASED ON THAT YOU CAN HARDLY CALL MAKE-UP UNMASCULINE. AND LOOK AT ALL THE OLD KINGS AND DANDIES.
>
> AND IF YOU LOOK TO THE ANIMAL WORLD, SO OFTEN THE MALE IS MORE BEAUTIFUL THAN THE FEMALE – LOOK AT PEACOCKS AND LIONS.
>
> REALLY MAKE-UP AND BEAUTIFUL CLOTHES ARE FUNDAMENTAL TO ME. IT'S JUST THAT WE LIVE IN SUCH A STRANGE SOCIETY.
>
> DAVID BOWIE 1972

Blinking the boy is unsure. Window light dimly illuminates a figure too big to fit in the boy's imagination. Undulating hips weave a pattern of sequins and seduction through the heaviness. They belong to a body that is keen to escape from the confines of a long and shimmering black gown. Heavy flesh moves with grace and poise in a dance the boy does not know. Disappearing, the figure leaves a sequinned hole on the edge of the horizon and a smoky shadow in the mind of the boy.

Many of the characters I have met throughout this journey, in both fiction and reality, have found ways to release themselves from the restrictions of gender. They have discovered that magical place on the edge, that border point, where suddenly there appears to be an endless freedom.

Perhaps it is this that has seduced me. Perhaps my exploration has been in search of a border where nothing is defined yet everything is possible.

?

Thesis, Central Saint Martins, 2004

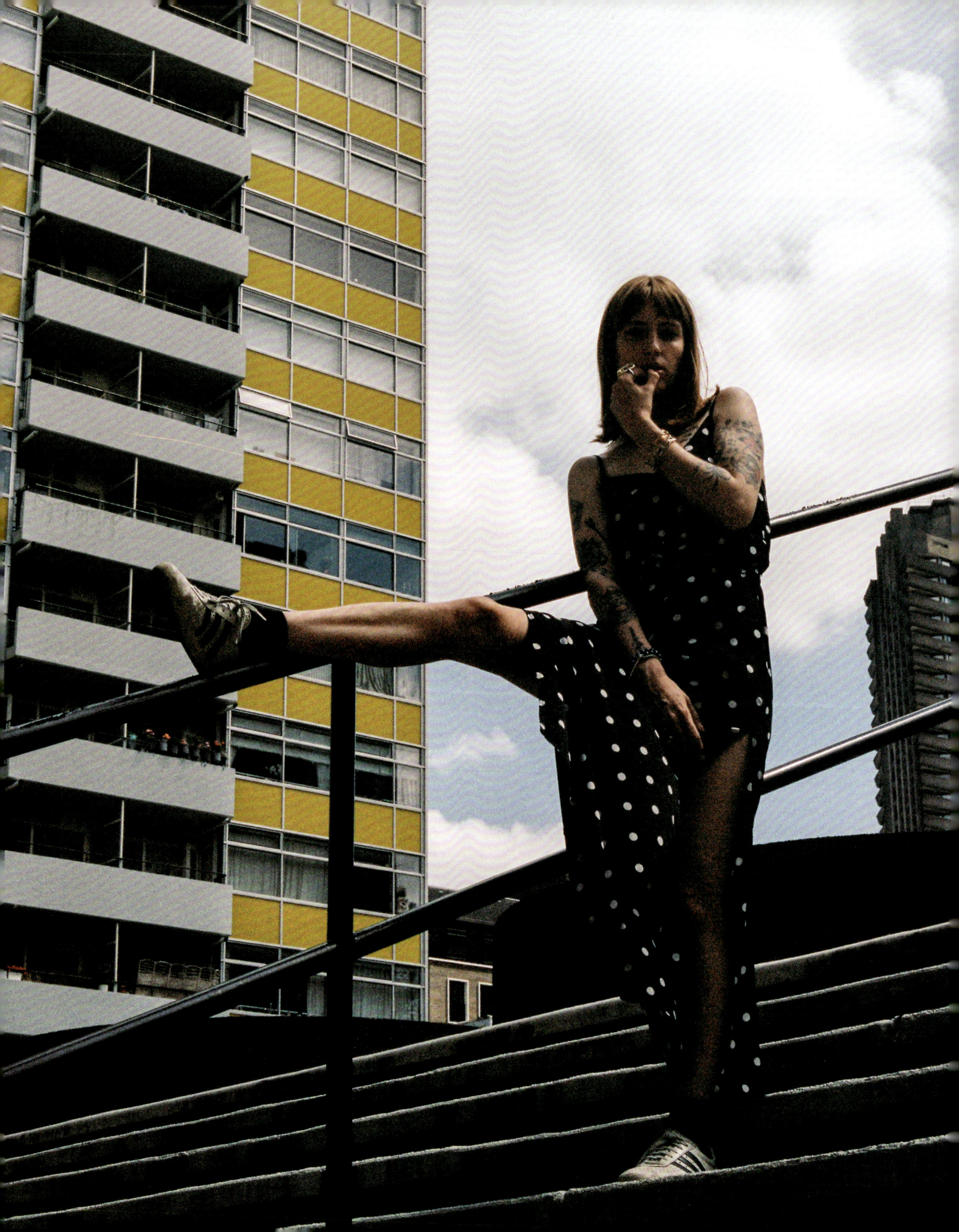

LONDON
CALLING

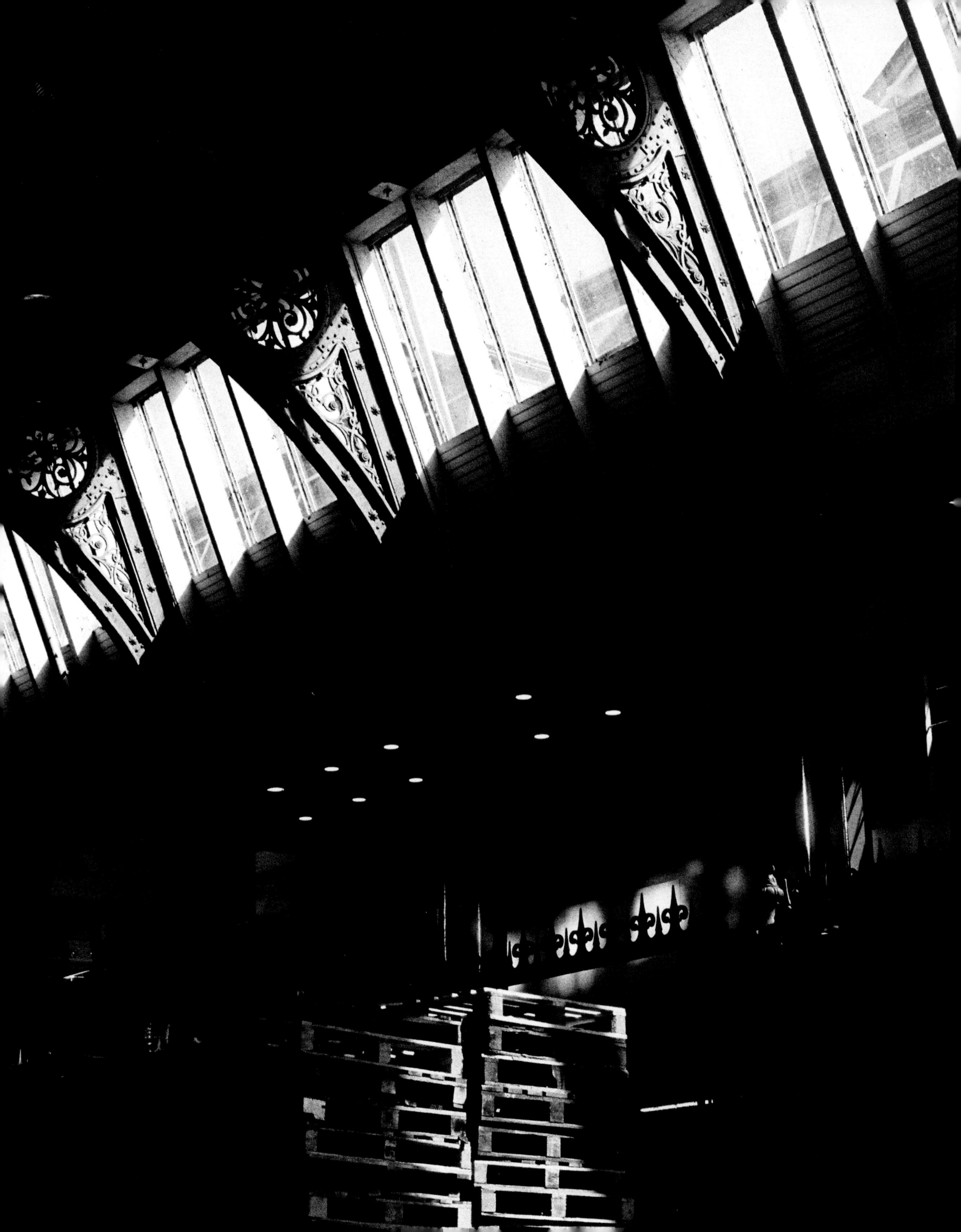

On the eve of the 21st century, London crackled with creative defiance as designers, artists and rebels reshaped culture directly in the shadows of its grand institutions. In fashion studios and jewellery ateliers, tradition was submitting to subversion, and reinvention was a way of life.

In 1999, Hannah moved to London to study at Central Saint Martins (CSM), which had produced many a rebel before her, among them personal idols like Pulp frontman Jarvis Cocker and the fashion designers John Galliano, Riccardo Tisci and – most of all – Alexander McQueen. 'That year changed everything for me; it laid the foundation for everything I am now. I feel like I owe my whole life to Saint Martins', she says.

Like many a small-town misfit, she found the capital a revelation, pulsing with creative energy and the promise of transformation. And she found her tribe immediately. 'Having been the "odd one out" your whole life, suddenly you find other "odd ones out". We formed a family. They're still my people.' With an emotional safety net in place, chasing creative risk became inevitable, vital. If the future was uncertain, the upside was a blank page, a chance to forge her own path.

At the bench, Hannah found her groove in goldsmithing; sharpened her instincts with stone-setting. 'It was rigorous and hands-on', she recalls. 'I learned that I could design my vision, and it could actually be made. You can't become a good jewellery designer without having spent a tonne of time at the bench.'

38 > london calling

THIS PAGE: Scenes from student days at Central Saint Martins.

OPPOSITE: First portrait, by Joss McKinley, 2005.

" I feel like I owe my whole life to Saint Martins. "

Gaining fluency in the language of materials – casting, soldering, setting, polishing – gave her confidence and enhanced her sense of community. 'My skills enable me to have a very different conversation with craftspeople', Hannah observes. 'I know what is possible and what isn't, and you can't have that conversation if you don't also possess those skills. I can sit down at a bench and show them how I want things done. As a woman, that's very useful because even today, jewellery is still very much a man's world.'

'That process is my favourite thing in the world. I love it! It's like experiencing the full spectrum of emotions but in this very contained, hyperreal moment. The thrill when I find something is so high, so intense. I think that's why I love selling jewellery. It means that I can make more jewellery.'

Simon Fraser – a bench-trained goldsmith, former fashion designer and course leader in the Design MA for ceramics, furniture and jewellery at Central Saint Martins – vividly remembers meeting Hannah for the first time.

In 1999, Hannah was a wide-eyed newcomer in a city brimming with the promise of reinvention. If students turned up in the capital as blank canvases, London quickly filled in the outlines, smudged around the edges, and offered up a whole palette of unexpected colours. Hannah took to the scene like an old soul who understood, instinctively, that transformation is the entire point of design.

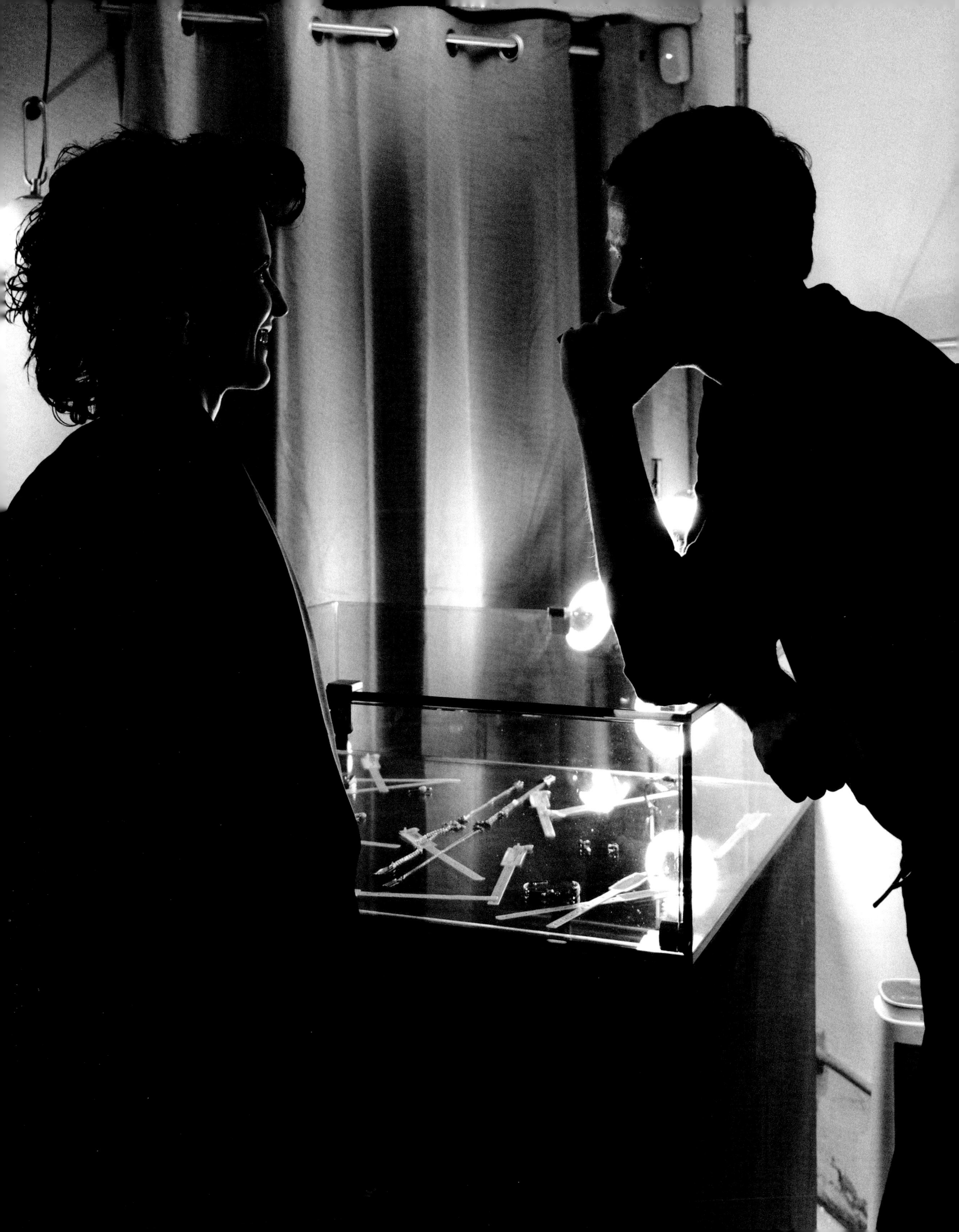

'It was a pivotal time for jewellery at CSM', Simon recalls. 'There was an urgency in the air, a sense that if you wanted to make a career of it, you had to commit completely.' As a goldsmith, silversmith and jeweller, he has, at various points in his career, eschewed traditional materials in favour of plastics, detoured into fashion via an eponymous brand in the 1980s, and chosen self-exile into the craft worlds of India and Japan.

To his mind, jewellery was never something fixed. It is more like a moving target. 'I was always interested in refining form and meaning', he explains. 'To me, it wasn't just about the object, or its preciousness: it was about what jewellery represented, and what it projected.'

Good jewellery speaks before its wearer does. Simon recognised Hannah's energy instinctively. Though it would take some time to hone her voice – and a few more years before she had her hair shorn into a signature mohawk – the budding designer exuded an unmistakable sense of purpose and direction. He sensed a kindred spirit. 'Her work was never going to be just adornment', he observes. Talent is one thing. Commitment is another. At CSM, the students partied and worked in equal measure, their edges gradually sharpened by shared ambition. At the bench, after hours, Hannah gave in to instinct and unyielding discipline.

It's Only Rock 'n' Roll.

ABOVE: Spur Ring, 18ct blackened gold and rubies, 2005.

OPPOSITE: Spiked Ring, 18ct blackened gold, sapphires and rubies, 2005.

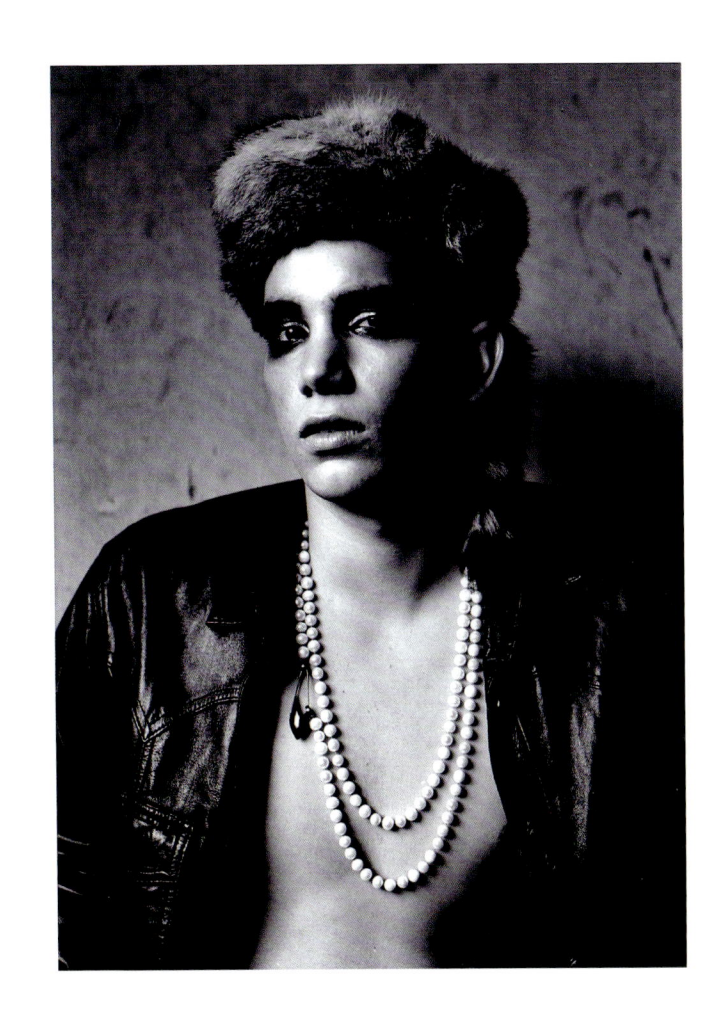

A Defining Journey - The City as Inspiration

Though driven, Hannah came to a point where she had to listen to her instinct and prioritise her own wellness. 'During my first year at CSM, I developed an eating disorder', she recalls. In retrospect, the pressures of school and stepping into adulthood had become overwhelming, a situation amplified by the loss of her beloved grandmother and an unhealthy relationship with a partner who was controlling.

'It's like I had been overloaded by life and I needed to stop it. I found myself needing to numb the feelings. That's what anorexia did for me. It numbed me. It's not unlike addiction to drugs or alcohol', she reflects. After a time of healing, she returned with renewed focus.

'When I came back to CSM, it's as though I had been "on pause" and suddenly someone had turned up the volume. I was greedy for life. I'm still greedy for life. I want to feel it all', she says. 'That was significant', observes Simon. 'Anyone can walk away. But to return willingly, purposefully? That means you're serious. And when she returned, she was no longer just part of the gang. She had become an individual on a journey.'

london calling < 43

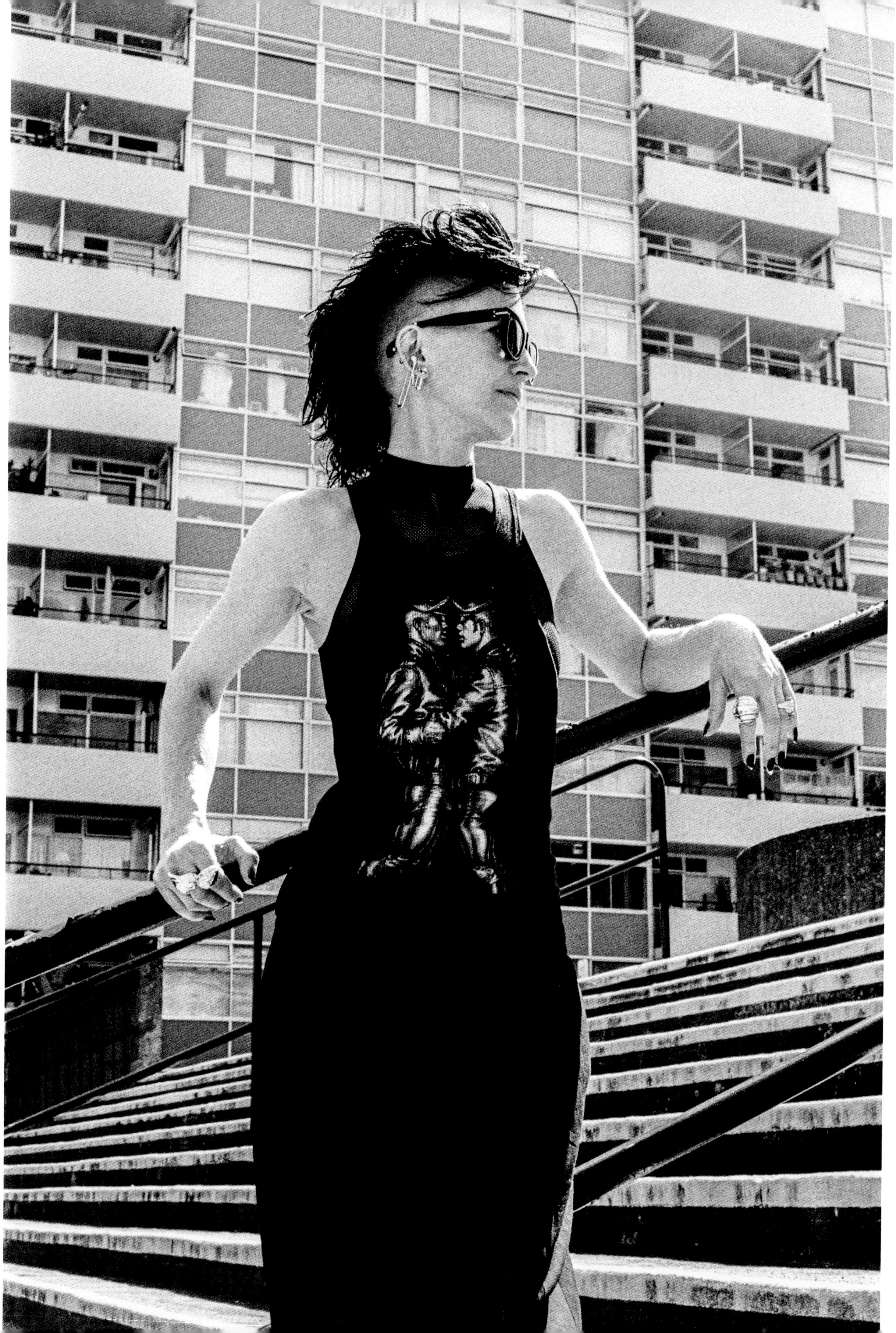

Competition is always fierce at CSM, but so is camaraderie. Students work hard, party harder, and push each other constantly. 'Her group was stylish, ambitious and unafraid of taking risks. It was a moment in time when they could immerse themselves fully in the creative process, figuring out who they were through the work they made. And Hannah, from the very start, had a clear aesthetic – bold, sculptural, unapologetic', he adds.

London offered more than just an education – it granted access to music, nightlife and an entire subculture of inspiration. 'This was where Hannah discovered mosh pits, underground clubs and the visceral energy of the city. That world fed into her work. Jewellery-making is exhausting, exhilarating. It's never just a solitary act – it's about being in the middle of things, absorbing, reflecting and then creating.'

In her second year at CSM, Hannah received the prestigious Cartier Award and moved temporarily to Paris to fulfill an apprenticeship in the world of high jewellery. 'Working there was an eye-opener for her', Simon recalls. 'She was surrounded by extraordinary craftsmanship, beauty and legacy. But something about it didn't feel quite right. She didn't belong on the Place Vendôme.'

london calling < 45

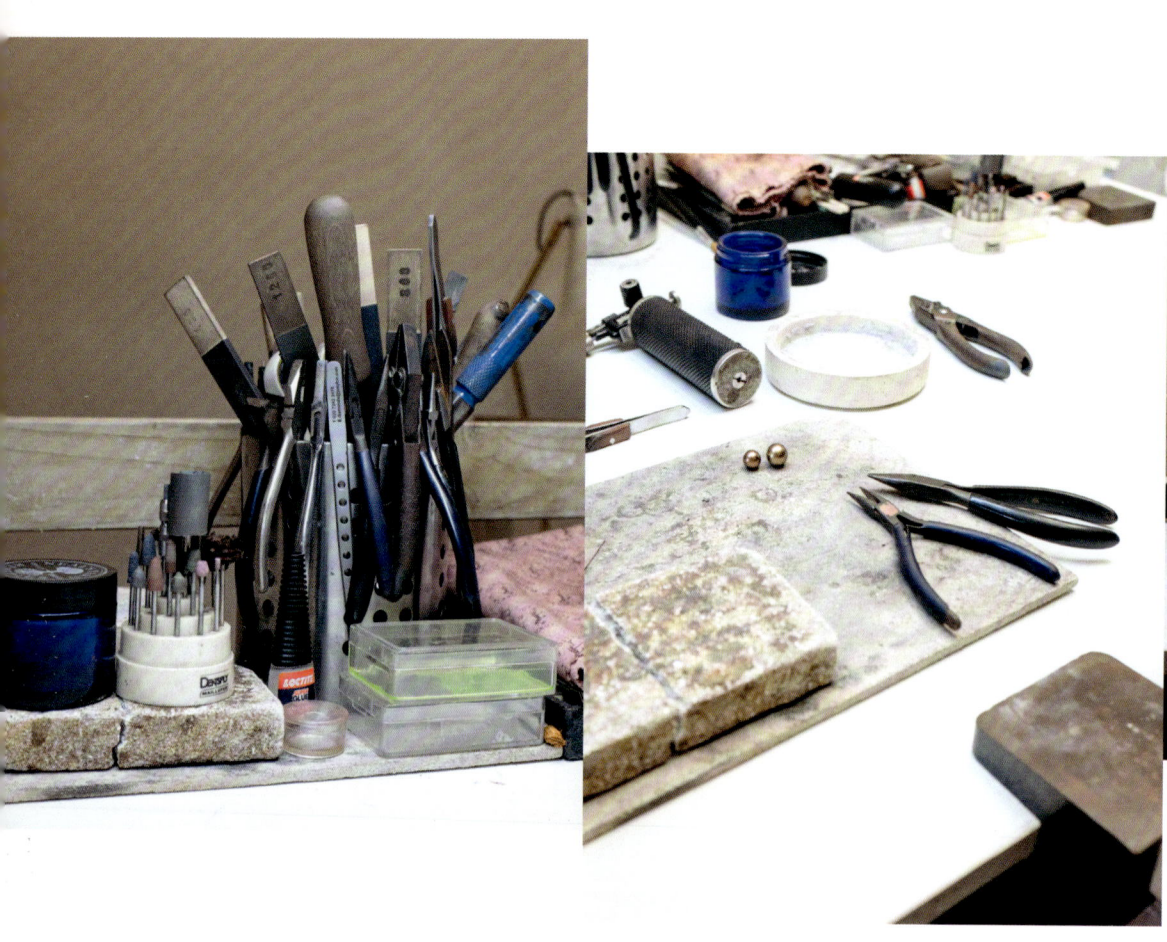

A single conversation with Simon changed everything. 'She credits me with the realisation that she could define jewellery on her own terms', he said. 'I'm not sure I deserve it, but I was glad to help her see that she didn't have to fit within an established mould. She had the power to make jewellery whatever she wanted it to be.'

Though head of the high jewellery atelier made it clear she wanted Hannah to stay on, the young designer declined. The moment was transformative. Hannah decided not to conform and returned to London determined to pursue her own vision. 'It takes courage to do that', Simon observes. 'There she was, being offered a place in a world that many designers would kill for, and she said, "No, I have my own ideas." That's when she truly stepped into herself.'

At the time when delicate, feminine, boho jewellery was all the rage, Hannah ran against the current, instead voicing a more imposing, angular, masculine aesthetic with her graduation collection. These were jewels that, at least nominatively, were designed for men, yet they were so compelling that girlfriends might co-opt them, as they would an oversized jean jacket or a man's shirt. Creative types, musicians first among them, took notice. In 2010, that stance would lead to the Albion Trinketry collection, a line designed in collaboration with Pete Doherty of The Libertines that was snapped up by other musicians, hellraisers, artists and creatives in art, architecture, design and fashion.

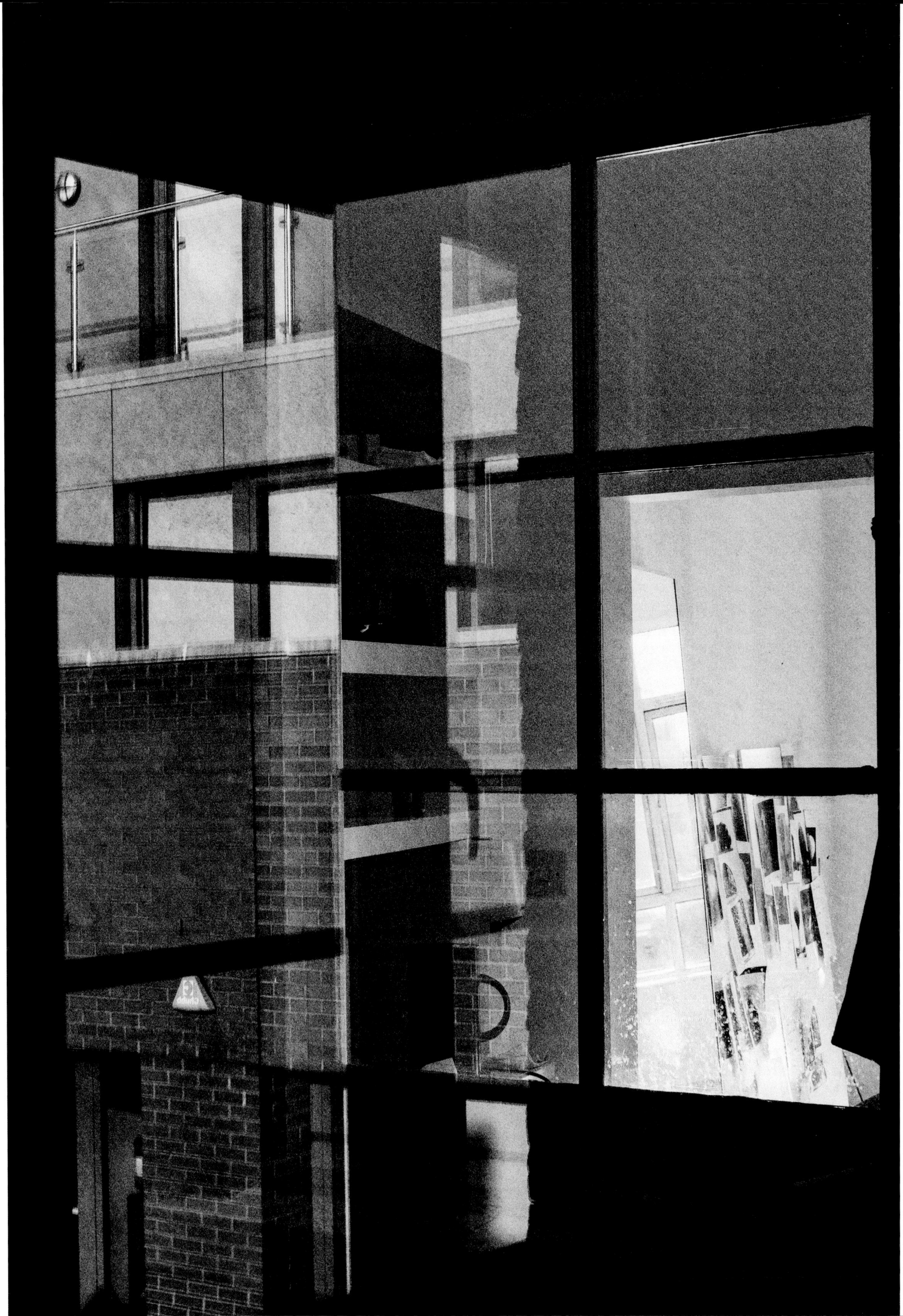

48 > london calling

Hannah's graduation collection of 2005 is what drew Michael Urbančík, Hannah's head of production and all-around right-hand man, into her orbit. 'One of the first pieces by Hannah that I ever encountered was her Spur Ring', he recalls. 'I had never seen anything like it. That's when I realised that jewellery could be made differently.'

In Hannah's creative explorations, one gleans a personal mappemonde that radiates outward from Central Saint Martins' former location, in Holborn.

'There was this core group of us who were just literally obsessed and wanted to be there all the time, making stuff in the workshop.' Struck by their dedication, some of the school's technicians, like Chris Howes and Campbell Muir stayed long after regular hours just to let the budding designers stay at the bench. 'They had all the time in the world for us', Hannah reminisces. 'That doesn't happen anymore.'

Above: Central Saint Martins graduate collection campaign, shot at The George Tavern, London, 2005.

Opposite: Spur Pendant on Pearls, 18ct gold & black pearls 2005, and Monumental Arc Ring, 18ct gold, 2014.

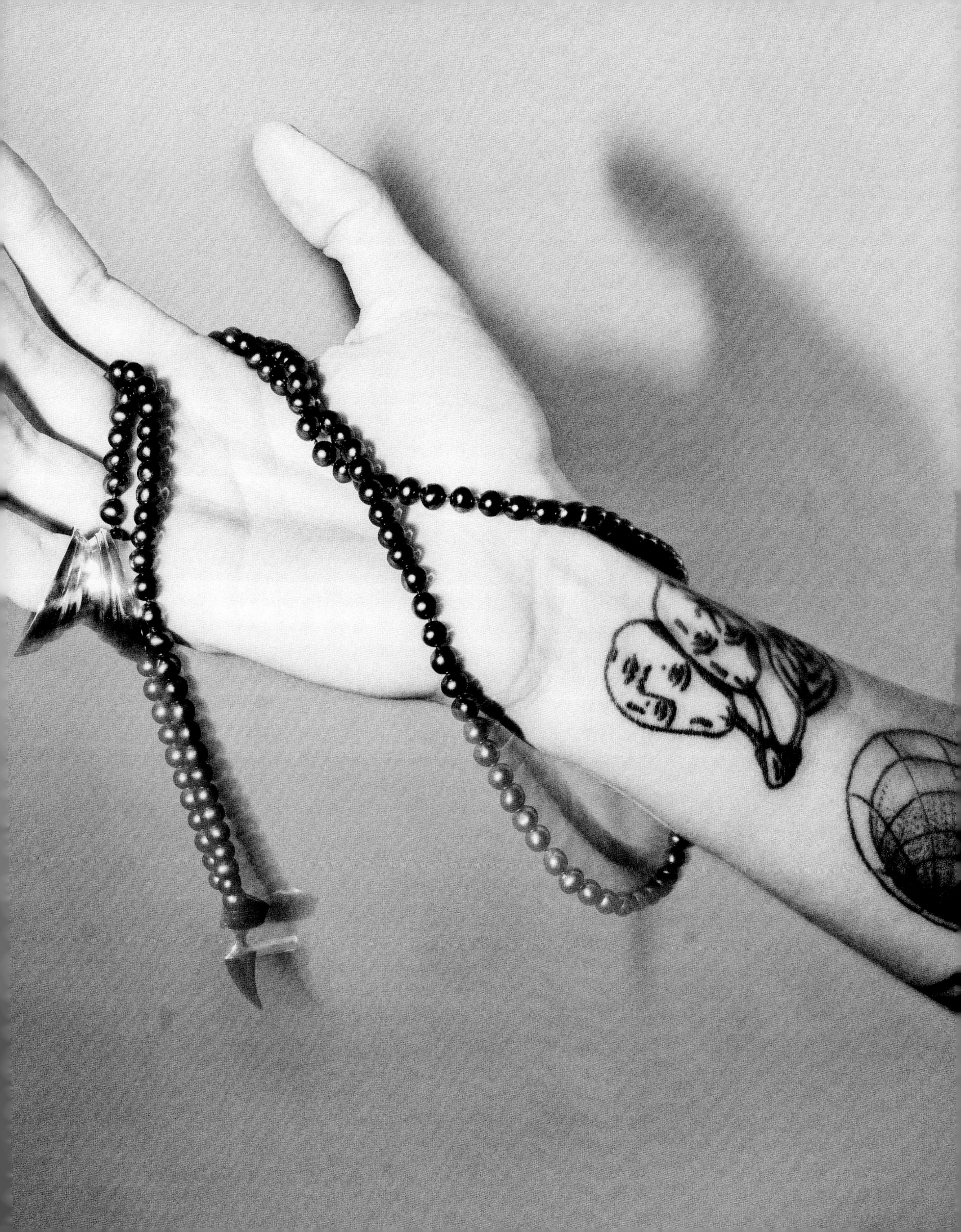

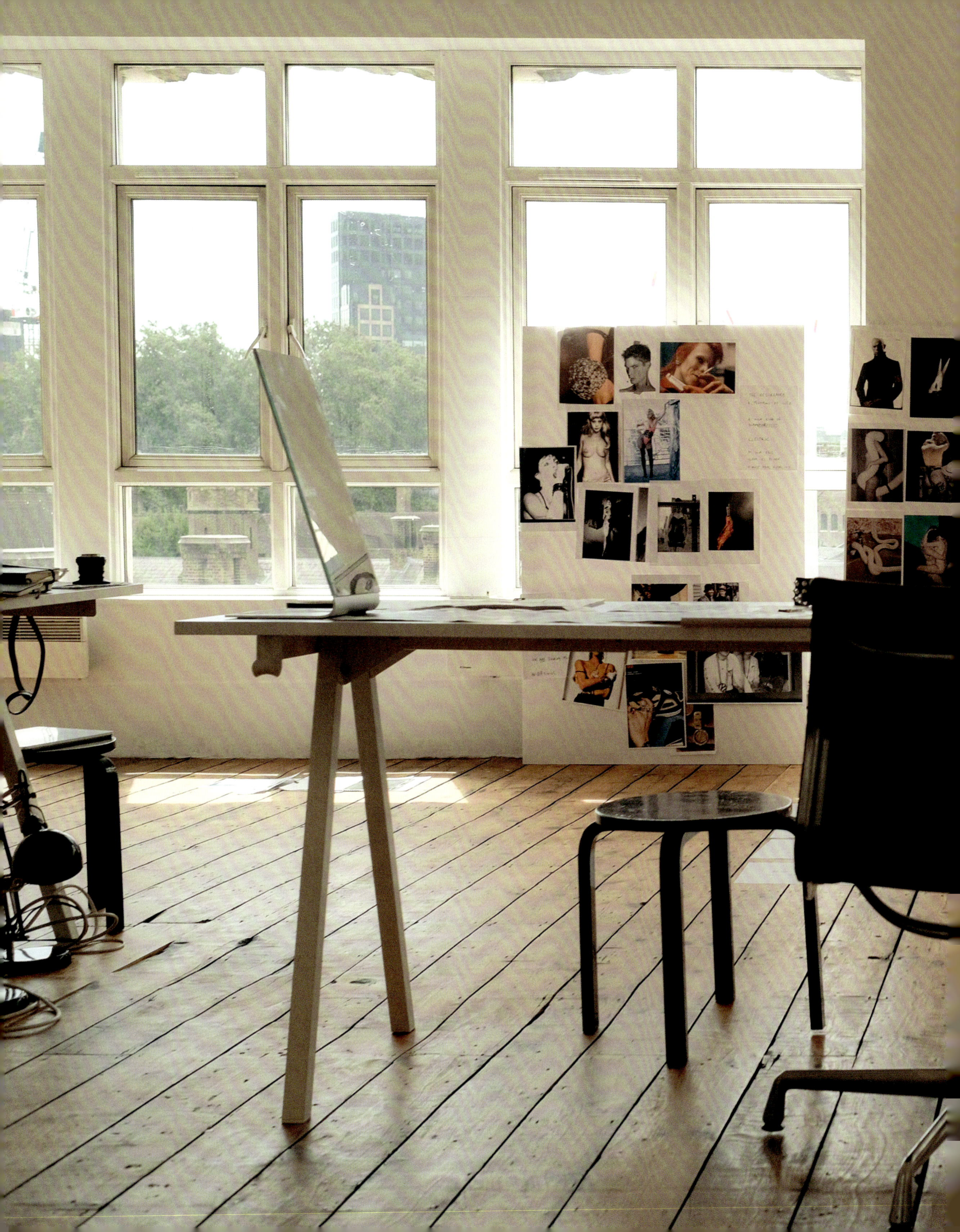

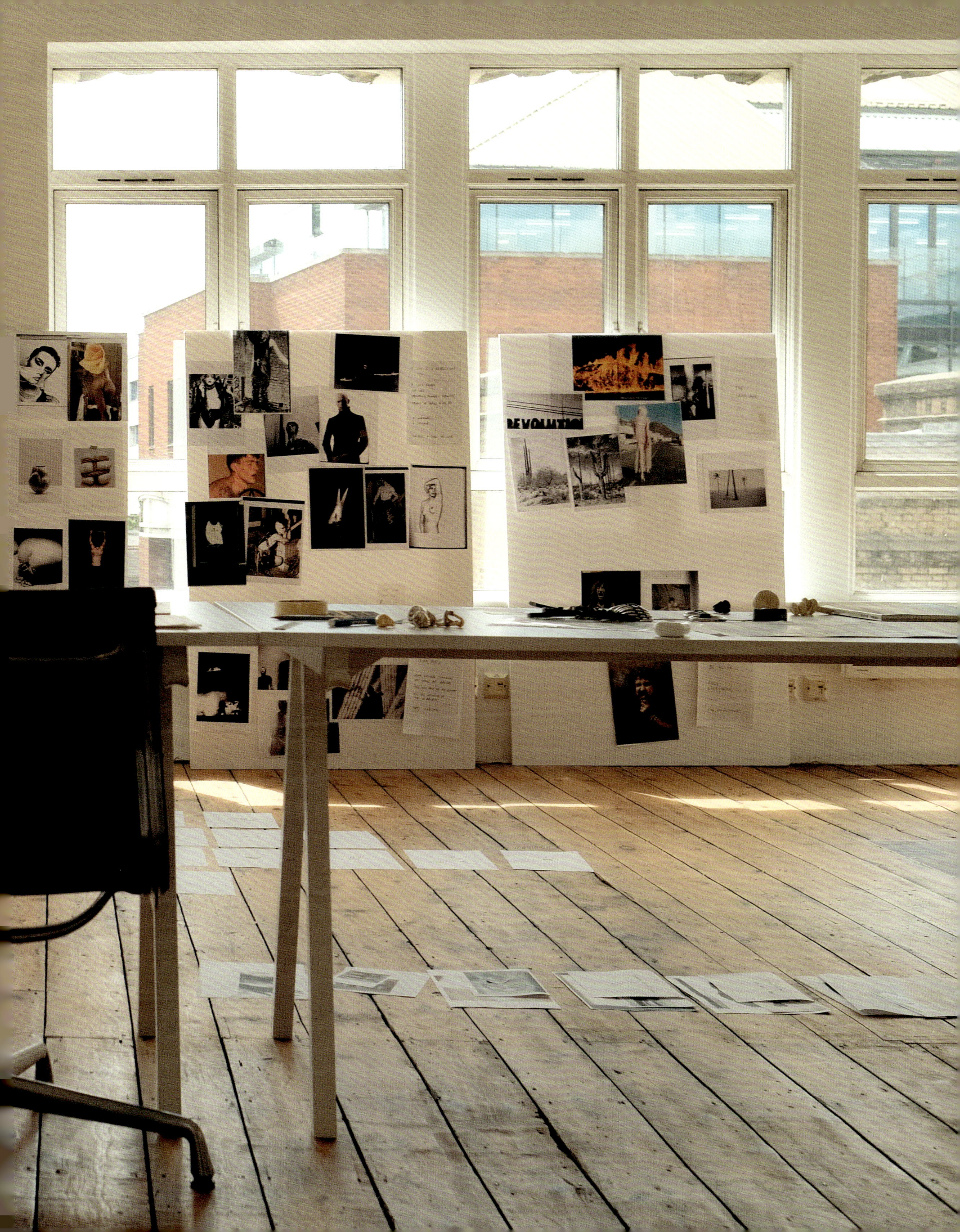

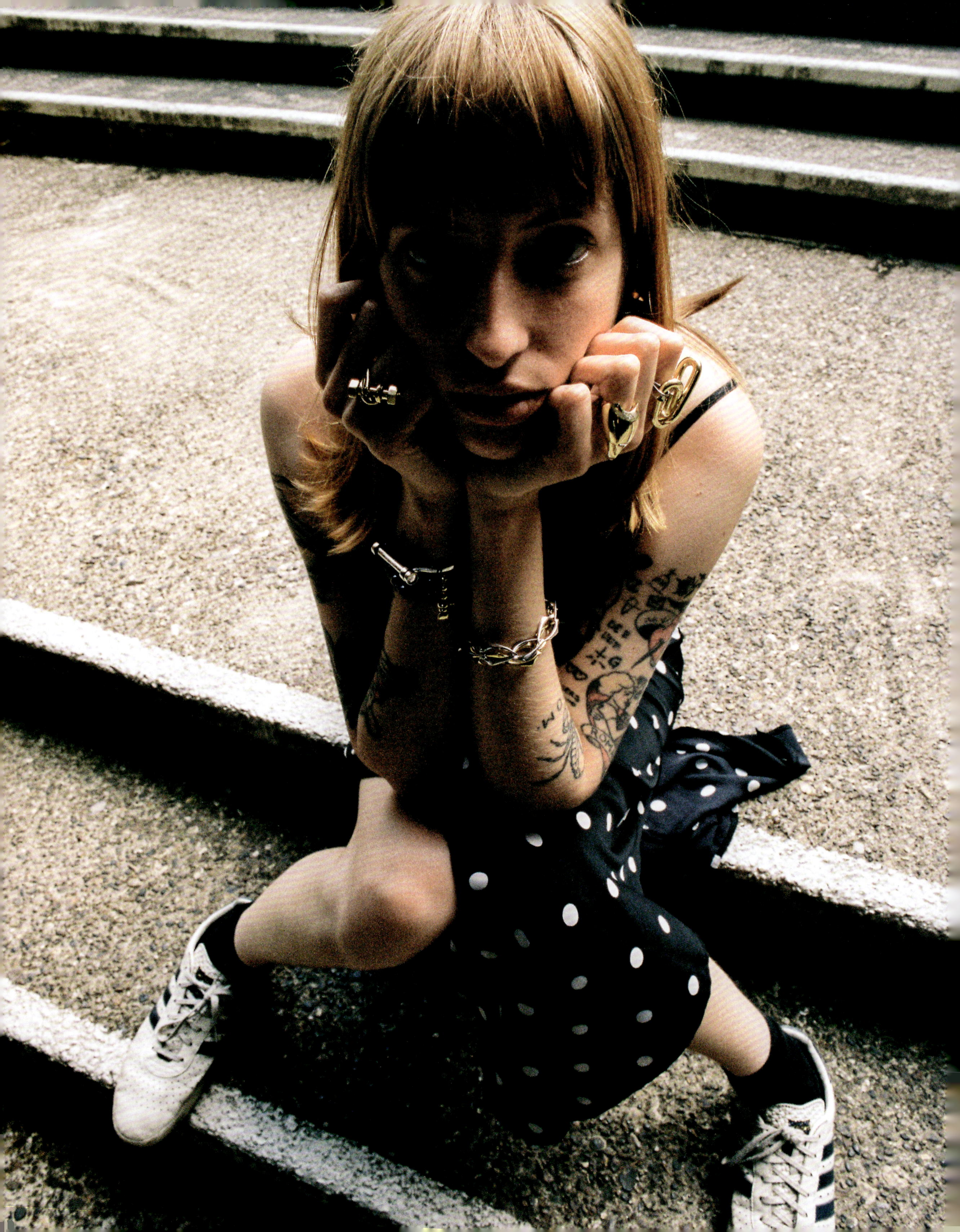

A New Act Of Rebellion, 2020.
Pierced Armour Ring and Rebel
Bolt Ring, 18ct gold.

It's Only Rock 'n' Roll, 2005.
Rock 'n' Roll Bracelet,
18ct gold.

Neighbourhood by neighbourhood, East London shaped her world. Home was Hackney, its streets vibrating with the kind of untamed creativity a young artist needs to thrive. Its markets and workshops offered up inspiration and room for experimentation; its pubs were packed with other fledgling designers likewise lost in their own world, free to make mistakes and learn from them.

Clerkenwell, by contrast, brought Hannah one step closer to structure, a bridge from the freewheeling improv of art school to the realities of building a business. 'My first studio at 1 Back Hill was tiny, but it was mine. I spent countless hours there, sketching, experimenting, failing, refining and trying again. That space became an extension of myself', she recalls.

Through word of mouth, she found a bigger space, a workshop in a late 19th-century building behind the historic Charterhouse. Eventually, a series of coincidences led her to a new apartment in the Barbican complex. From her perch in that monument of Brutalist architecture, Hannah need only gaze out over her balcony to commune with a skyline that – like her – thrives on contrast.

london calling < 53

54 > london calling

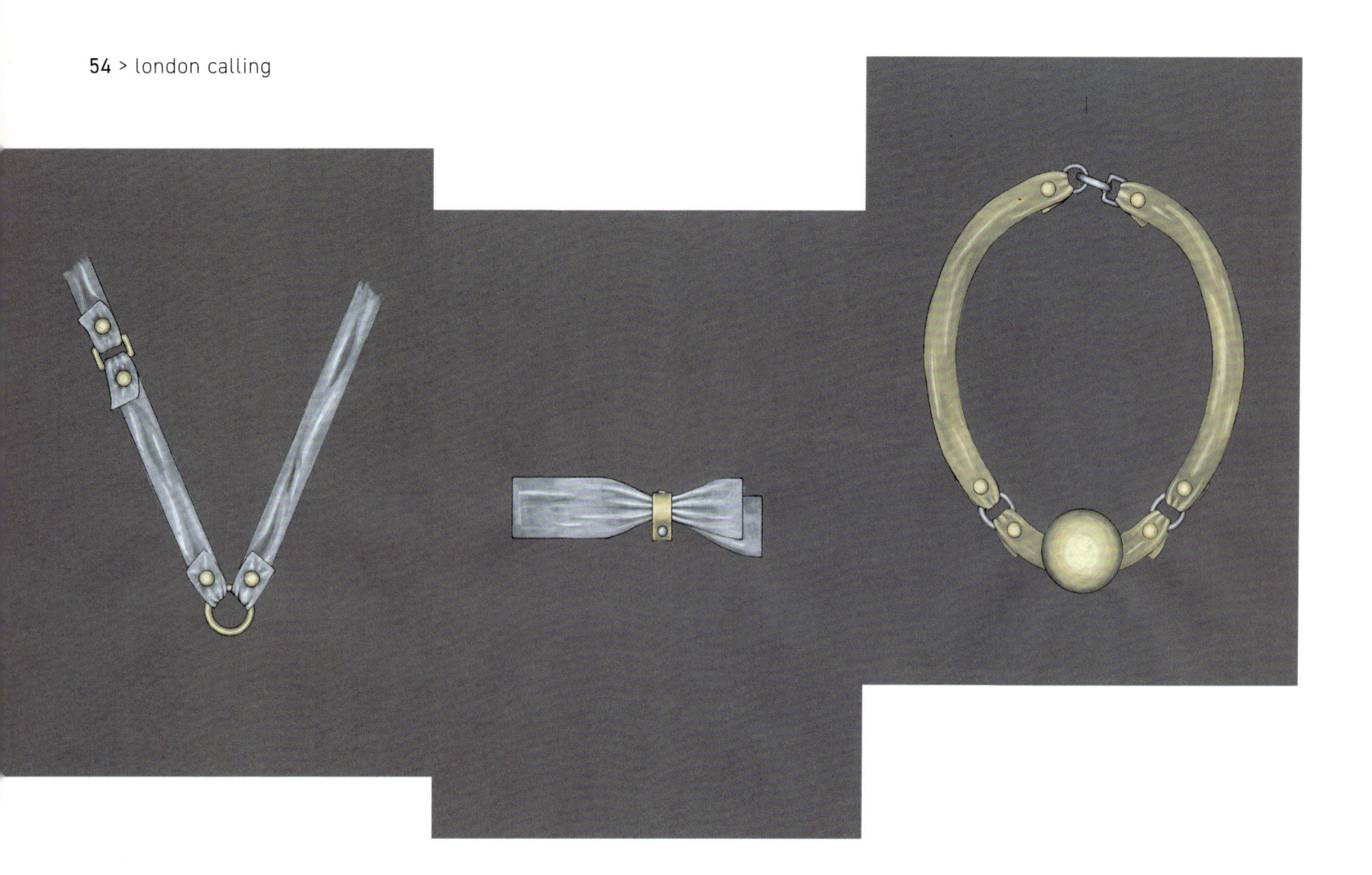

From Graduation to The Perfect Drug

For Hannah, jewellery-making is not only about aesthetics, it's about authorship. 'I make my jewellery in London so I can control the whole entire process. When you produce overseas, you have less control over who makes it, how it gets made and under what conditions', she notes. Producing locally lets her be uncompromising about every piece and detail.

Even so, she'll cross borders in search of the right kind of craftsmanship. Hannah and her team spent months scouring the globe for craftsmen able to develop chainmail with a ribbon-like suppleness to use for pieces in The Perfect Drug, a line introduced in autumn 2024. They found them in a tiny workshop in a remote part of the U.S.

'It's delicate and sensual and exquisitely made', the designer notes of the chainmail she worked into bracelets inspired by the all-access wristbands that are badges of honour among music fans everywhere. 'When you're working with artisans in the same city, you can touch the metal, feel the weight, make instant adjustments. That level of control is something I wouldn't trade for anything in the world', she says.

The Perfect Drug, 2024.

Above: Hand-painted gouaches.

Opposite: Fluid Strap Two-Tone Chain, sterling silver chainmail and 18ct gold, 2024.

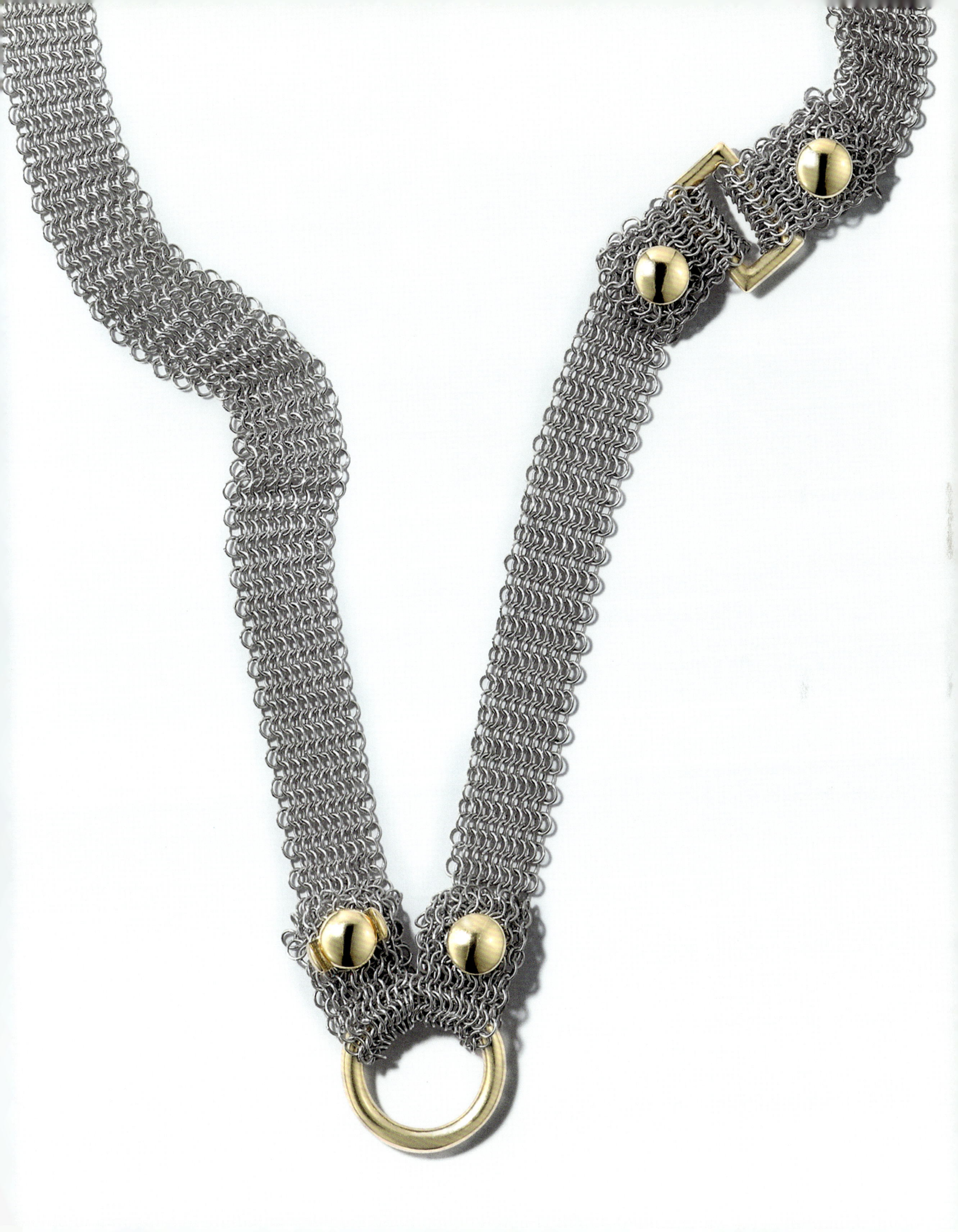

> london calling

At the bench creating
The Shamans Triangle Bangle,
2010.

Hannah's jewels are never just about ornamentation, let alone status. They are studies in precision, passion and deep technical expertise. Every piece she creates reflects the lessons learned at CSM, the streets she has walked, and the hands-on dedication that sets her apart in an ever-more crowded field. If London made her, now she holds up a mirror to the city she loves most and, through her jewellery, gives something back.

The Philosophy of Making

Beyond the technical mastery is an emotional component to her process that remains unchanged since her early days at CSM. The act of making is deeply personal – an extension of herself.

'There's something sacred about sitting at the bench, about physically shaping metal into something tangible. It's meditative. It's where I feel utterly connected to my work', she says.

That sense of connection resonates throughout Hannah Martin London collections, with each piece conveying a narrative, an energy, an essence of the city that shaped her. While beautiful, her designs eschew conventional beauty; while fashionable, they are unconcerned with trends, and though weighty, they do not speak to status. Rather, they elicit a sense of shared meaning.

'Every piece I design has a history, a purpose, a real backstory', Hannah explains. 'It connects back to the craftsmanship, the thought, the energy that went into its creation.'

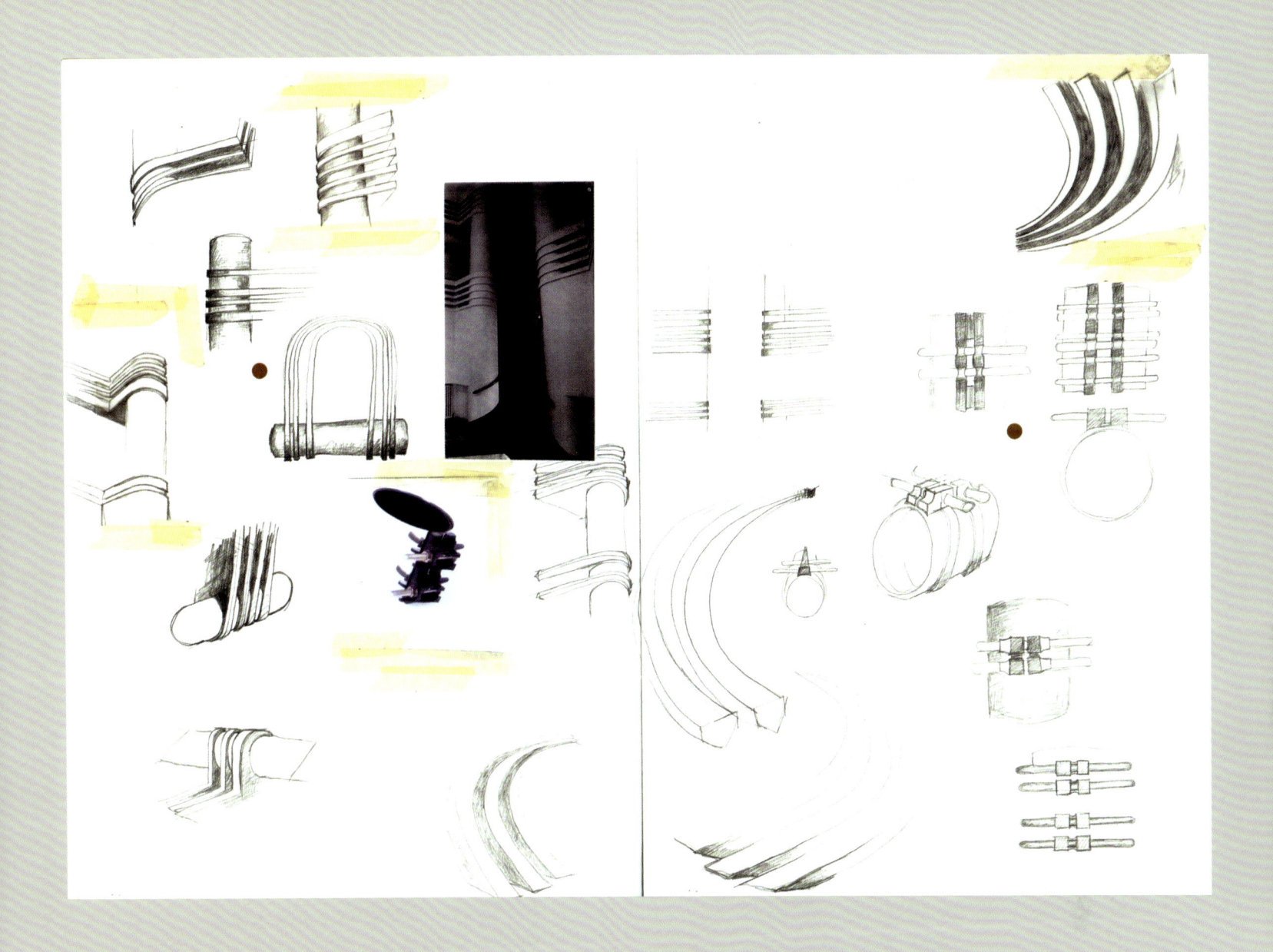

'If I exist as a designer, it's because all I have ever wanted is to make people feel something', she adds.

'I don't want my pieces to be disposable. I want them to mean something. To outlive me.' These are jewels to be worn constantly, to carry stories forward and be passed down.

Despite her deep roots in London, Hannah is always looking ahead to new collections, fresh collaborations, other ways of pushing the boundaries of her craft. But no matter where her work takes her, the foundation remains the same: an unwavering commitment to skill, to integrity, to the city that made her.

More than a backdrop, London has shaped the contours of her journey. Its twists, turns, and detours are a part of Hannah's identity, as intrinsic to her art as the metal she works.

'Every piece I make carries a bit of London with it. The energy, the history, the craftsmanship – it's all there, in every detail. That's something I will never lose.'

london calling < 57

The Art of Restraint

As Hannah's work evolved, so did her understanding of holding back. 'Young designers want to put everything into a single collection', Simon Fraser observes. 'They want to show every idea at once. But great design requires editing. It's about knowing what to hold back, understanding that there's a lifetime ahead to explore different directions.'

Hannah mastered this balance early on. 'Her sense of scale and form is exceptional. It took time for her to refine it, but now it's completely sublime. She learned by watching people interact with her pieces – how they wore them, how they moved in them. That's the ultimate test.'

Asked what makes Hannah stand out beyond her talent, Simon offers an unexpected insight. 'She has a rare ability to trust. She hands over creative control when necessary, but she also trusts herself. That's powerful. It allows her work to evolve naturally.'

Double Pearl Shackle Choker, 18ct gold and black Akoya pearls, 2006.

That power has given her a presence as unmistakable as her jewels. 'Hannah still has the same energy I remember from her student days, but now it's magnified. Her confidence, her vision – it's all there. She's created a body of work that speaks for itself, that acts as her voice even when she isn't in the room', notes Simon.

Like every true creative, for Hannah the act of making is just as important as the final product. 'You have to live with your pieces, test them, understand how they interact with the world. She never stops experimenting.'

When an approach is this immersive, a designer can't help but inhabit her work. More than an aesthetic, Hannah Martin pieces tell stories. Each piece is an evolution of the one before it, reflecting a point in a life's journey. 'For Hannah, jewellery is more than an accessory. It's a statement, a philosophy, an identity. And that's rare', Simon concludes.

Red Silk

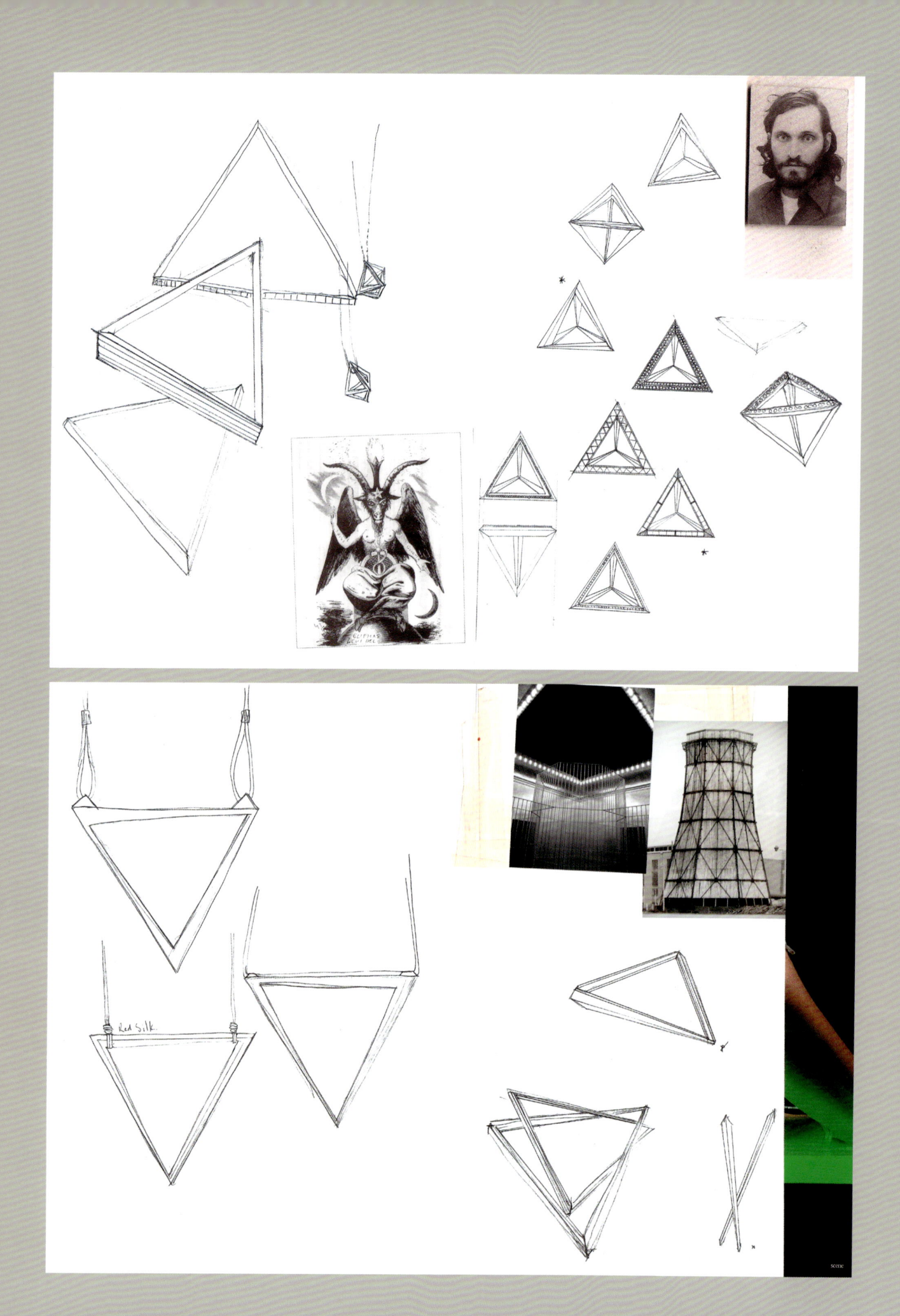

The Shaman's Triangle, 2011.
Series 01: The Man Who
Knows Everything.

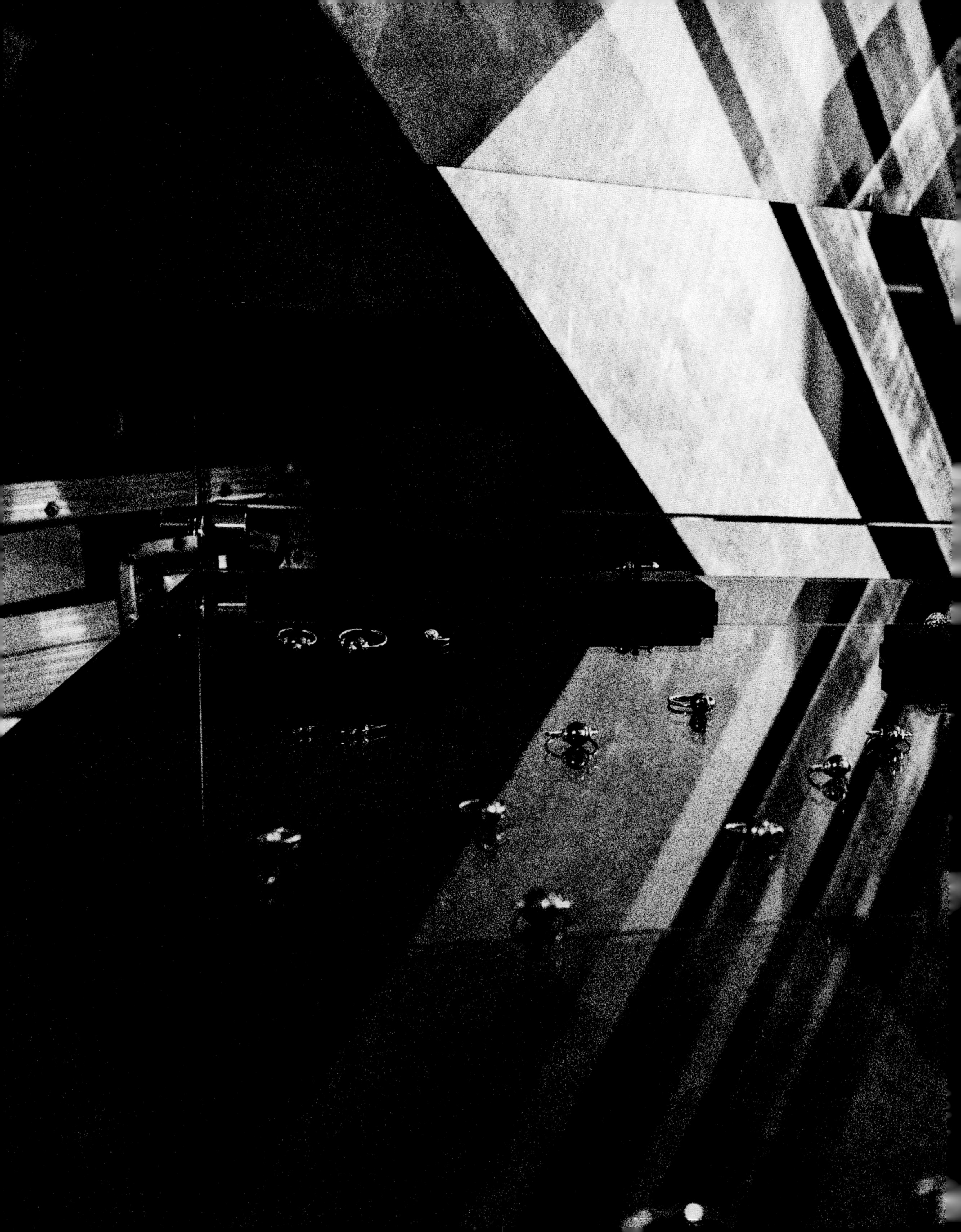

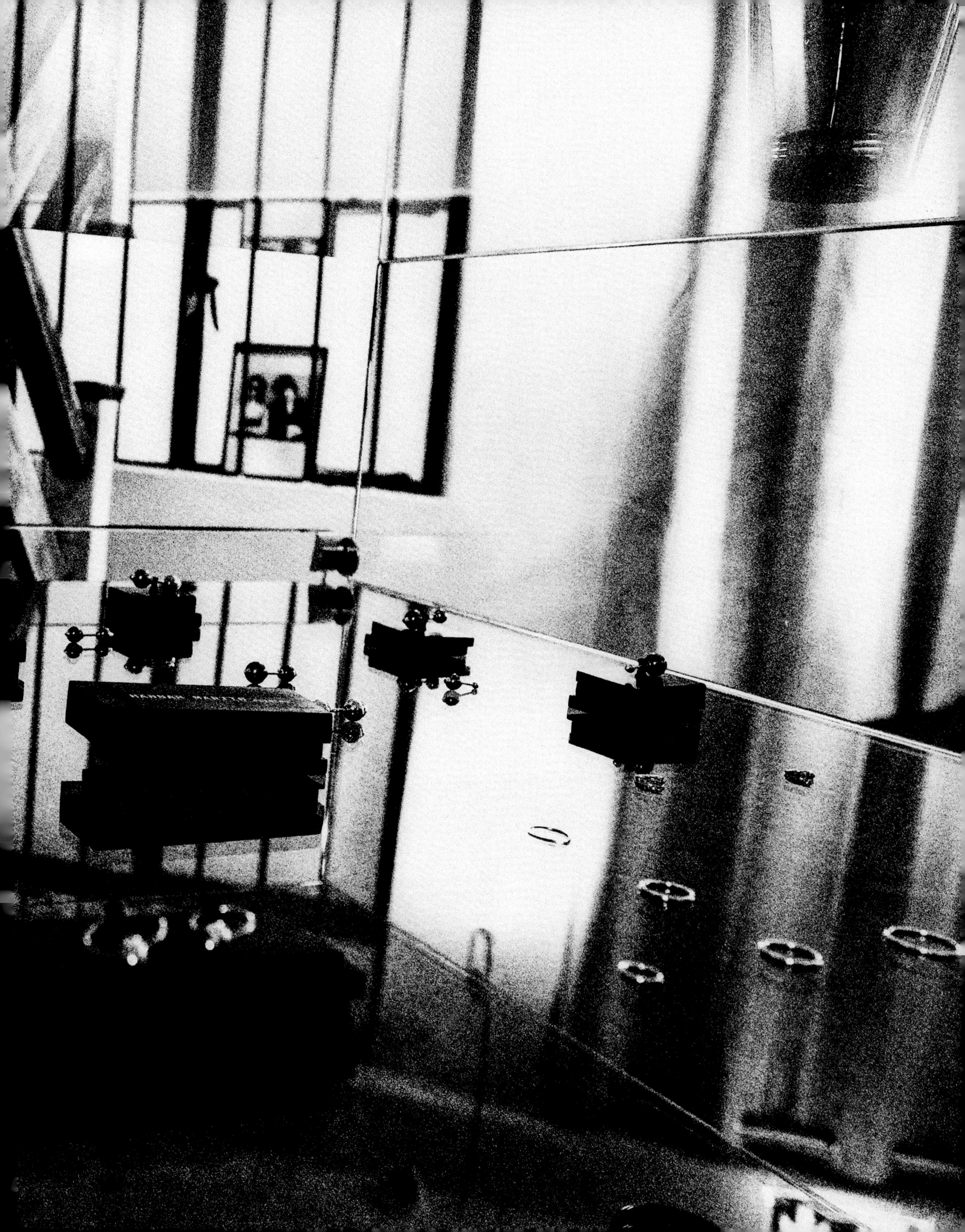

Delirium, 2014. Series 03: The
Man Who Knows Everything.

Somebody's Sins, 2016.
Possession Ring and Cuff,
18ct gold and cognac diamonds.

66 > london calling

A Vanitas, 2023.
'Remember you will die
(Please act accordingly)'.

' This collection sprung from a chance encounter on a Los Angeles to London flight when I met a man wearing one of my earrings, and both our lives changed. It's a rather extraordinary story. The 17th-century Dutch Masters created *Vanitas* paintings to evoke the fleeting nature of life. This collection takes that concept and expands it into a call to arms to make the most of every living moment. You never fucking know what's round the corner (or on an aeroplane). '

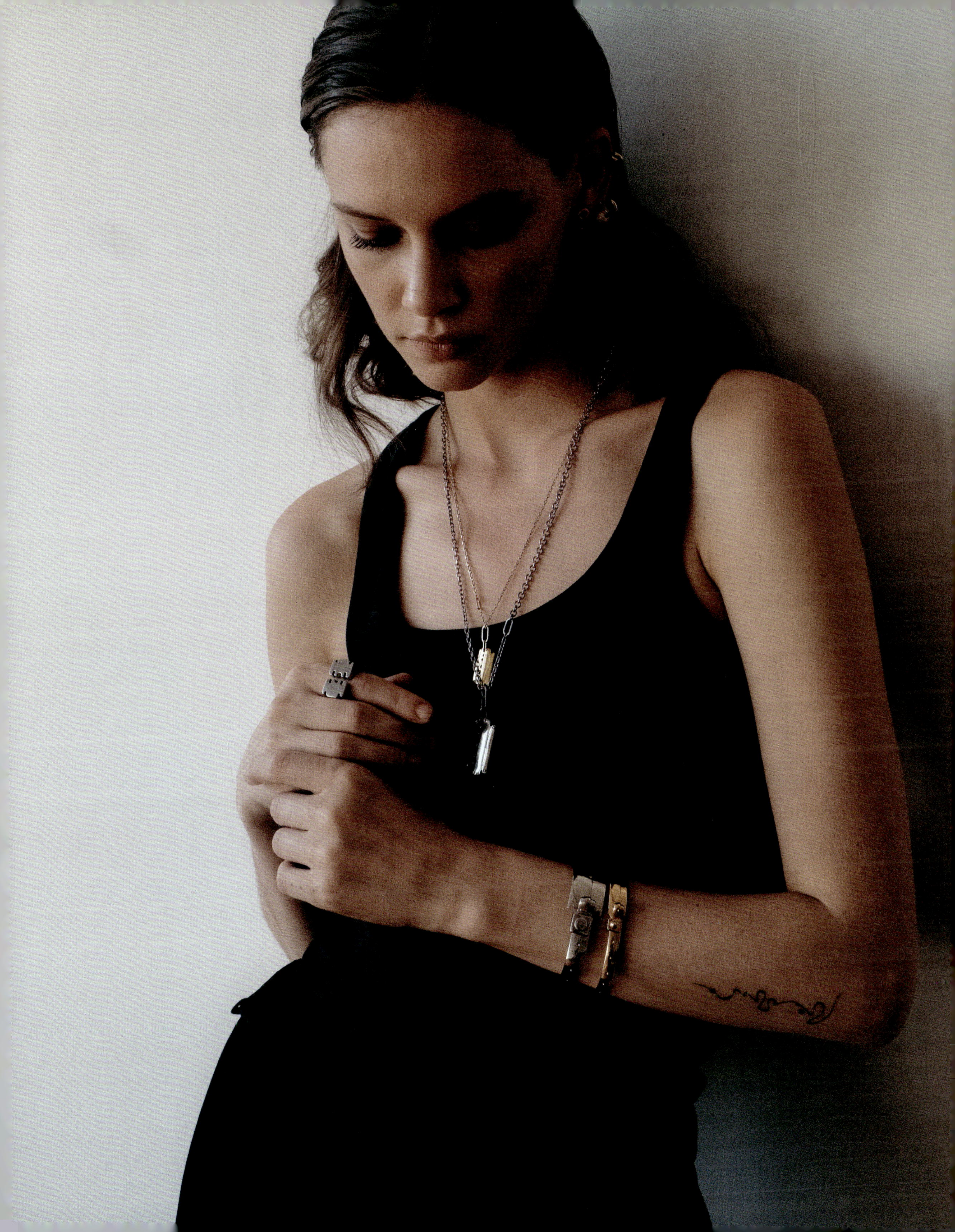

68 > london calling

Baxter Dury shot by Stewart Baxter, Barbican, 2021. Warrior Chain Necklace, 18ct gold, 2020.

london calling < 69

'Every piece I make carries a bit of London with it. The energy, the history, the craftsmanship – it's all there, in every detail. That's something I will never lose.'

london calling < 71

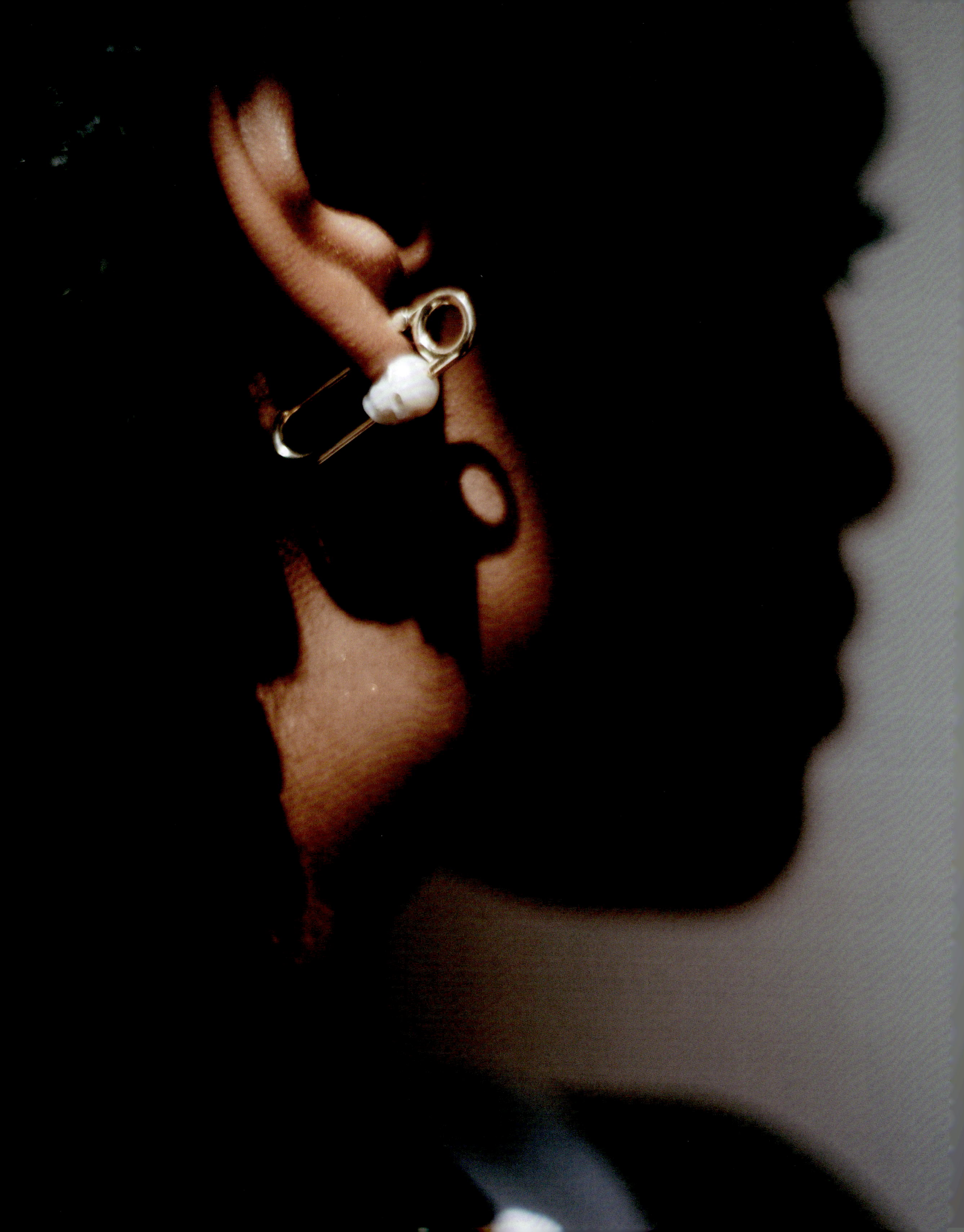

THE
MAKER AND
HER MUSIC

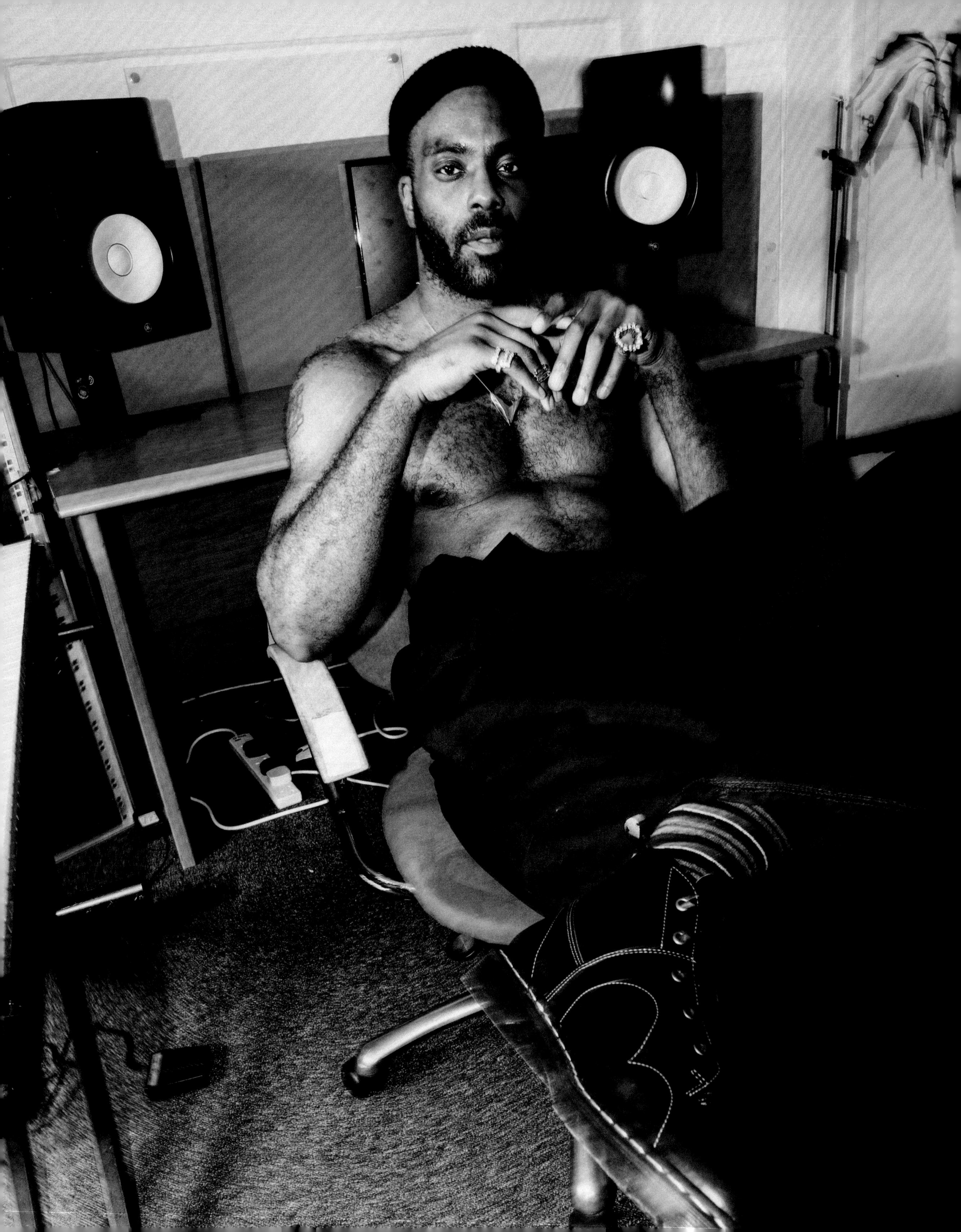

Chiedu Oraka shot by Stewart Baxter in the studio, Hull, 2024.

F or many designers, regardless of discipline, music is a creative spark. But for Hannah Martin, sound is even more elemental: music is her vital energy, her true north, a compass, a bridge for family divides, a way to access emotions that otherwise would lie forever out of reach.

Growing up in a rural neighbourhood on the outskirts of Bristol, she learned from her father – the son of a navy officer and an Argentinian immigrant, a graphic designer by trade and DJ by night – to embrace the fire of Sid Vicious and the Sex Pistols, the Rolling Stones.

'Dad dabbled in rebellion, but he was too much of a family man to be a true rebel', she says. 'Even so, he loved the bad behaviour.'

Her mother was a teacher, who would sit at the piano and improvise intricate melodies on a whim. From her, Hannah absorbed the power of self-invention/self-expression. In the evenings, she and her sister, Rosie, would sing along as their mother reprised tunes by Tom Paxton, Bob Dylan or June Tabor by ear. If school was a drag and dynamics of extended family were tangled, home was a haven, a loving space where self-invention was welcomed and encouraged.

For teenage Hannah – the doe-eyed, soft-spoken, odd-kid-out – punk and grunge provided armour against bullies, a way to forge an identity, a refuge, a means of tearing things down and staking out

the maker and her music < 75

76 > the maker and her music

her own place. An early infatuation with Nirvana anthems such as 'Love Buzz' and 'Sliver' brought Kurt Cobain to her bedroom, where he stayed, if only in poster form. When the singer died by his own hand, on 5 April 1994, Hannah boycotted school, instead locking herself in her room to mourn.

'I lit candles', she recalls. 'The music you're into at that stage in your life is deep in your soul. You're busy finding yourself, weaving your tapestry. I was convinced I'd lost the love of my life.'

The grunge scene coincided perfectly with her teenage angst and raging hormones. 'I probably fancied Courtney as much as Kurt', she said. 'The way she could rip up a ball gown and throw on a cheap tiara was a perfect way of saying, "I mock you and your references."'

Other musical acts filled out her personal landscape, among them Nine Inch Nails and Radiohead, Nick Cave and Patti Smith. To Hannah, these were not just artists, they were architects, builders of a wild and visual world.

They also personified, in their art and life, how pain could be reshaped into something compelling and powerful. Even as eyeglasses and orthodontia fell away and a swan began to emerge, Hannah refused to place stock in her own beauty. Instead, she craved escape.

The experience of embracing something extraordinary, far from the mainstream, someplace where she could find her people. Her tribe.

She found it in the mosh pit. There, amid a sea of writhing, sweating bodies, waves of relentless sound, Hannah experienced catharsis, transcendental moments, a salve for heartbreak, hurt and all the emotions she has always felt more keenly than most. Suddenly, pain morphed into something sublime.

Among artists, no one embodied transformation and what was not yet known as 'gender fluidity' more than David Bowie. His presence loomed large in the Martin landscape thanks to a favourite uncle. A miner turned forensic photographer, he was also the rock star's most ardent fan. 'Even when everything else in the world shifted, Bowie always remained', she recalls. 'Music has this staying power that connects people.'

Transcending nostalgia and interpersonal relationships, Bowie's work grew into a shared lexicon, a thread drawn from the family tapestry and rewoven into Hannah's work. Shapeshifting and audacious reinvention resonated with her taste for exploring sexuality and seduction, disruption and metamorphosis.

the maker and her music < 77

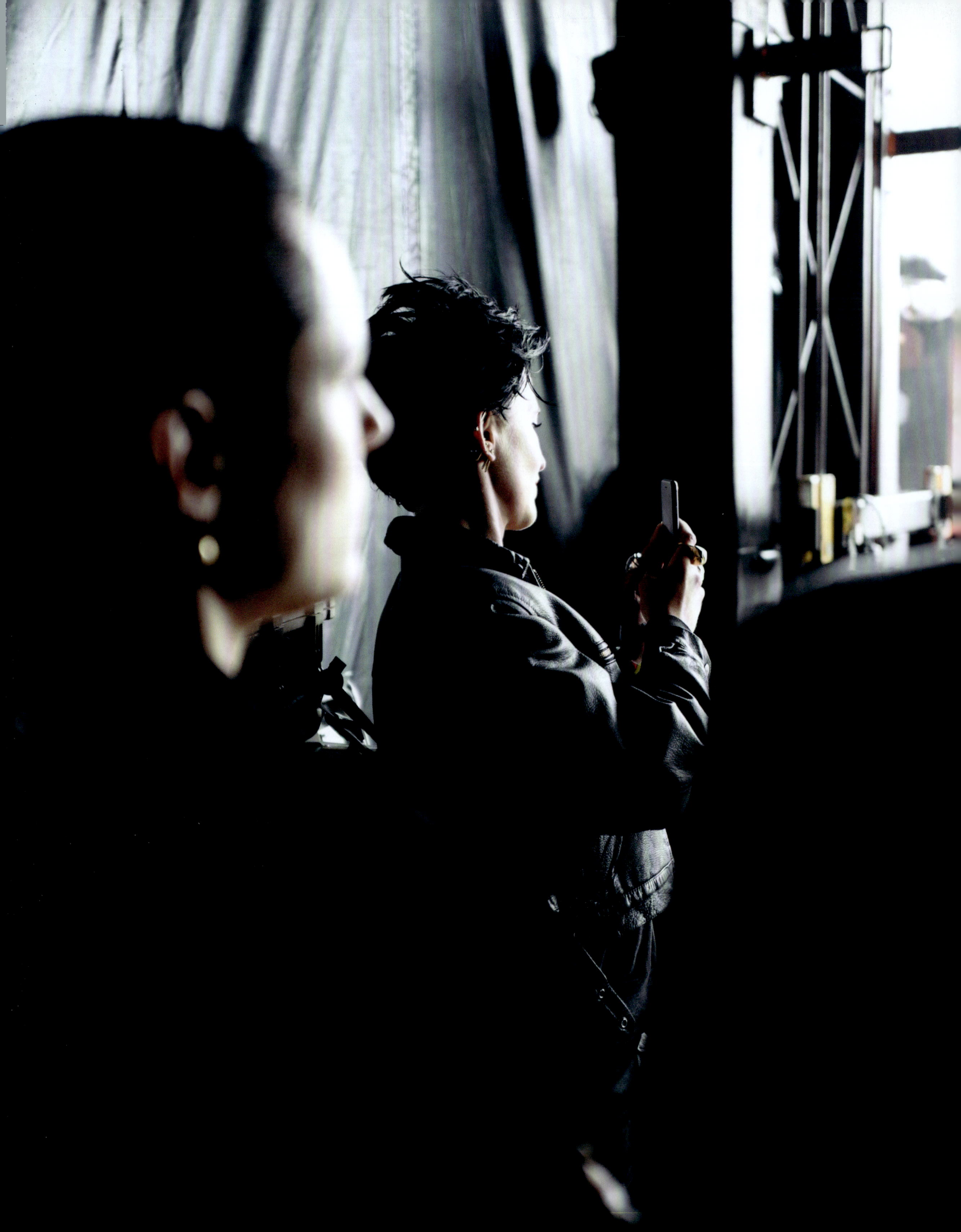

"Even when everything else shifts, music has this staying power that connects people."

80 > the maker and her music

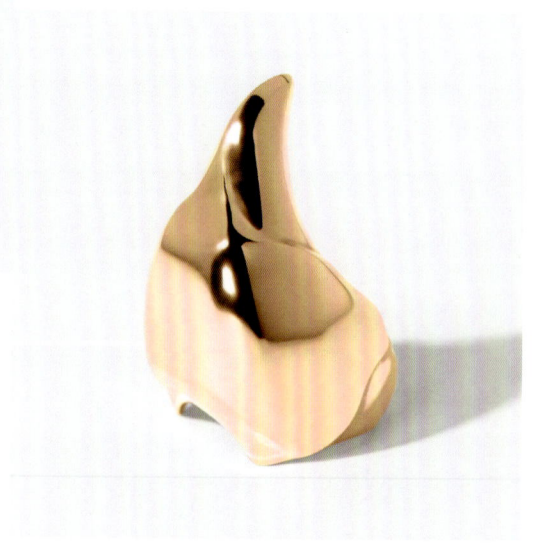

Her personal dialogue between the sacred and the profane took shape at the bench. There, her reverence for precious materials fused with irreverence for the status quo. Like the artists she admires, Hannah wanted to say something that mattered while also subverting convention through her work. *You want precious? I'll give you that – and more.*

But if rebellion forged her persona, the designer's relationship to music was also, essentially about finding the courage to connect. She'll describe one of her countless playlists with the same bright fervour that inspires her to trawl the internet for the perfect ball gag or cock ring to subvert it into a necklace in 18ct gold. Jewellery-making, like music, represents an act of defiance that provokes, awakens and demands a response.

'It's naughty, but that's the point', she says. Take a closer look and behold the power of becoming, the ecstasy of connection.

'It's all about feeling. It jars you. It's about creating something that didn't exist before, something that changes how you look at the world. And, like heartbreak, it reminds you that you're alive', Hannah says.

If you know, you know. You hear the music and you feel it – or you don't.

From left, The Monumental Arc Ring, 18ct gold, 2014; Secret Stud Ring, 18ct gold and sapphires, 2005; Imperial Eagle Icon Ring, 18ct gold, 2009.

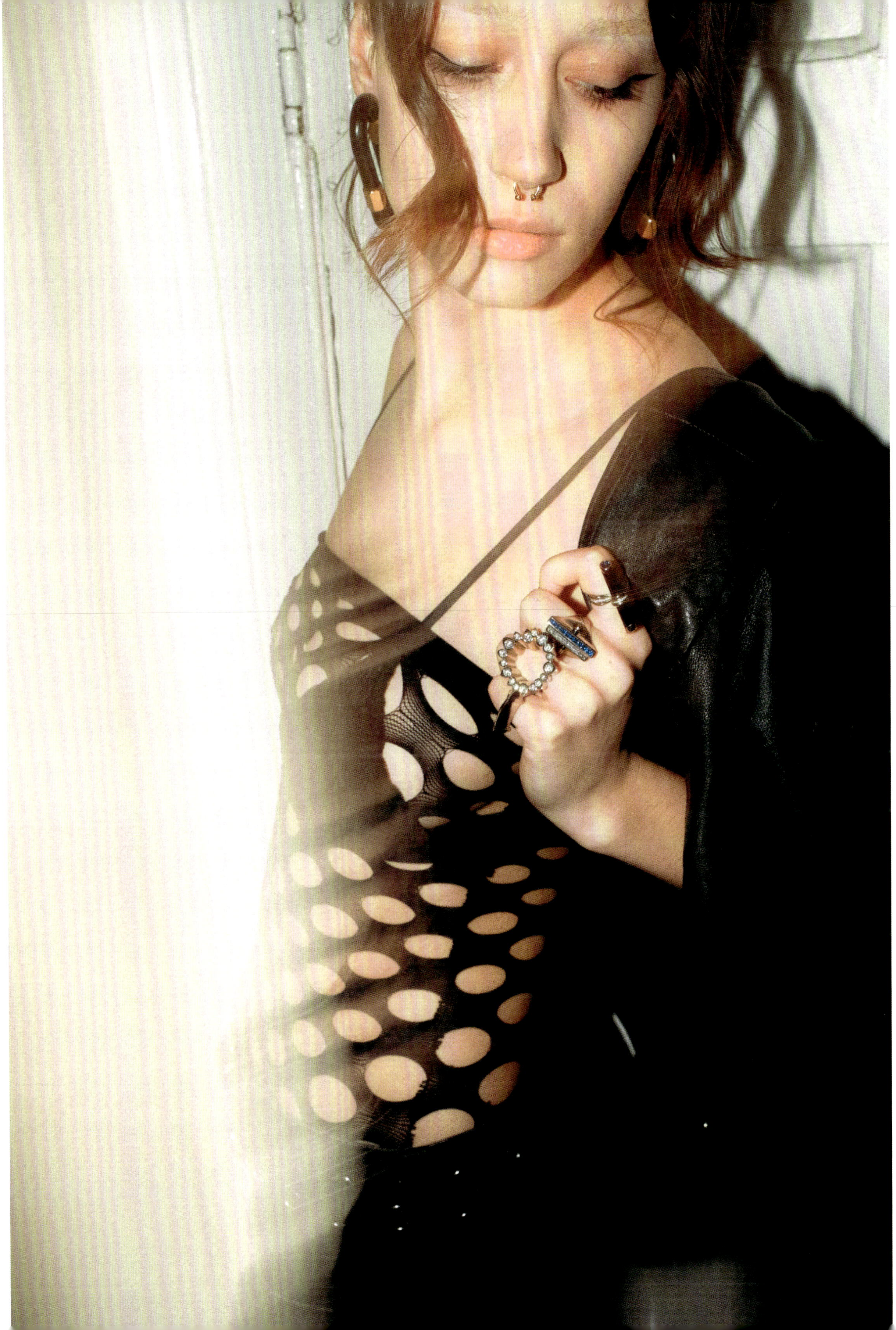

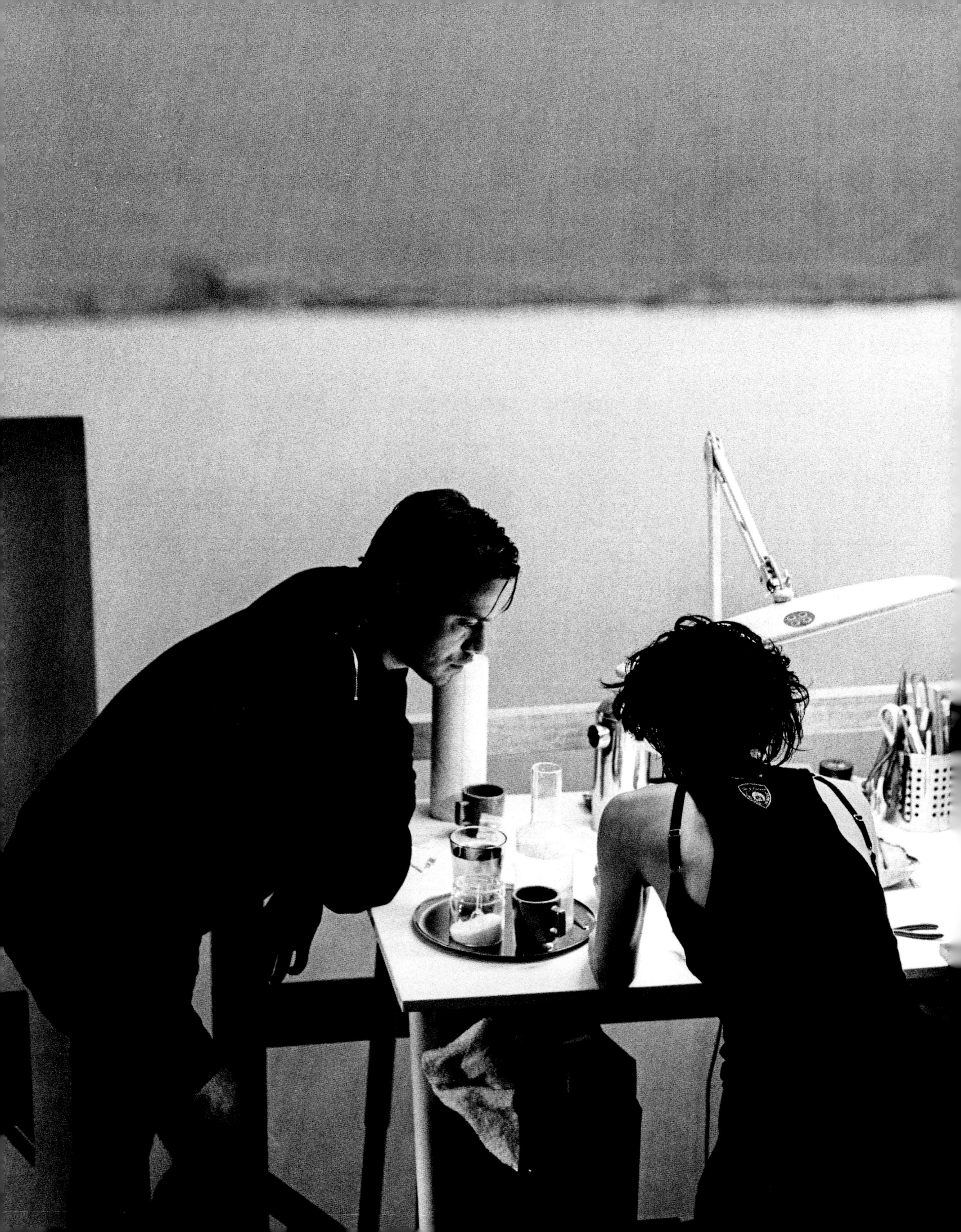

A Rhythm All Her Own

Hannah's lifeline – her strength, her personal wellspring – is music. Her relationship to it is layered, complex and, ultimately, transformative, much like her designs.

Before a collection has a name, a theme, a look, it has a soundtrack. Eventually, those songs will be released as a playlist to accompany the jewels, like a bonus track for added context and depth. But mostly, these compilations are an act of generosity, a tradition in the Hannah Martin studio since 2005, well before playlists became common currency, let alone marketing tools.

Hannah's longtime collaborator, Michael Urbančík, is as close to his boss as anyone who is not a lover can be. He describes her creative process with quiet admiration: jewellery people are more comfortable expressing themselves through their gestures, not words.

'She basically locks herself away with music and images, and then two weeks later she comes out with sketches', he says. Like a portal, music lets her access a place where the ordinary melts

Sketches for The Perfect Drug, 2024.

the maker and her music < 83

84 > the maker and her music

away and bold, provocative ideas take form. 'It's not a passive relationship; it's an active exchange. The music feeds her spirit', he explains. Like the bands she admires, sound sharpens her focus, emboldens her designs and helps her resist conformity.

What most might hear as a sequence of sounds, Hannah feels as texture. As emotion. A shapeshifter, not unlike the precious metals she melts, casts and solders into jewels that are more wearable art than status symbol, though they are that, too. Wrought in chainmail or set with carved stones, they occupy space on the skin with the intensity of sound. Honest, raw, unapologetic and utterly unforgettable, they are like a song that swells into an anthem. Pretty soon, you can't imagine living without it.

If Hannah hadn't become a jeweller, Michael reckons she might have found her way from the mosh pit into the music industry. 'It just oozes out of her, so whatever the endeavour is, it would always have to be creative, almost primal', he observes. An expression of desire, of joy, of longing, of lust. 'It's like her work resonates with the energy of whatever she's been listening to. The songs that fill the studio fuel her vision. It's a total osmosis.'

Though their tastes in music do not always align, its power to bring disparate elements together into a cohesive whole mirrors their dynamic: a rare partnership based on trust and mutual challenge.

Mez Sanders-Green, *LIFE* shot by Stewart Baxter in the studio, Hull, 2024.

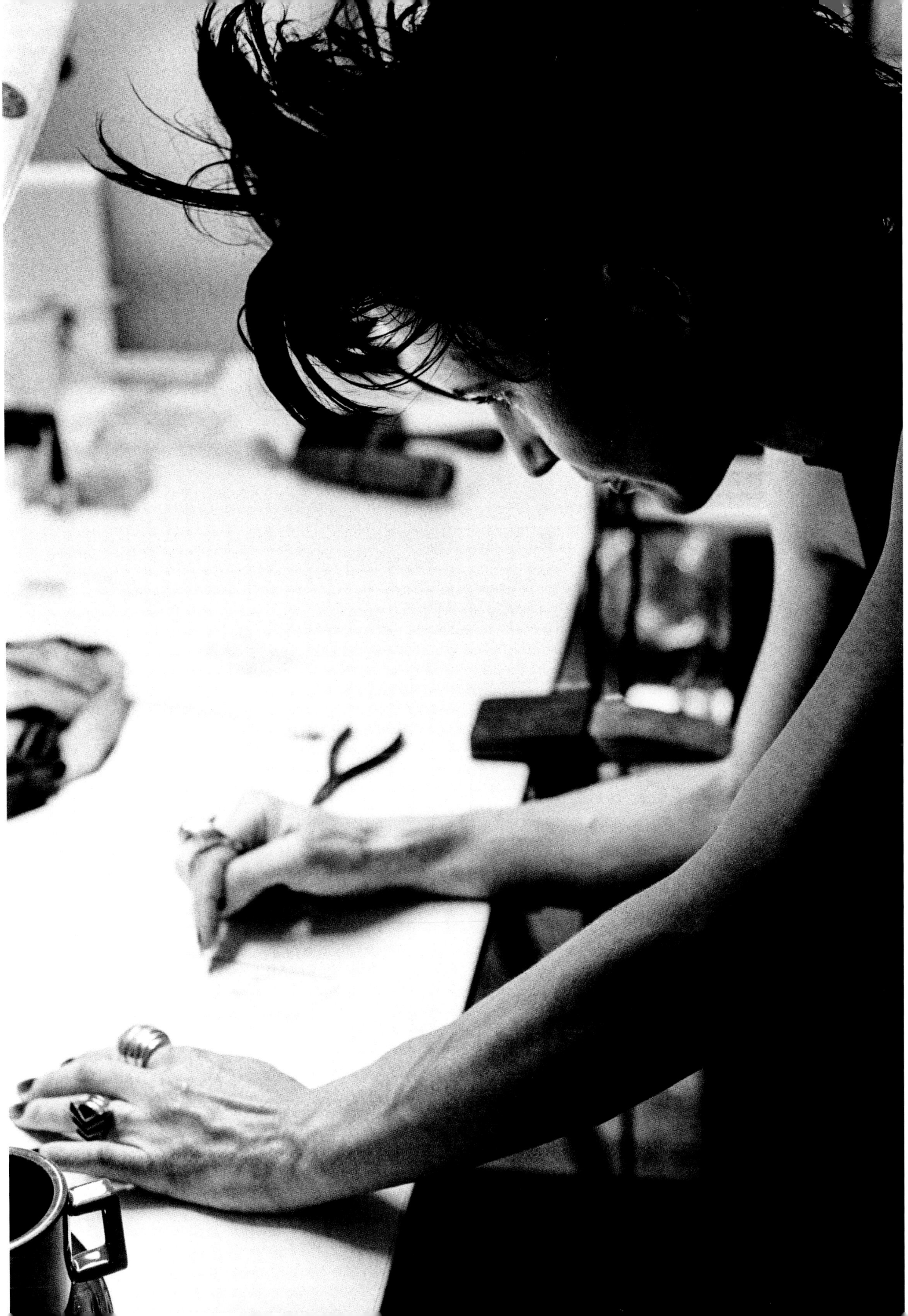

86 > the maker and her music

In the studio, with music rolling through the space, Hannah's creativity shines bright. 'She works intuitively, fearlessly, always striving for something that resonates not just visually but emotionally', notes Michael, likening Hannah to the sculptor who patiently pares away to reveal a truth that's invisible to everyone else. If each new design is Hannah's alone, they fine-tune the details together, honing down one-tenth of a millimetre at a time until a piece is ready to go out into the world.

Being an independent designer comes with a unique set of pressures: there is the business aspect to manage, and the constant expectation of newness, of conjuring something out of nothing that is distinctively yours. Michael sees Hannah's ability to compartmentalise as both a coping mechanism and a creative necessity. By immersing herself in music, she can shut the door and connect with the essence of her work. It's in those private moments, that her most daring ideas are born.

Opposite top: Sketches for A New Act of Rebellion, 2020.

Bottom: Sketches for It's Only Rock 'n' Roll, 2005.

the maker and her music < 87

88 > the maker and her music

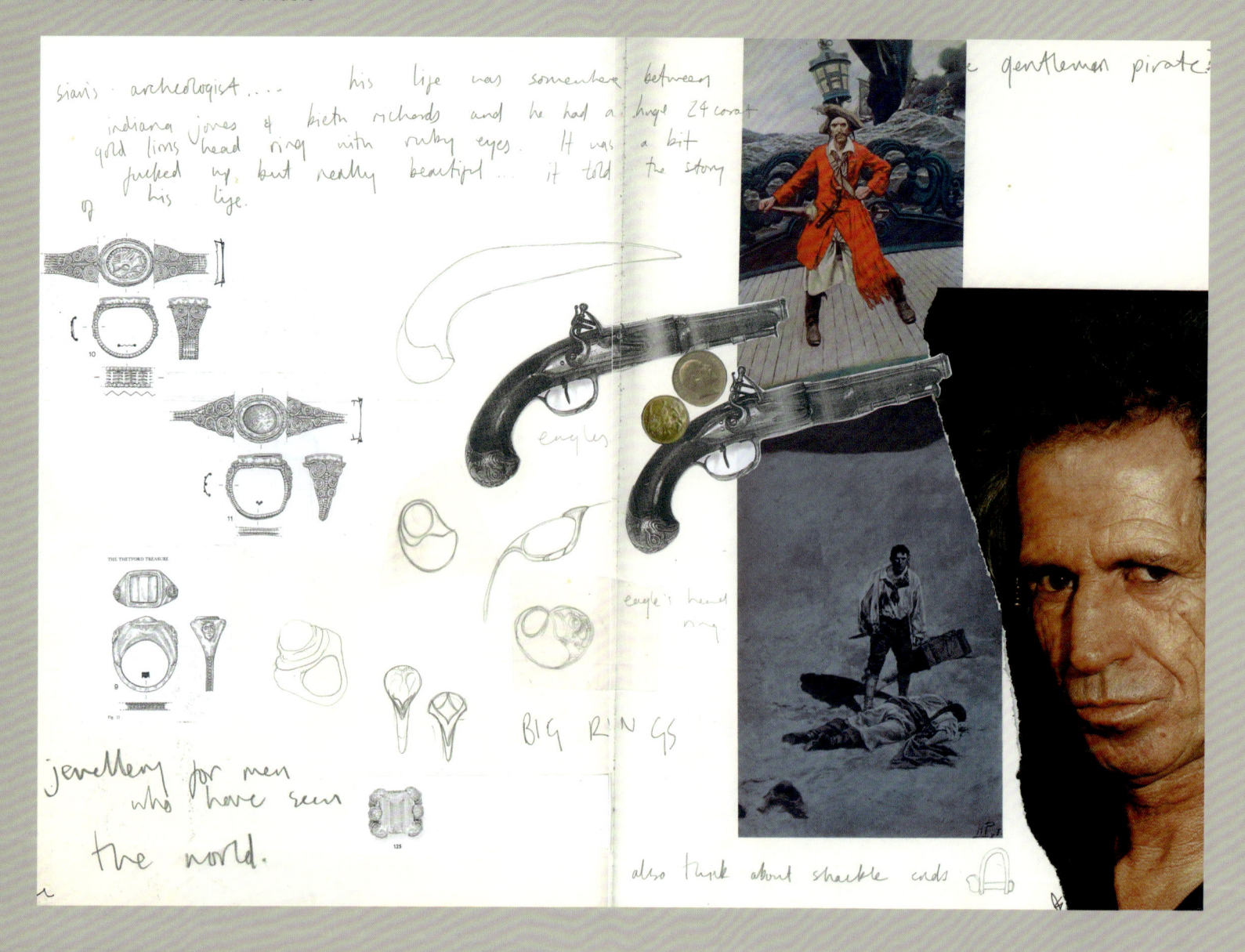

The Forgotten Treasure of The Infamous Aguila Dorada, 2007.

Eagle Gun Icon Ring, 18ct gold.

'It's difficult to explain but over time, I've learned to recognise that little thrill of excitement that happens when I hit on something sketching. It's intense, like a turn-on. I feel it through my whole body.'

Out in the World

Hannah Martin jewellery is not for everyone, but she wouldn't have it any other way. Her pieces speak to those who are ready to listen, to feel. Her designs are for the bold, the thoughtful, who appreciate substance and nuance – and who speak her language.

'She wants to grab the right people', Michael observes. 'She never thinks about the masses.' And yet, the broader audience of jewellery-lovers know Hannah without knowing her. It might be through the occasional gig as a ghost designer. But more likely it's because her work has been brazenly picked up and copied up and down the price scale. But those who know, know. Hannah Martin jewels find their tribe, and that tribe recognises one another at a glance. Opulence for its own sake holds no sway here; they are most interested in intent. Creating things that matter. Eliciting an emotion that lingers in the mind long after the final note is gone.

While jewellery design has a glamorous aura, for Hannah it is a responsibility – a high-stakes dance of risk and reward. The reward is almost sexual in its ecstasy: the glow of molten metal, the soldering rod that insists, again and again, until everything gives, the spark of life in a newly polished surface. 'It's fear and excitement at the same time, and it's totally addictive', says Michael. Something like the visceral thrill of a live performance. A precarious balance of precision and passion that, ultimately, produces a true work of art. An anthem rendered in metal and stone.

Above: Shadow Trance Amulet Delirium, 2014.

Opposite: Jehnny Beth wearing the Perfect Drug shot by Stewart Baxter at The 100 Club, London.

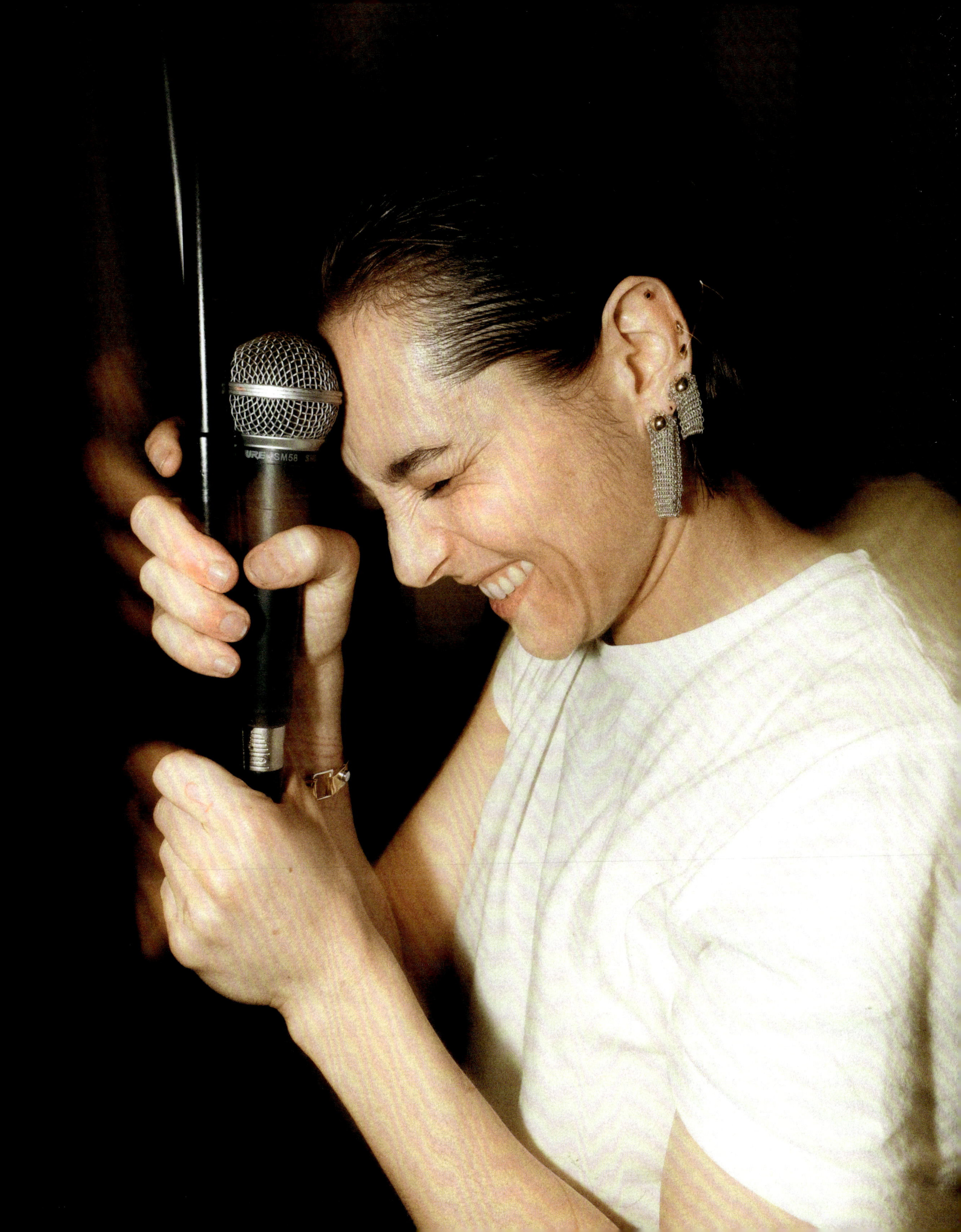
SM58

' During my apprenticeship at Cartier, I was spending my days on the rarified Place Vendôme and my nights at sweaty punk gigs in gritty clubs. I put these two worlds together, and the seed of my brand was born. '

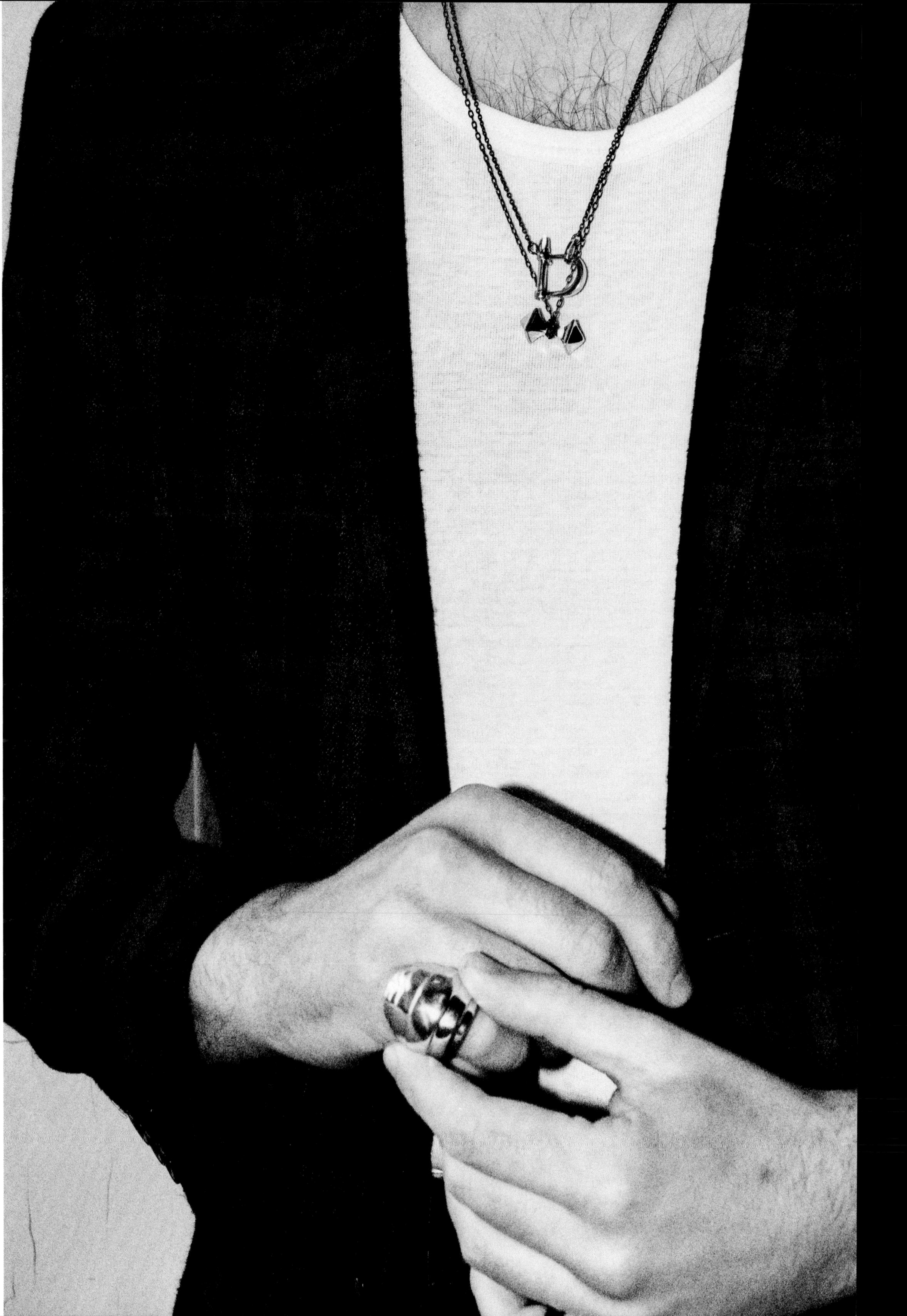

94 > the maker and her music

the maker and her music < 95

"Jewellery should reflect dignity, not just in its beauty, but in how it's made."

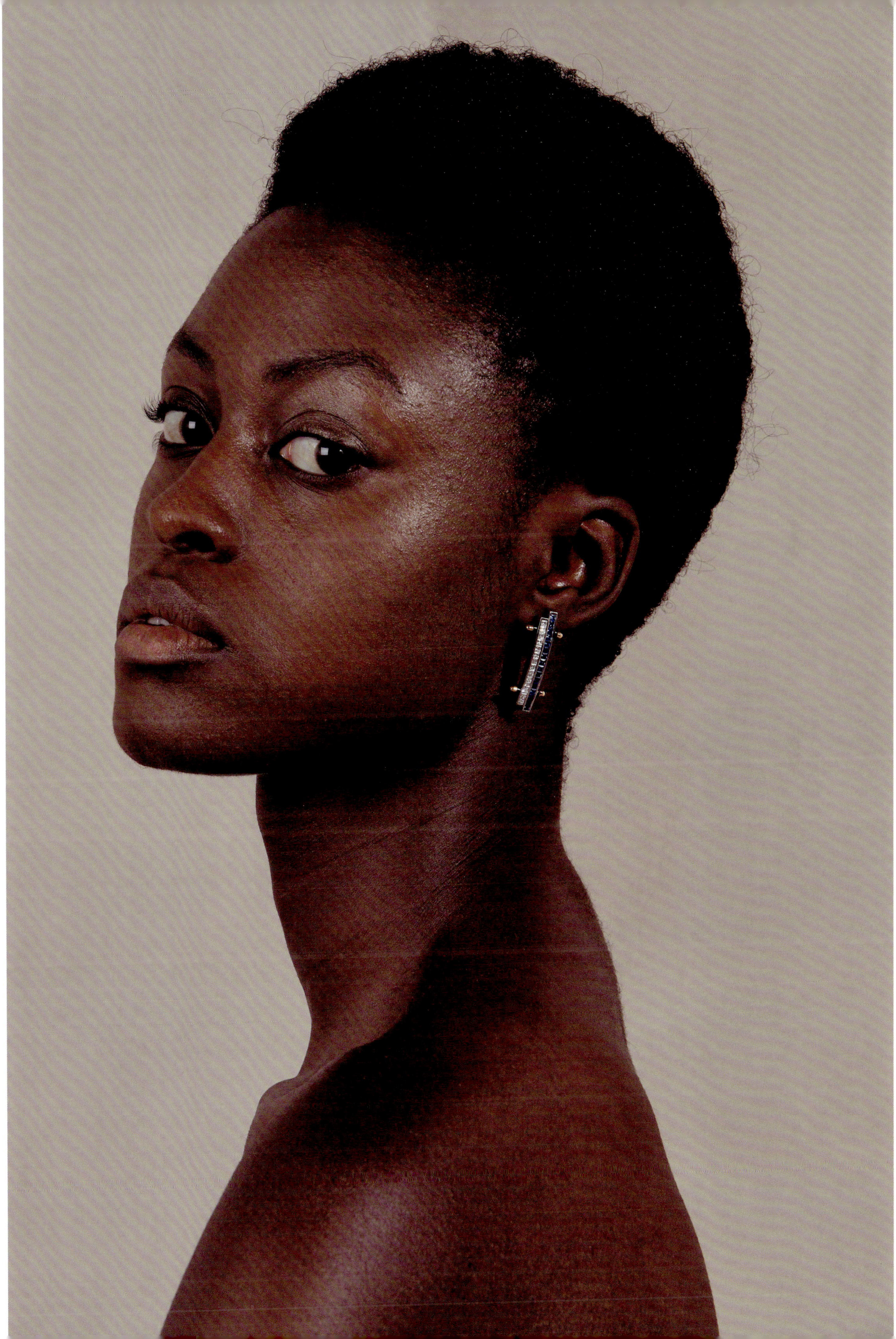

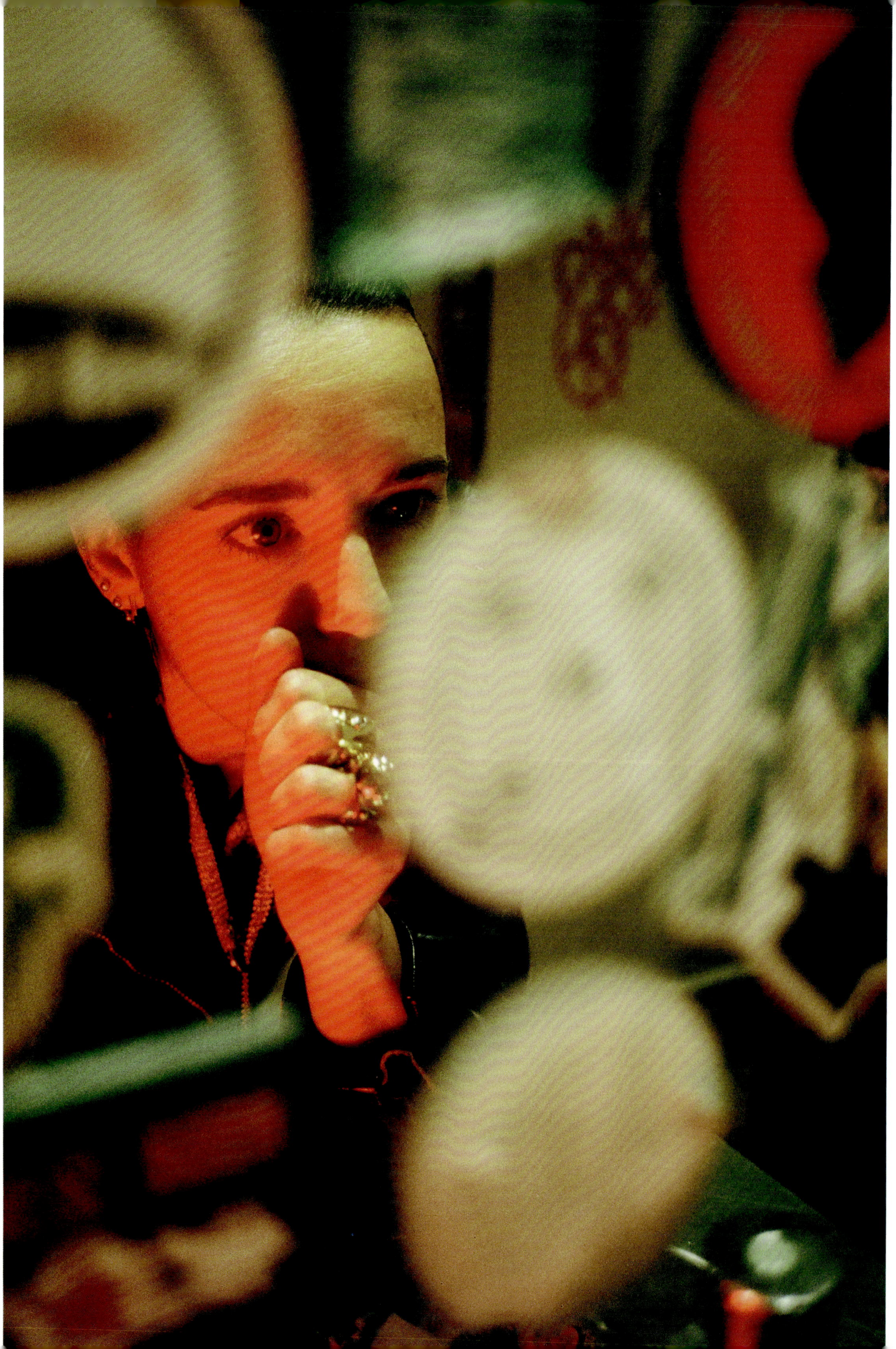

‘ I want you to want to touch it with your skin. To stroke it. To lick it. ’

❛ The process is visceral. I immerse myself in a room full of images I've collected, there are literally hundreds all over the floor and on the walls. I put on music and I sink into some dark, calm, beautiful place. And then I try to stop thinking. I let my gut, or whatever part of me contains that germ of the idea, sift through it all. ❜

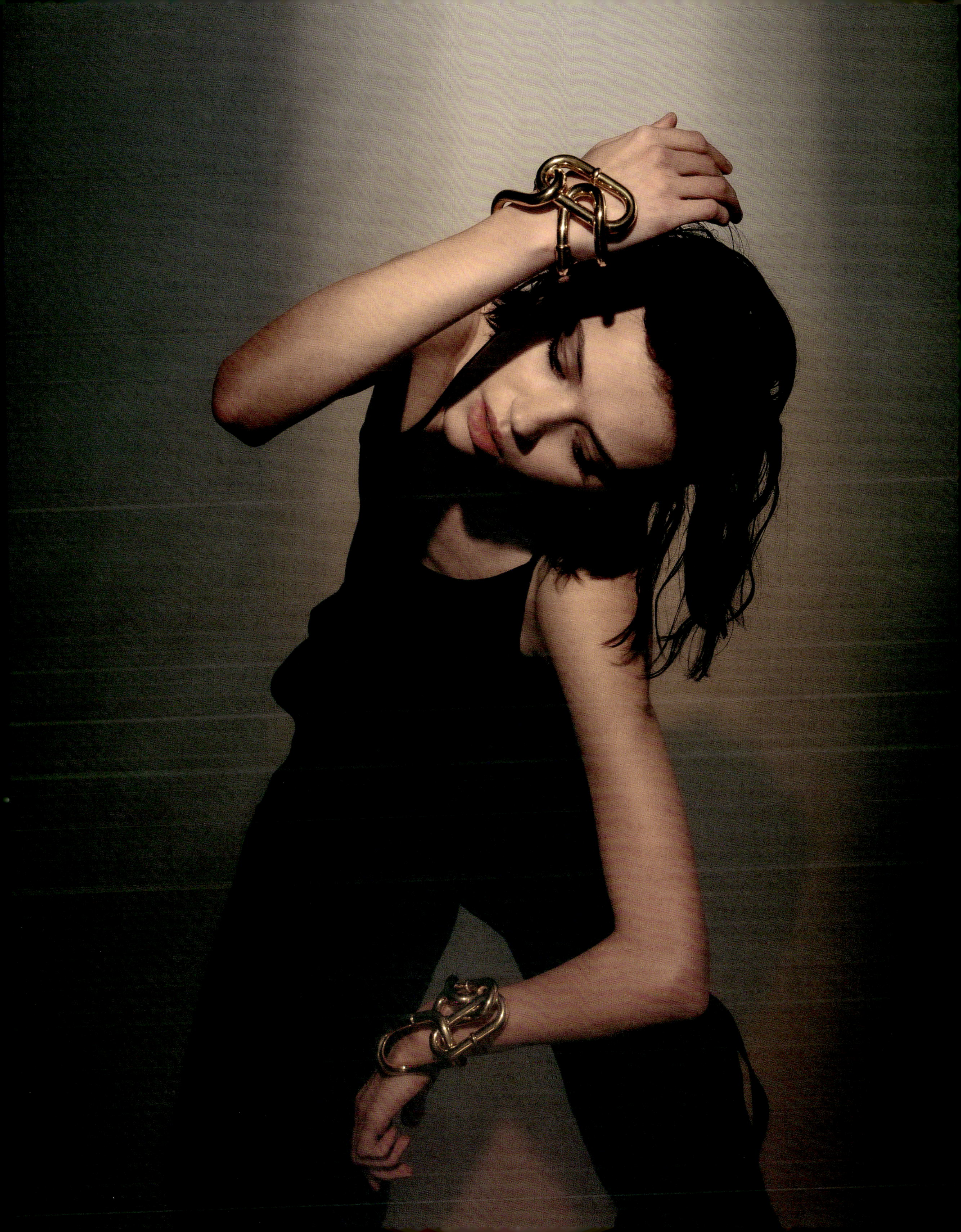

102 > the maker and her music

The Perfect Drug, 2024.

From left: All Access Bracelet, 18ct gold; Fluid Strap Chain, 18ct gold; Strapped Orb Ring, 18ct gold.

‘ Making jewellery is storytelling. Every piece I design has a history, a purpose. ’

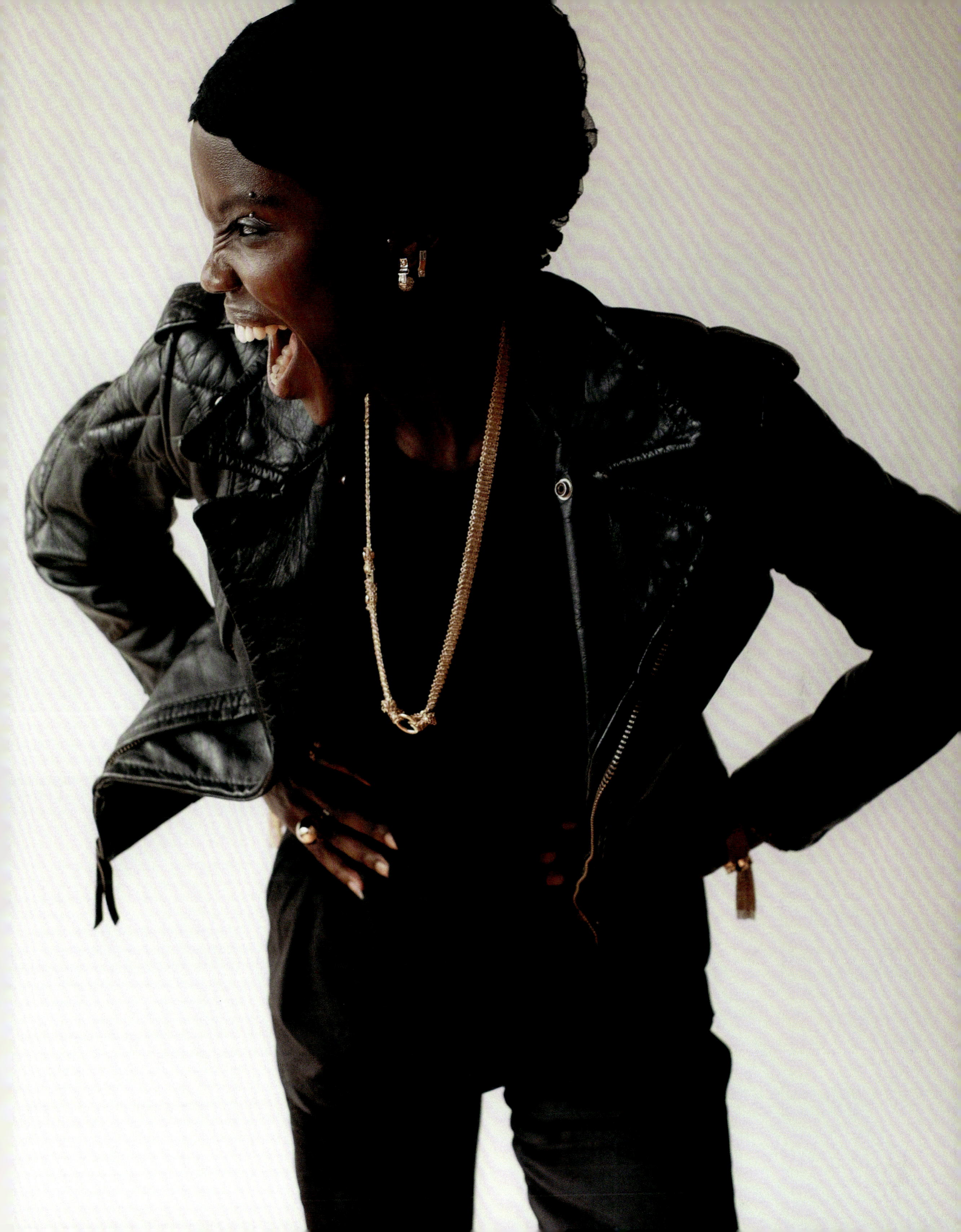

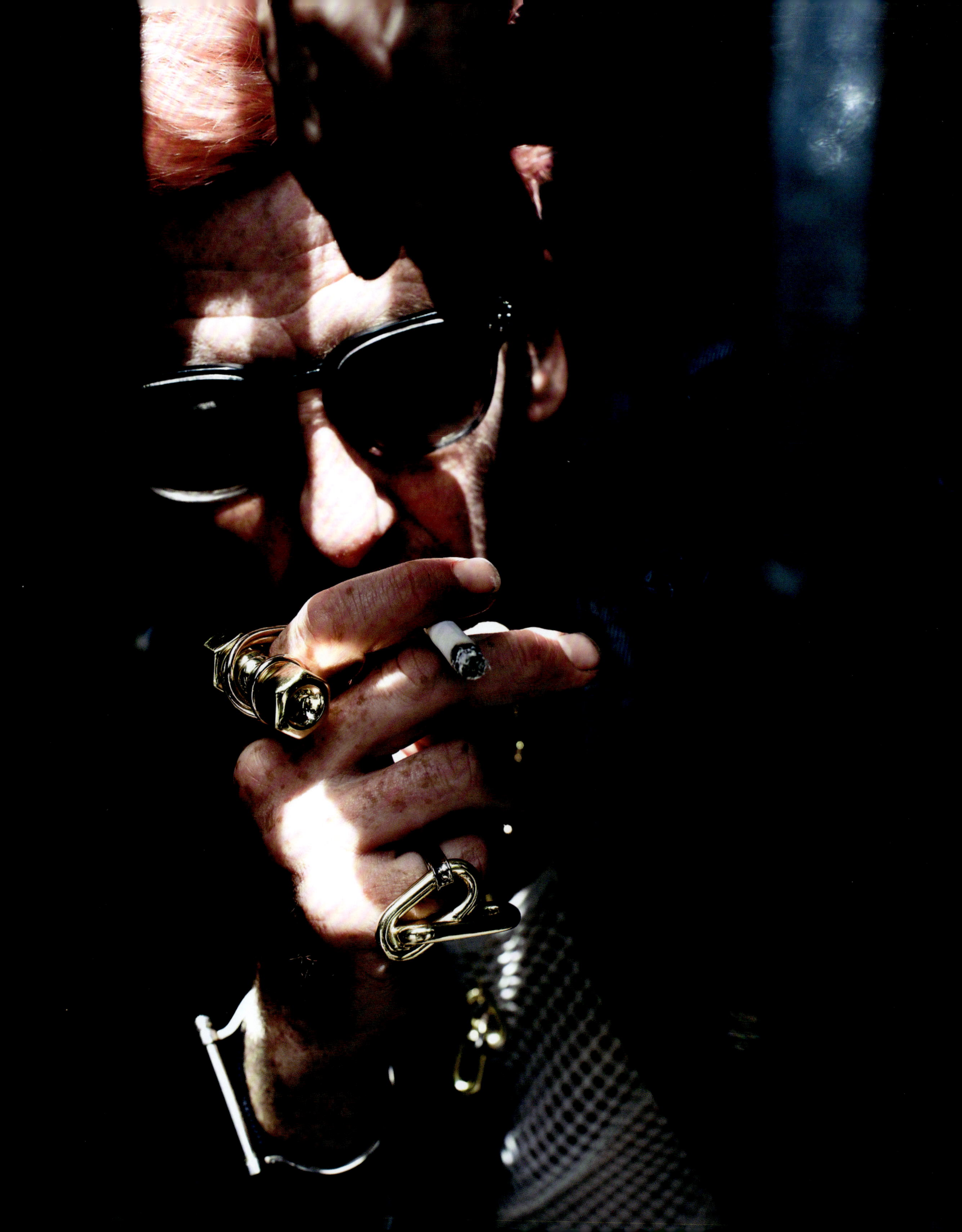

Seye Adeleken shot by Stewart Baxter, Soho, London, 2024.

OPPOSITE: Paul Anderson shot by Anthony Byrne, Smithfields, London, 2021.

> ❝ I live my life relishing moments of feeling and intensity – amazing food, amazing music, amazing sex – because I LOVE being alive. It is this that I want to transmit in the work that I make. ❞

the maker and her music < 107

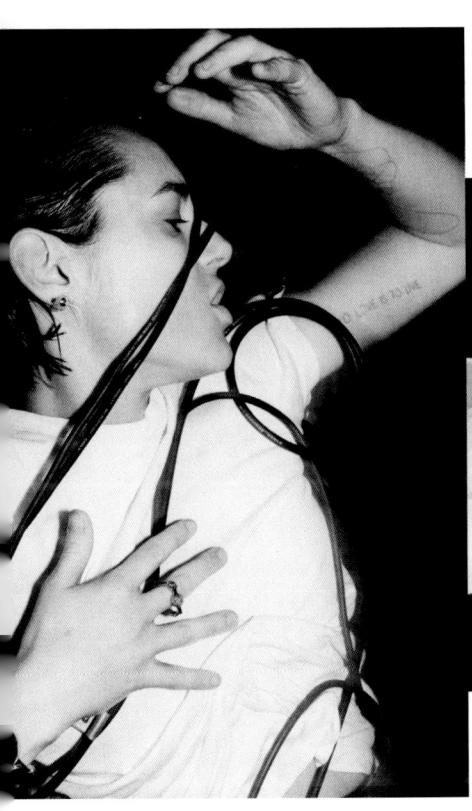

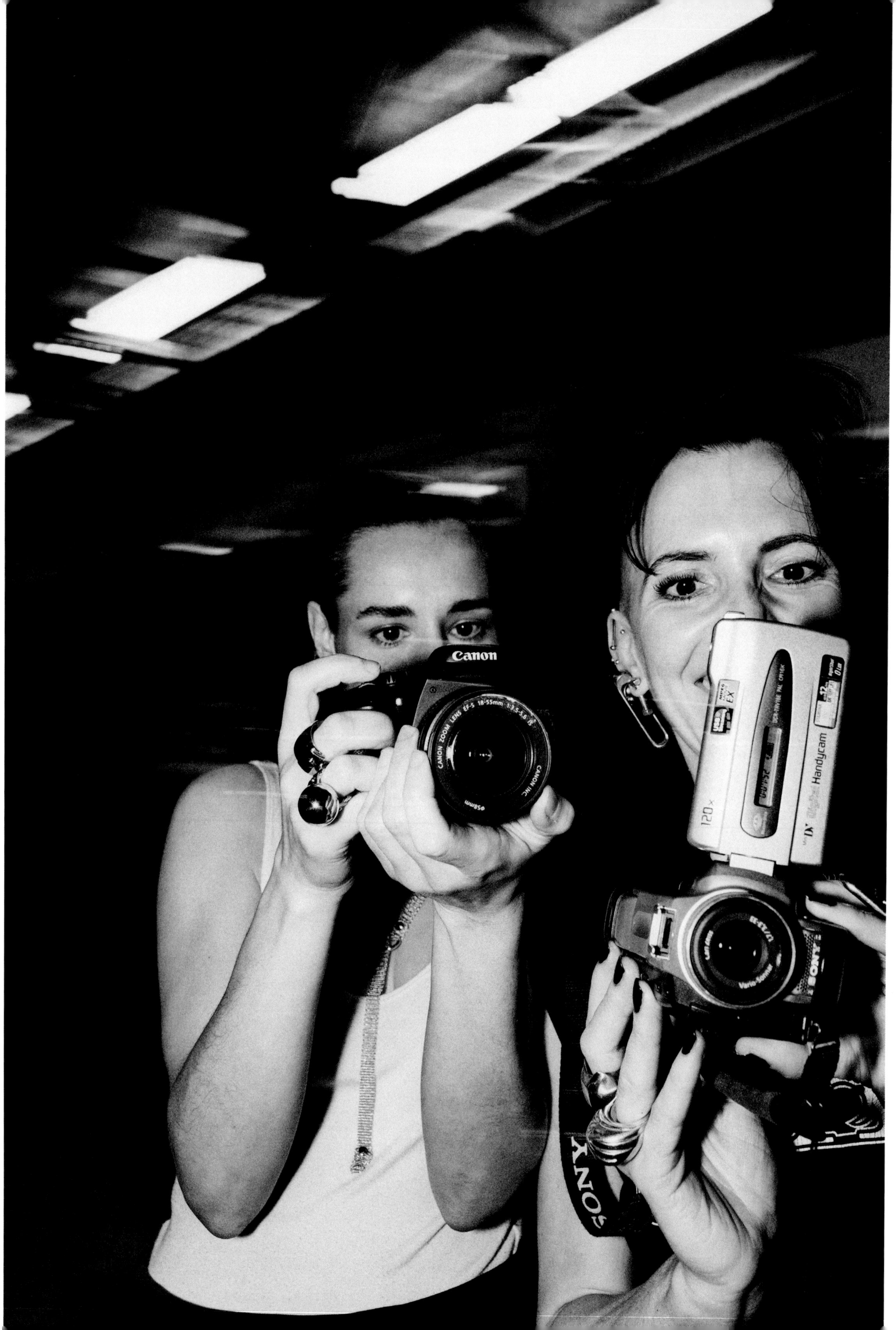
Canon
Handycam

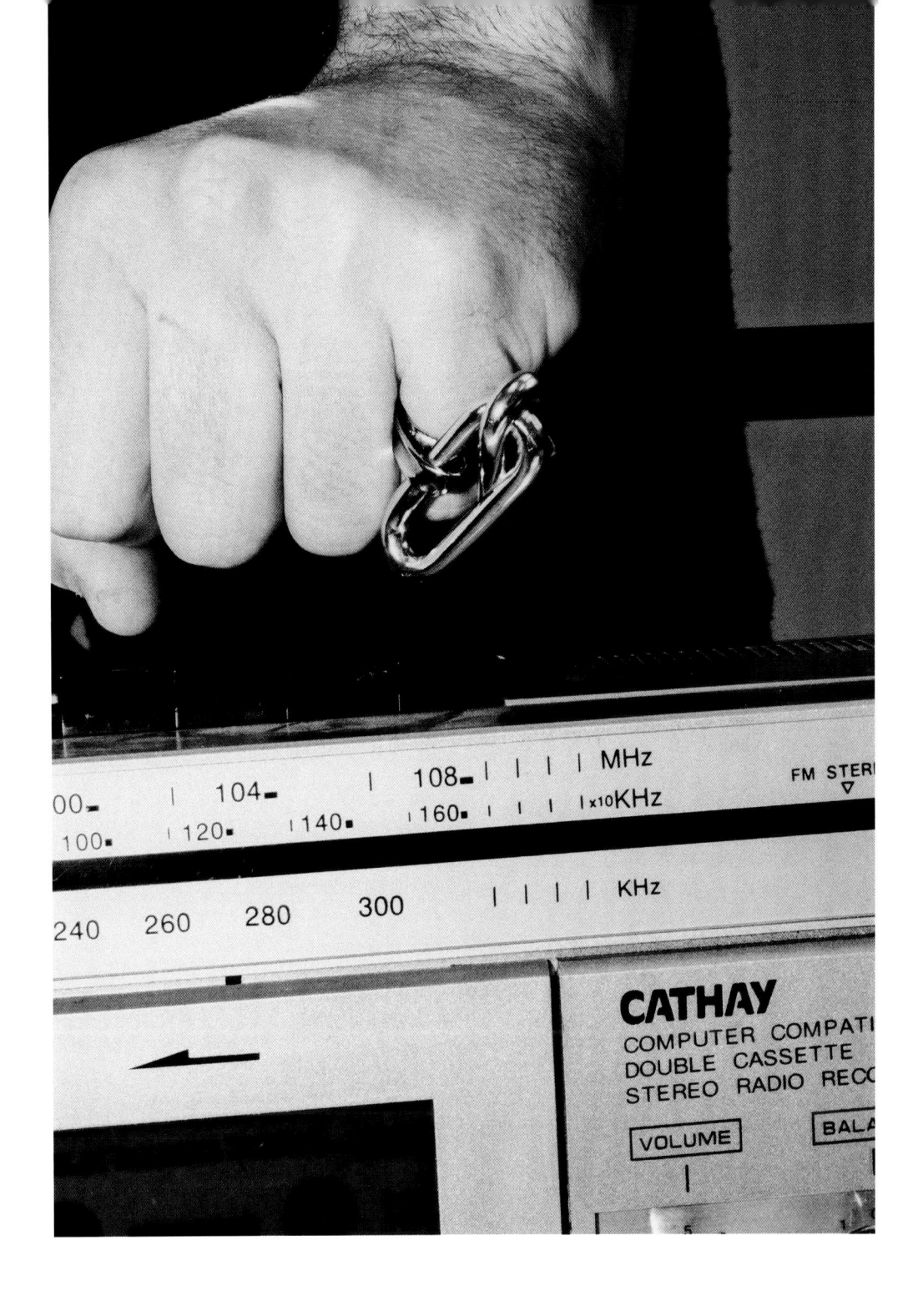

❛ It still feels to me like I'm this kid in a world that's not totally mine.
It feels naughty, like I'm taking something sacred and subverting it. ❜

110 > the maker and her music

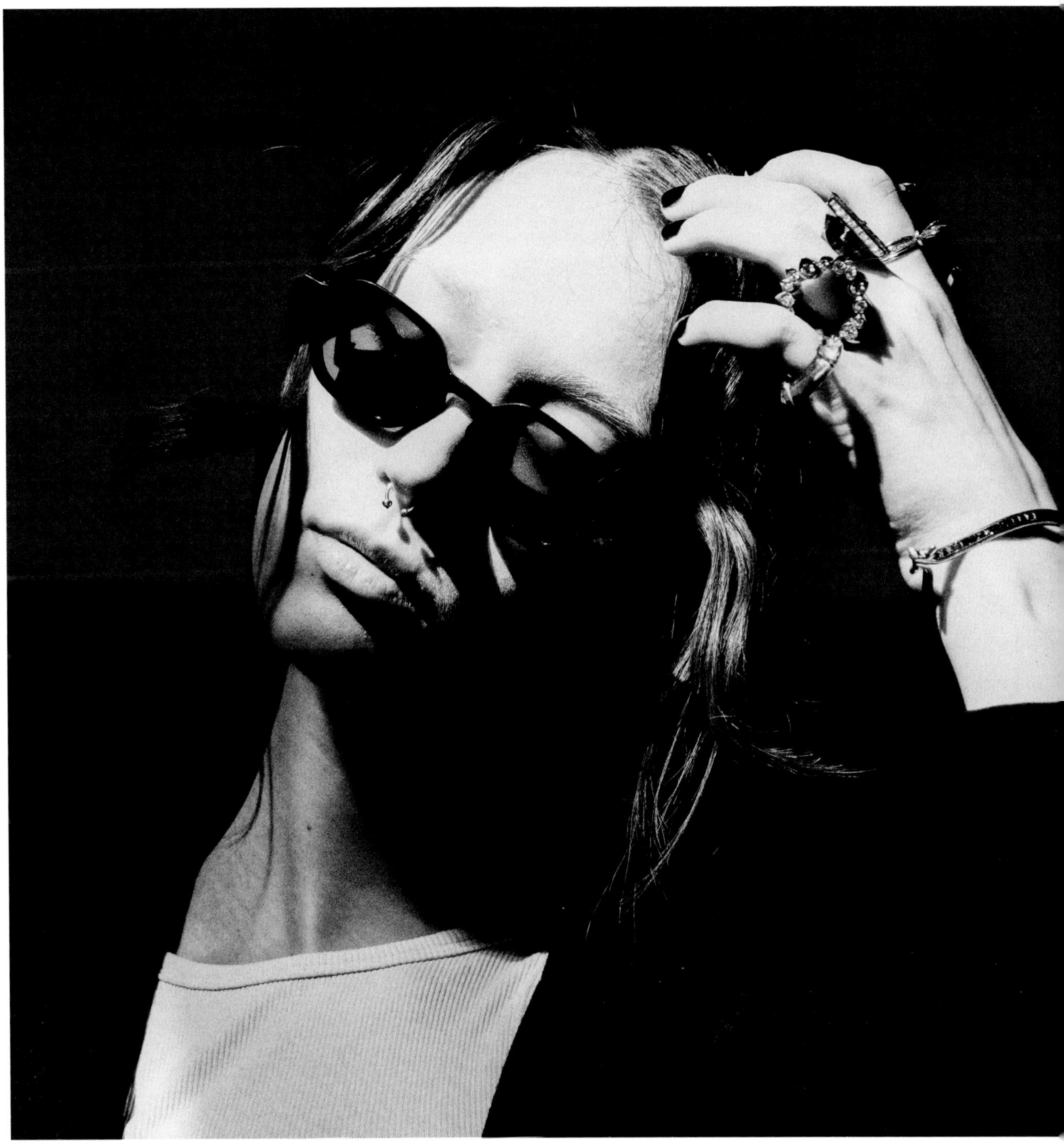

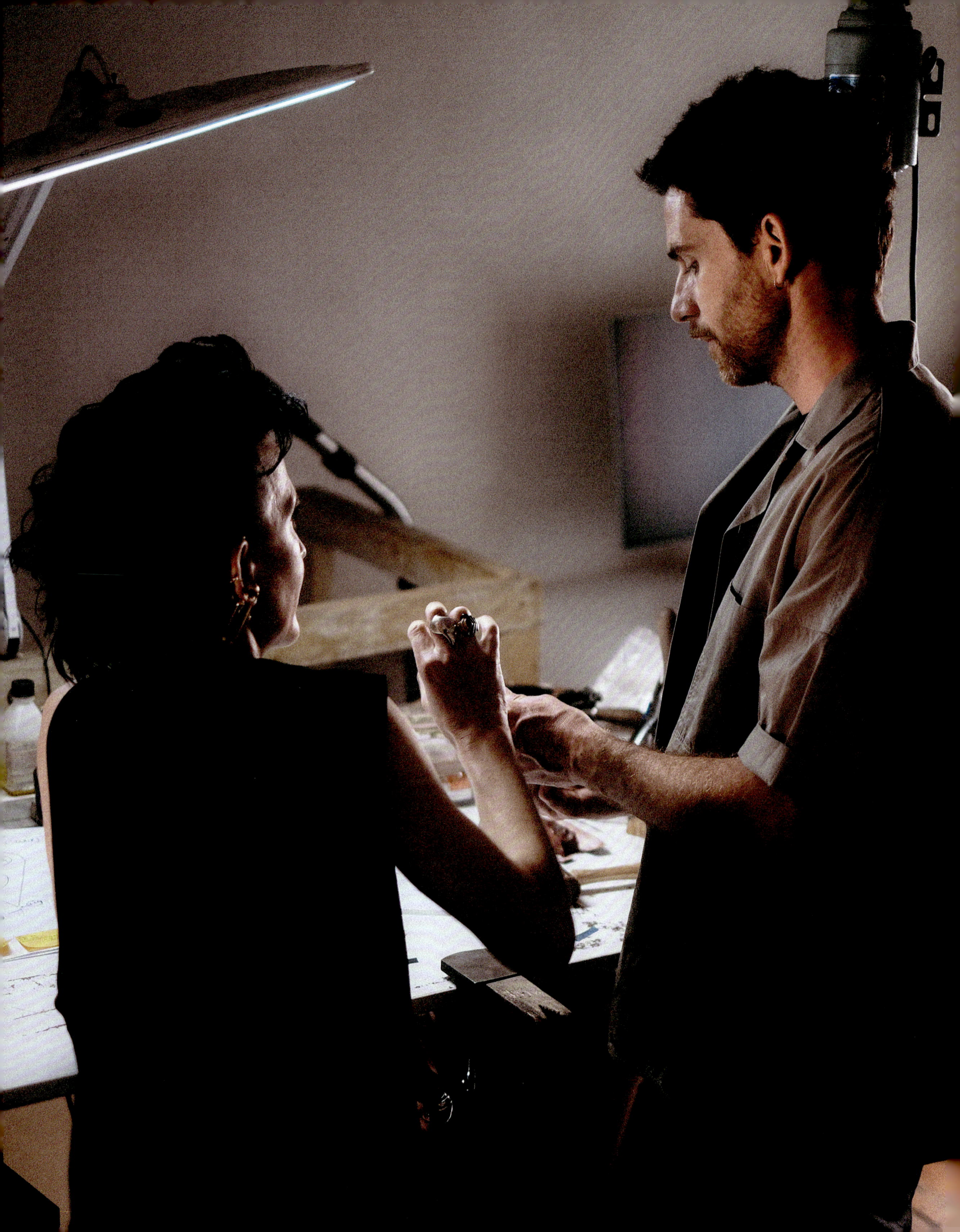

❛ Her work resonates with the energy of whatever she's listening to. The songs that fill the studio fuel her vision. It's a total osmosis. ❜

Michael Urbančík

The Making of the Brit Awards

The Brit Awards – chaotic, electrifying, impossible to ignore – always carried a certain mythology for Hannah. When she was invited to design its nominee trophy in 2022, the project arrived like a storm: urgent, demanding, irresistible. She envisioned it like a relic from a lost civilisation, pieced together from fragments of the past. Its molten, battered form took shape in hand-sculpted plaster and jesmonite. Working with a storied London foundry, she had the 'B' cast in bronze, its curves deliberately sensuous, its heft weighty in the palm. The base – in ebony salvaged from the UK's last snooker cue factory – made each piece quietly unique. The 'B' does not simply perch on the plinth; it appears to have fallen and lodged at an angle, held upright through sheer balance. Part sculpture, part talisman, part artefact of a dystopian world, it is an elegant memento – luxurious, tactile and undeniably alive.

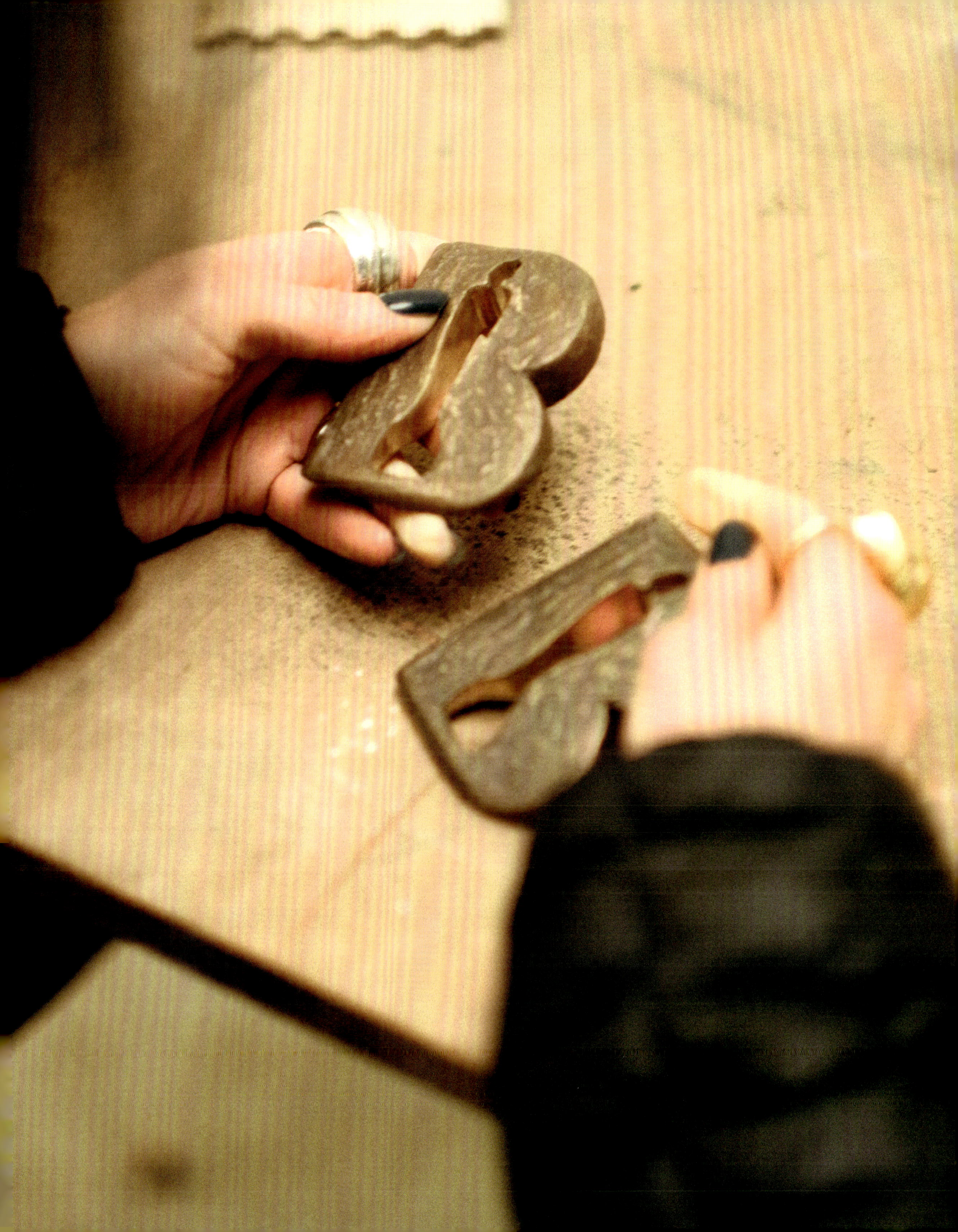

NOGUCHI
MALEVICH
TATTOO
TASCHEN
FRANCIS BACON
The Complete Marquis de Sade
HOMME+
YOGA FOR MEN
PUNK LOVE
PUNK PIONEERS
JENNY LENS
SPIKE ISLAND
LONDON LIFE
OLYMPIA
LENI RIEFENSTAHL
JACK PIERSON
Variety
MORE EGGS
Sometimes Overwhelming
THE AMERICANS
Faces of Africa

REPLICA
STUDIO 54
DISCO
Carlo Mollino Polaroids
the dark carnival
PURIENNE
HOLIDAY
Eadweard Muybridge
BRUCE DAVIDSON
CABINETS OF CURIOSITIES
TARKOVSKY
RYAN MCGINLEY
SOVIET MODERNISM
CALATRAVA
CCCP
ENLIGHTENMENT
LEE BROOM FASHIONING DESIGN
TIM WALKER STORY TELLER
DAVID KING

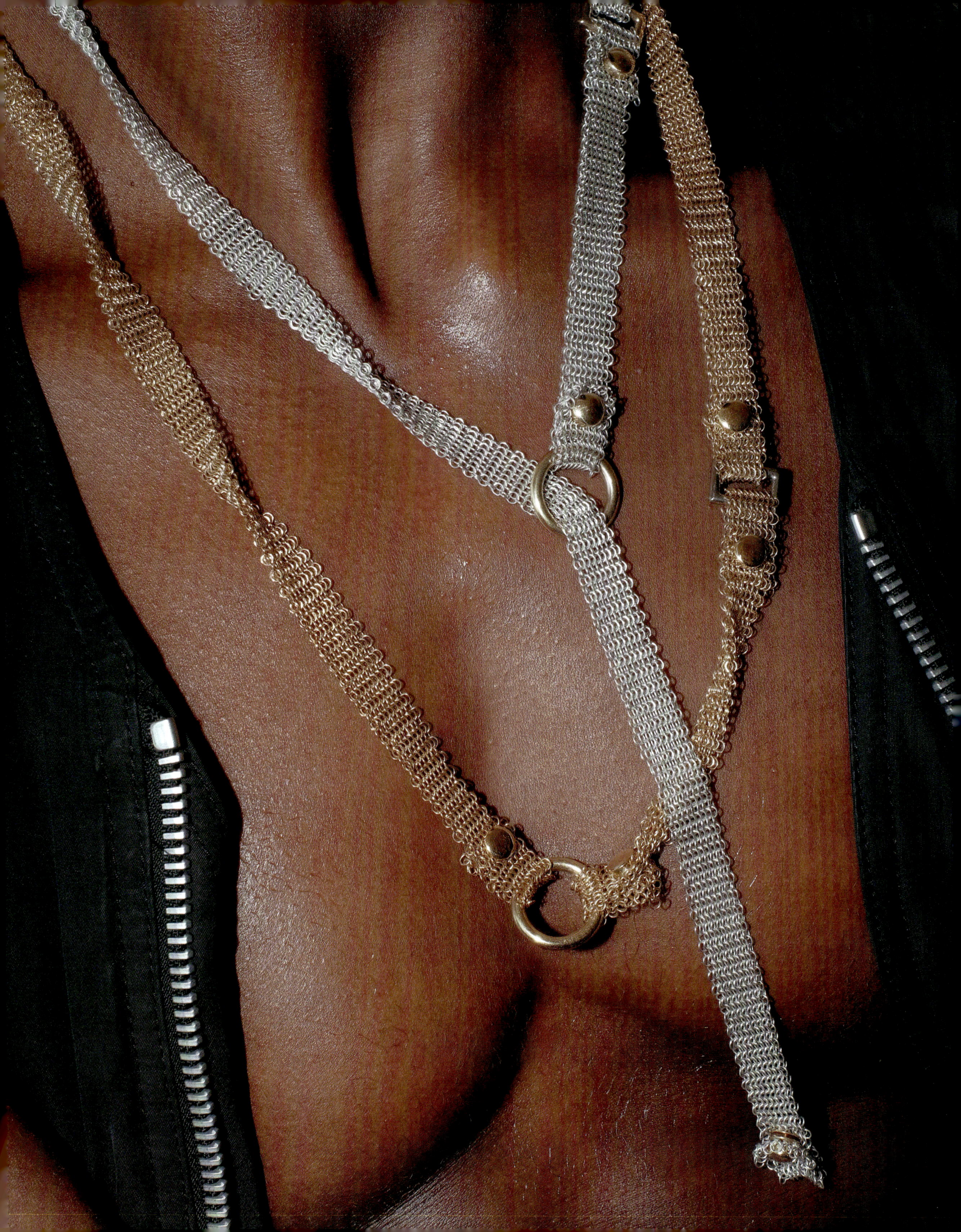

THE ALCHEMY OF ADORNMENT

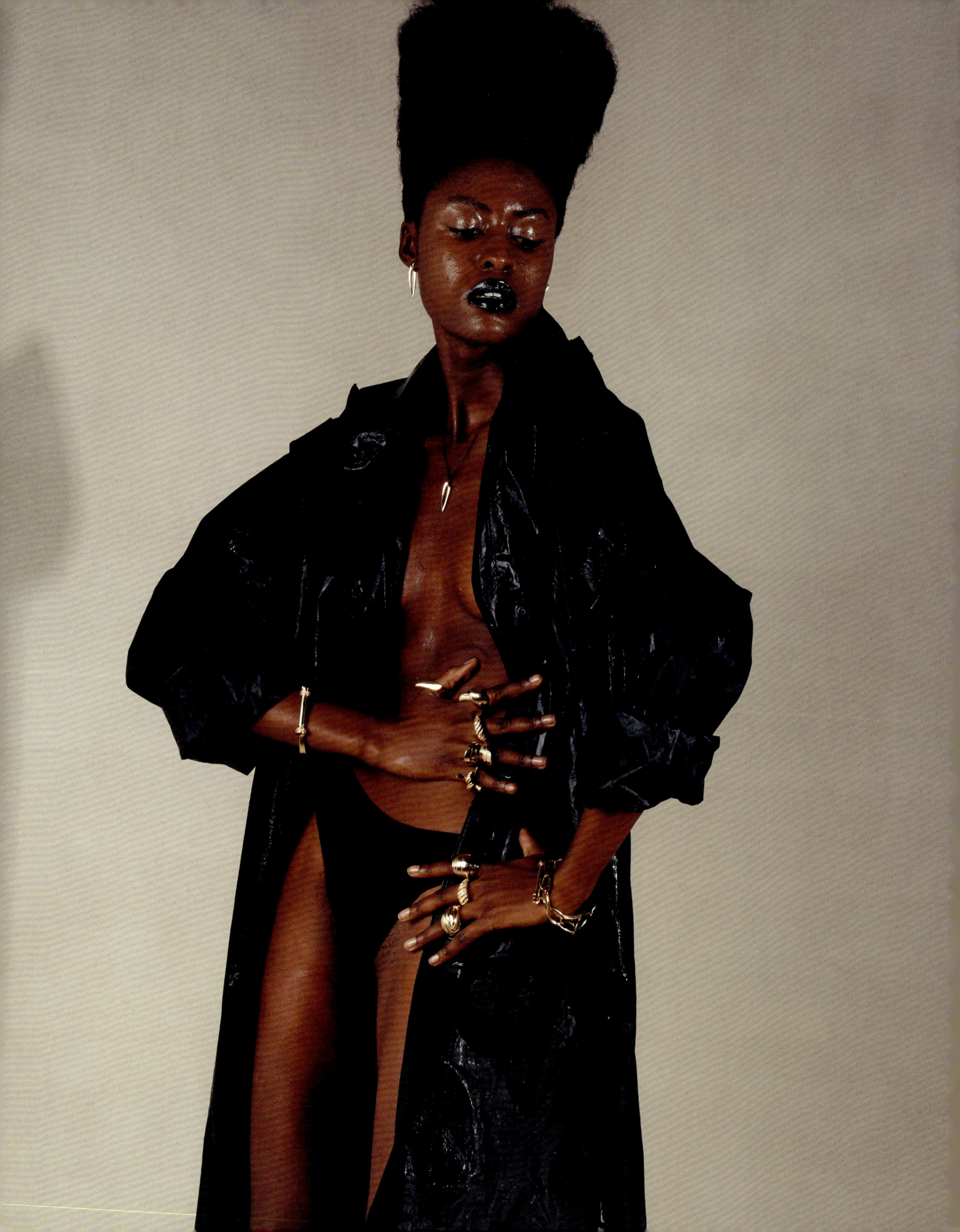

Jewellery, for those who understand it, is never merely an object. It is history distilled, an identity wrought from humble materials or precious metals and gemstones. In the right hands, it is an act of defiance.

For Hannah Martin, jewellery is not just a craft – it is a dialogue, a tension between the sensual and the cerebral, between gender and expectation, between the body and the mind. 'My sexuality occupies a big place in my creativity. I think the freedom aspect and the rejection of boundaries has powered my work. In the same way I never understood why my jewellery had to be specifically for one gender, I've never accepted that my sexuality had to be for one gender because those boundaries just don't feel normal to me', she says.

From the outset, her work has resisted categorisation. Beauty and luxury, as she sees them, are not static ideals but provocations. Having grown up far removed from the codes of high luxury, Hannah approaches them with an outsider's irreverence, a freedom to – as she puts it – 'fuck with them.'

Sex, connection, freedom and intimacy all converge at the bench.

'I've always been curious about sexuality and the world of fetishism', Hannah explains. 'I find it exciting but not even necessarily in a sexual way. It has more to do with an awakening of the senses. It's the same reason I love going to music gigs and being in the mosh pit of people and sweat and bodies. It's why I love hot yoga.'

122 > the alchemy of adornment

Sensuality at the Bench

The Hannah Martin studio is a space of tactile intimacy, where jewellery is as much about feeling as it is about form. Fire bends metal to will, raw material transforms in an alchemy that is at once technical and deeply sensual.

'Soldering is one of the sexiest things I do', Hannah says, describing that moment when heat touches metal, transforms it, and controlled chaos gives way to new structure. Her work carries the same balance: curves defy rigidity and movement is embedded in every jewel. Her sketches are often spontaneous, capturing the instant before form becomes fixed, when a ring or a pendant exists in potential rather than permanence. As Hannah sees it, jewellery should never sit there passively; it is the protagonist in an intimate, ongoing performance. It should never simply lie there against the skin: It must be felt deeply by its wearer and beholders alike.

'Someone who has an eye for line is drawn to her jewellery regardless of the inspiration', says one collector and industry insider. 'They respond to the form first. They don't need to buy into the backstory or even know about it. Hannah leaves you the space to invent your own story so that wearing it becomes a personal expression. The design allows you to do that. The wearer takes ownership of the design.'

Above: Sketches for Somebody's Sins, 2016.

Opposite: Sketches for The Perfect Drug, 2024.

the alchemy of adornment < 123

124 > the alchemy of adornment

Above: Bound Ring, 18ct gold, black jade, diamonds and sapphires, 2016.

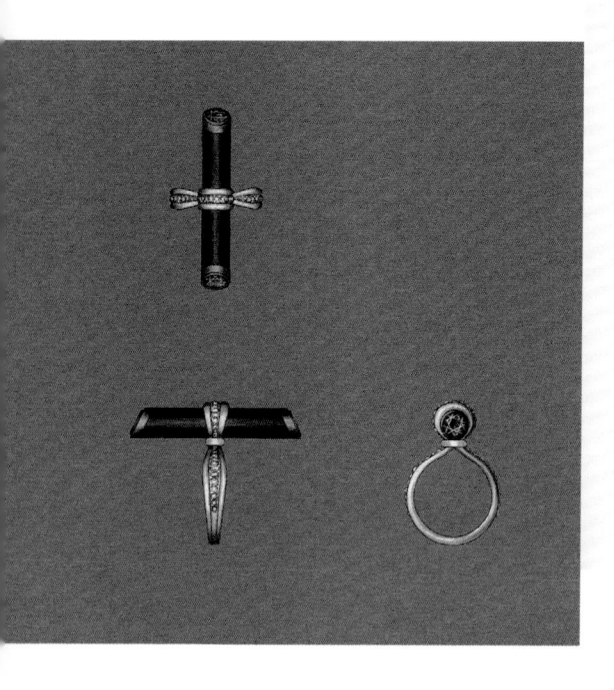

Breaking the Binary

'I suppose I started really exploring my bisexuality or leaning into it in my early twenties but it was always something I kind of accepted about myself. My exploration of sensuality and sex over the years is really about finding my power as a woman and not feeling bad about it or ashamed', Hannah notes. 'Along the way, I've learned that a woman finding her power scares some people.'

In Hannah's world, jewellery's traditional, gendered descriptions/designations – delicate chains for her, weighty signets for him – feel antiquated, a relic of a bygone era. Her designs resist prescription, speaking to identity rather than expectation. 'There's something deeper in my pieces', she allows. Indeed, her high-jewellery clientele is arguably the most diverse in the industry, spanning young professionals and rebels, accountants, entrepreneurs, actors, rock stars and couture regulars. 'Gender has little to do with it. I've seen my designs on people I'd never have imagined', Hannah observes.

Comments one collector and industry insider: 'In all my years of working in this field, I've rarely seen such a diverse range in a high-jewellery clientele. Her jewellery is obviously rock 'n' roll yet it's just as likely to be worn by the haute-couture set. It's the strength of the design that ties everything together.'

The genesis of Hannah's aesthetic owes much to a fascination with masculinity, albeit a stylised, cinematic one. At the centre of her creative mythology stands Vincent, a fictional Russian gangster – a vision of hyper-masculinity that, in her hands, dissolves into something altogether more fluid. A ring might carry an air of toughness, but its contours invite softness. A cuff may evoke power, but its fit is intimate, its weight a whisper rather than a directive.

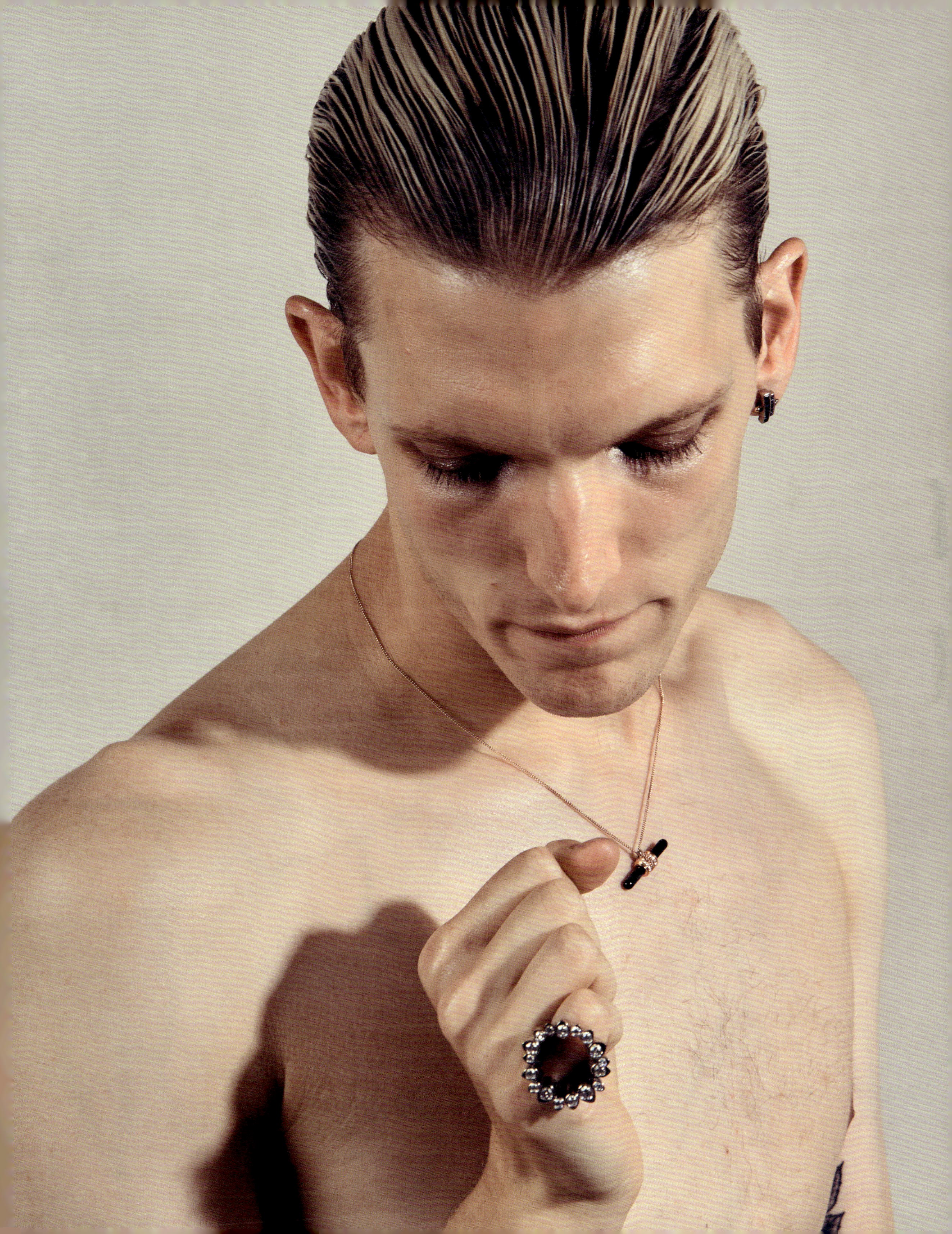

' There's something a bit unsafe about these pieces – that are also so full of love. '

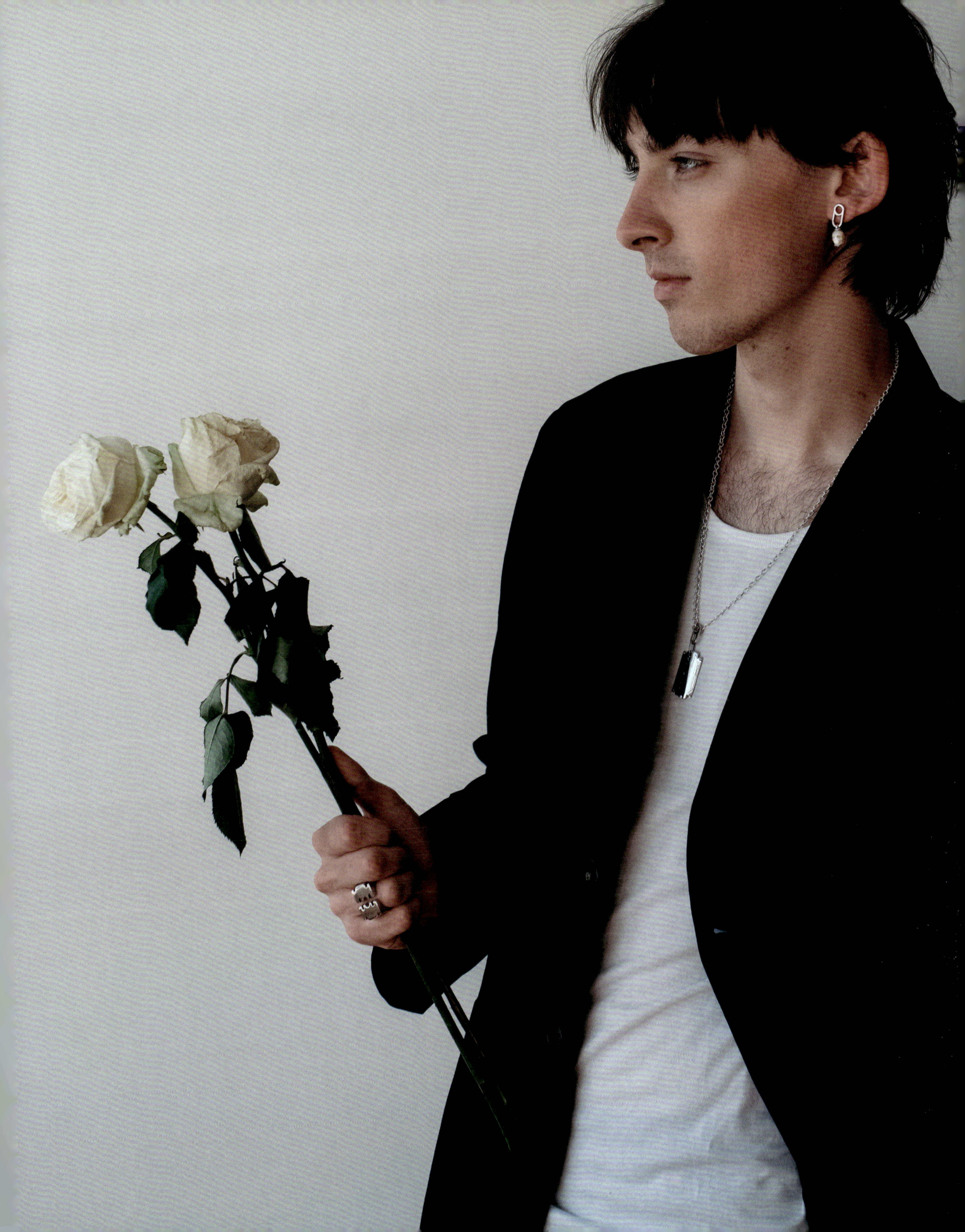

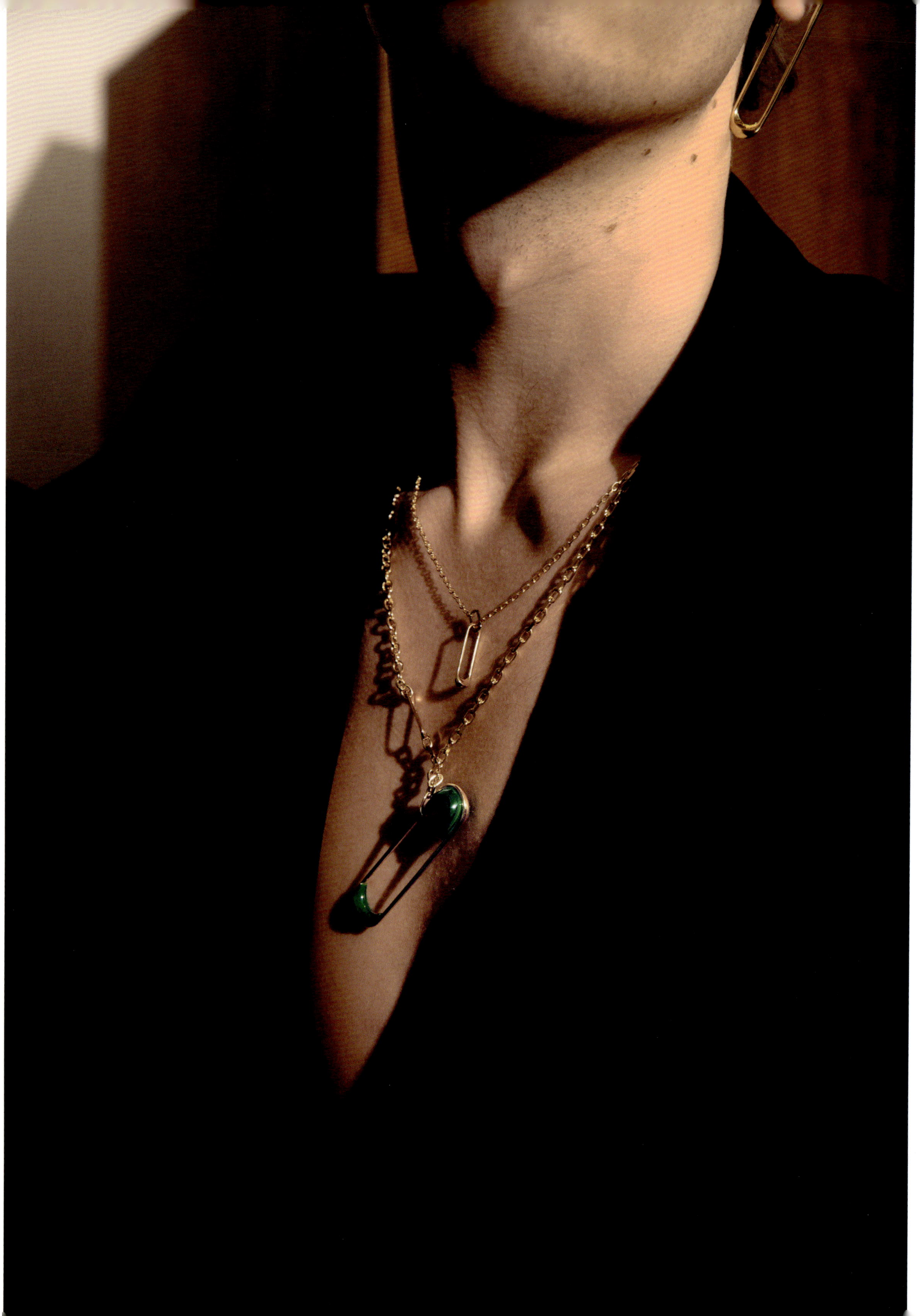

Touch Me, Feel Me

Jewellery and sex share a fundamental language – both elevate and expose, both mark and transform. Hannah understands this instinctively. Her work does not merely acknowledge intimacy; it revels in it. A number of pieces draw unselfconsciously from fetish culture, appropriating sex paraphernalia with a jeweller's exacting eye. A cock ring is transformed into sculptural adornment, an object for public display. This is no gimmick. It is a deliberate provocation, a challenge to the notion of jewellery as mere ornament rather than intrinsic expression. 'Jewellery is an extension of the self', Hannah asserts. 'It's anything but merely ornamental.'

Hannah Martin designs emphasise the interaction between jewellery and skin – the way a ring deliberately weights a finger, how a chain drapes languorously over a collarbone. In these encounters, sensuality is proactive; it is the whole point. These accessories demand engagement, awareness, exposure.

'Good or bad, all I have ever wanted is to make people feel something', says Hannah.

ABOVE: Creative collaborators (aka The Crow Appreciation Society aka the pervy art duo) Hannah Martin and Stewart Baxter, Chateau Denmark, London.

OPPOSITE: A New Act of Rebellion, 2020.

the alchemy of adornment < 129

130 > the alchemy of adornment

The Power of the Object

Jewellery has always symbolised power – whether through the regalia of royalty, religion and stardom or the quiet significance of a simple gold band. For Hannah, power isn't status – it's presence.

Her creative approach is immersive, almost ritualistic. She withdraws into a private world where ideas take root and mood boards accumulate, where images and textures coalesce into form. Some pieces borrow from history – chainmail armour reimagined as a delicate all-access bracelet – while others are thoroughly modern, their sharp edges tempered by organic movement. Yet all share a sense of intention, of meaning that surpasses mere adornment.

'Jewellery should feel like it could last forever', notes Hannah. 'Not just its materials. Its meaning.'

ABOVE: Process, The Perfect Drug, 2024.

OPPOSITE: Moodboard, Somebody's Sins, 2016.

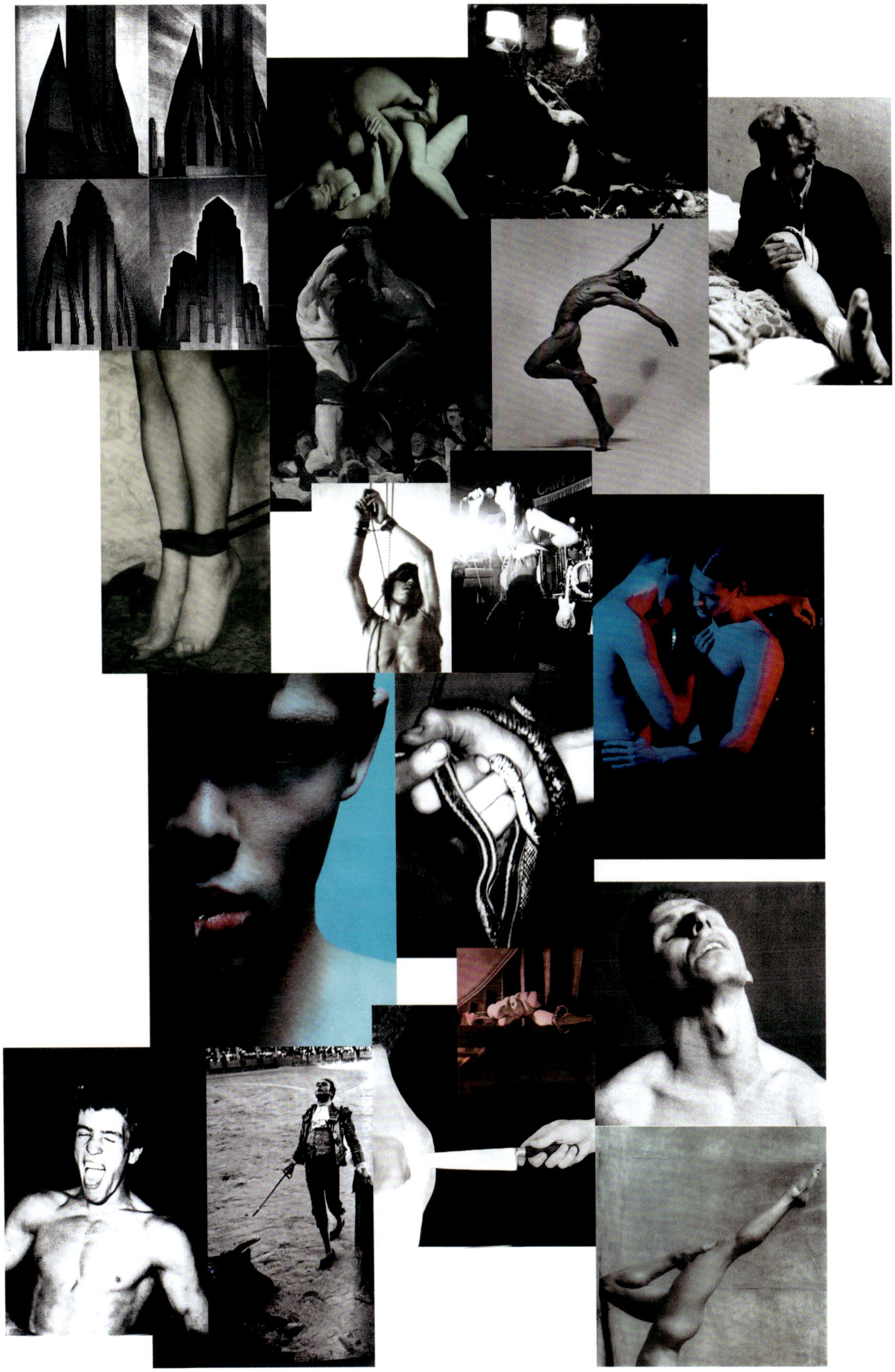

THIS PAGE: The Perfect Drug, 2024, hand-painted gouaches.

OPPOSITE: Strapped Stone Ring, 18ct gold and obsidian, 2024; Orb Harness Ring, 18ct gold, 2024; All Access Ring, 18ct gold, 2024; Spur Cufflinks, 18ct gold and black diamonds, 2005; Studded Orb Harness Ring, 18ct gold and steel diamonds, 2024.

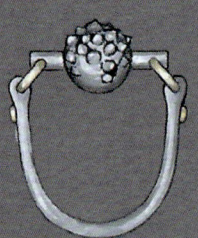

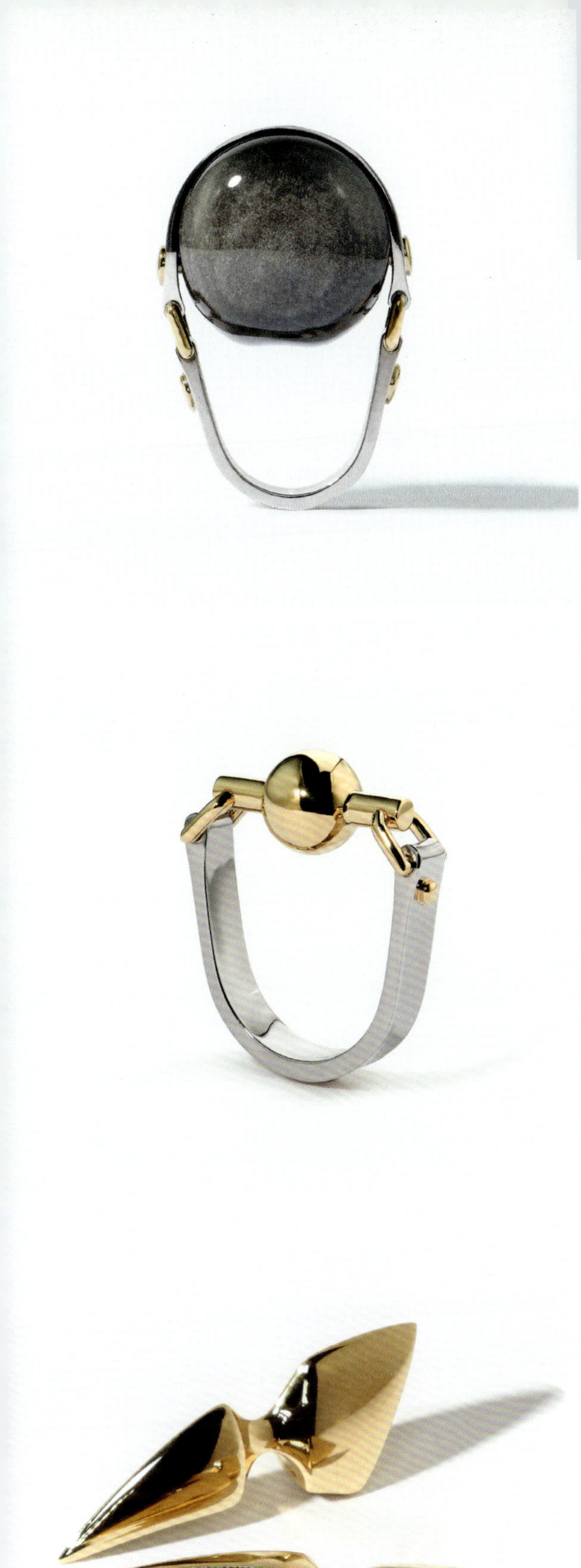
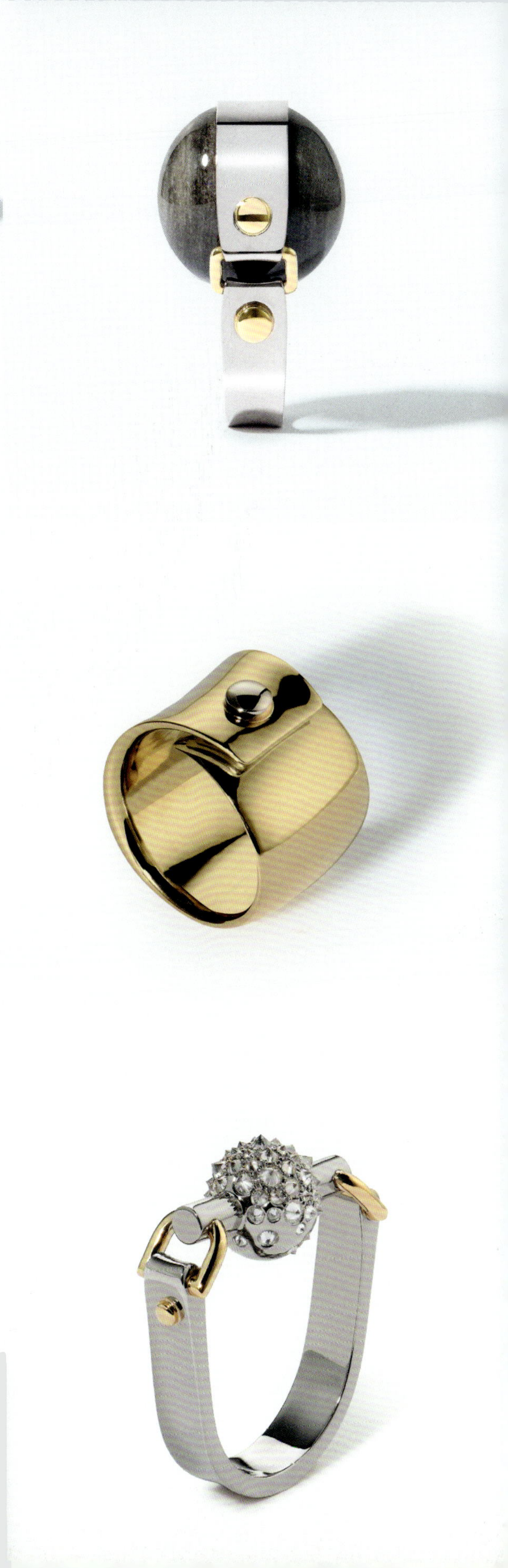

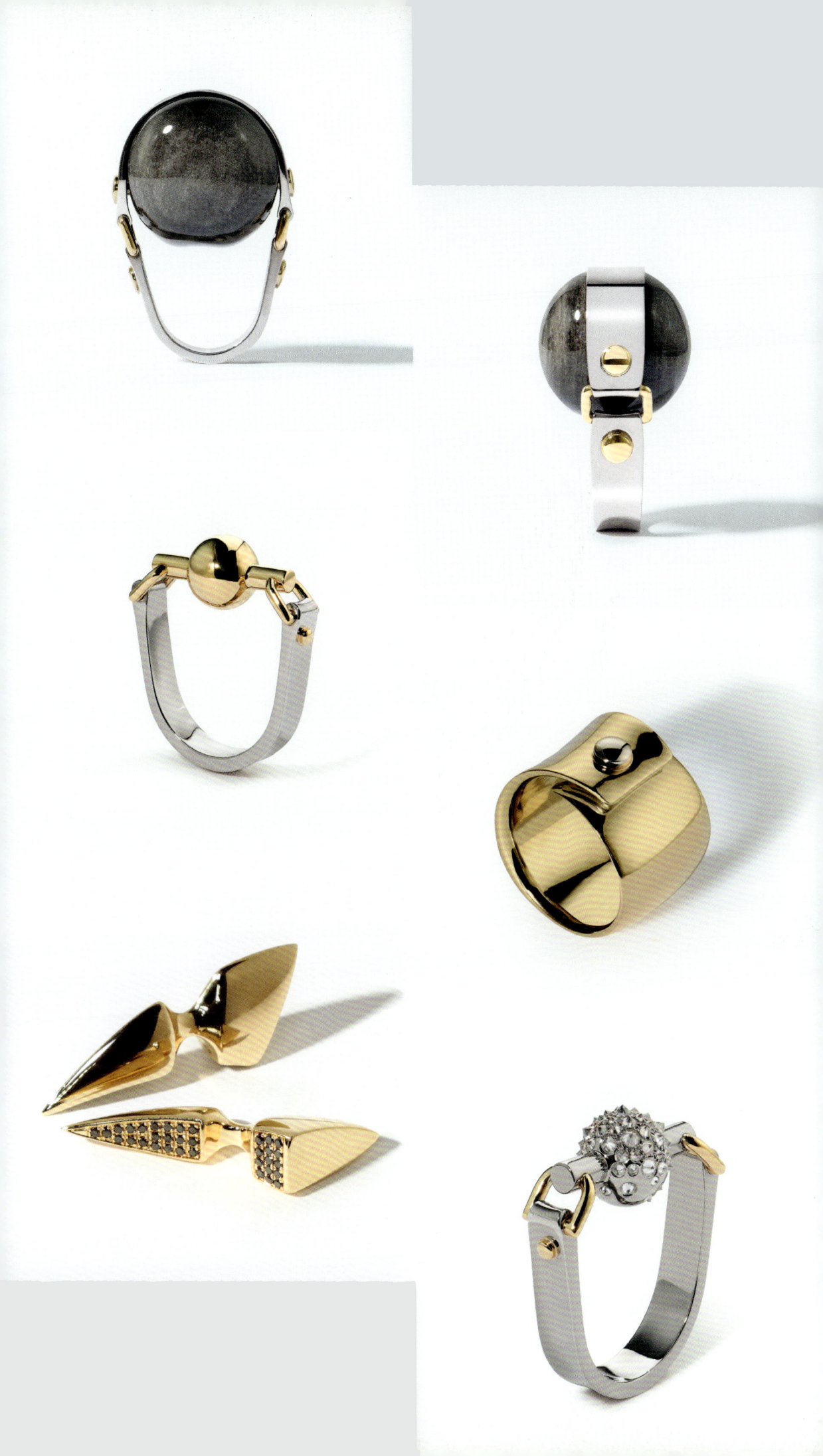

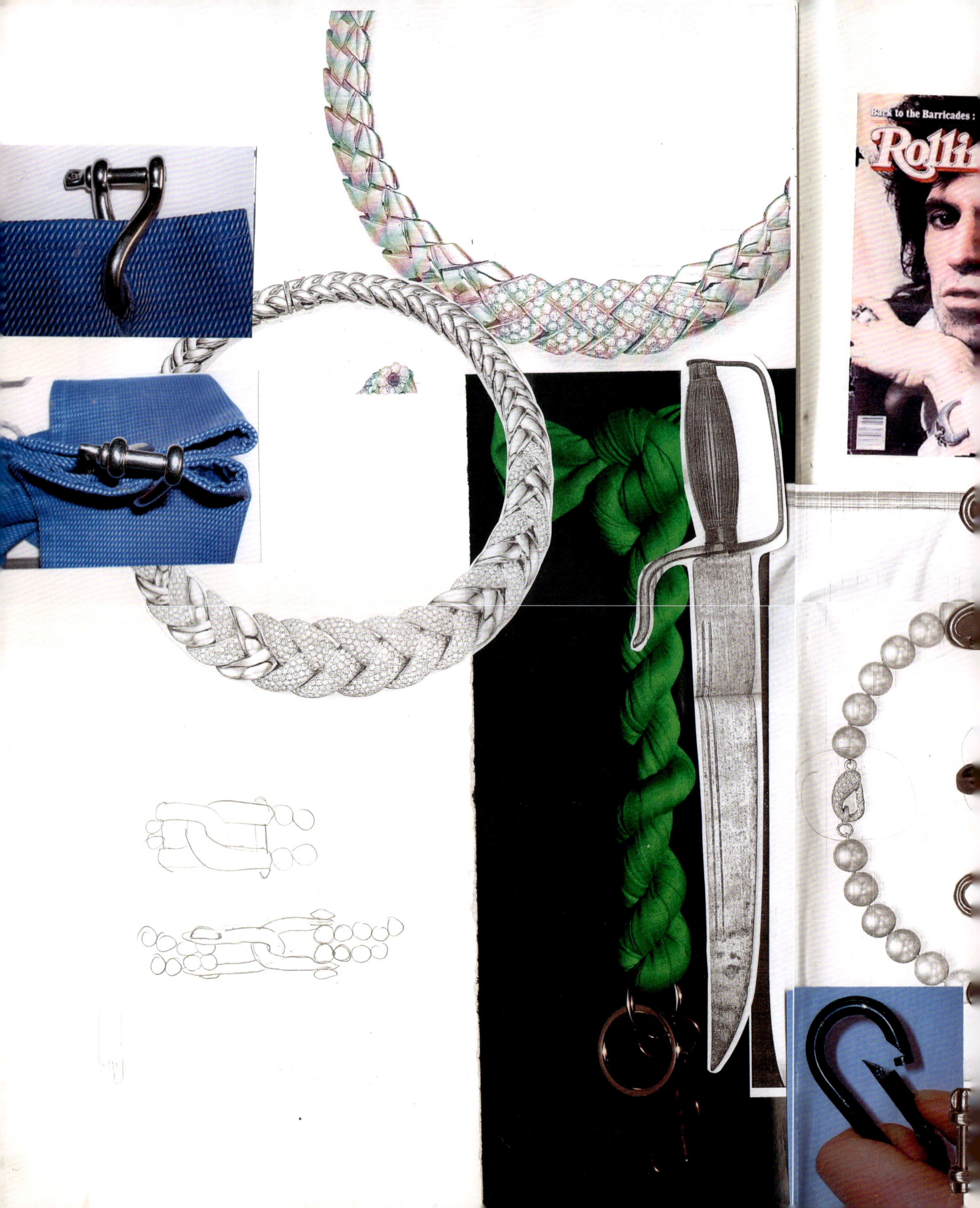
Back to the Barricades :
Rolli

Aguila Dorada, 2007. Double
Pearl Shackle Bracelet,
18ct gold and black pearls.

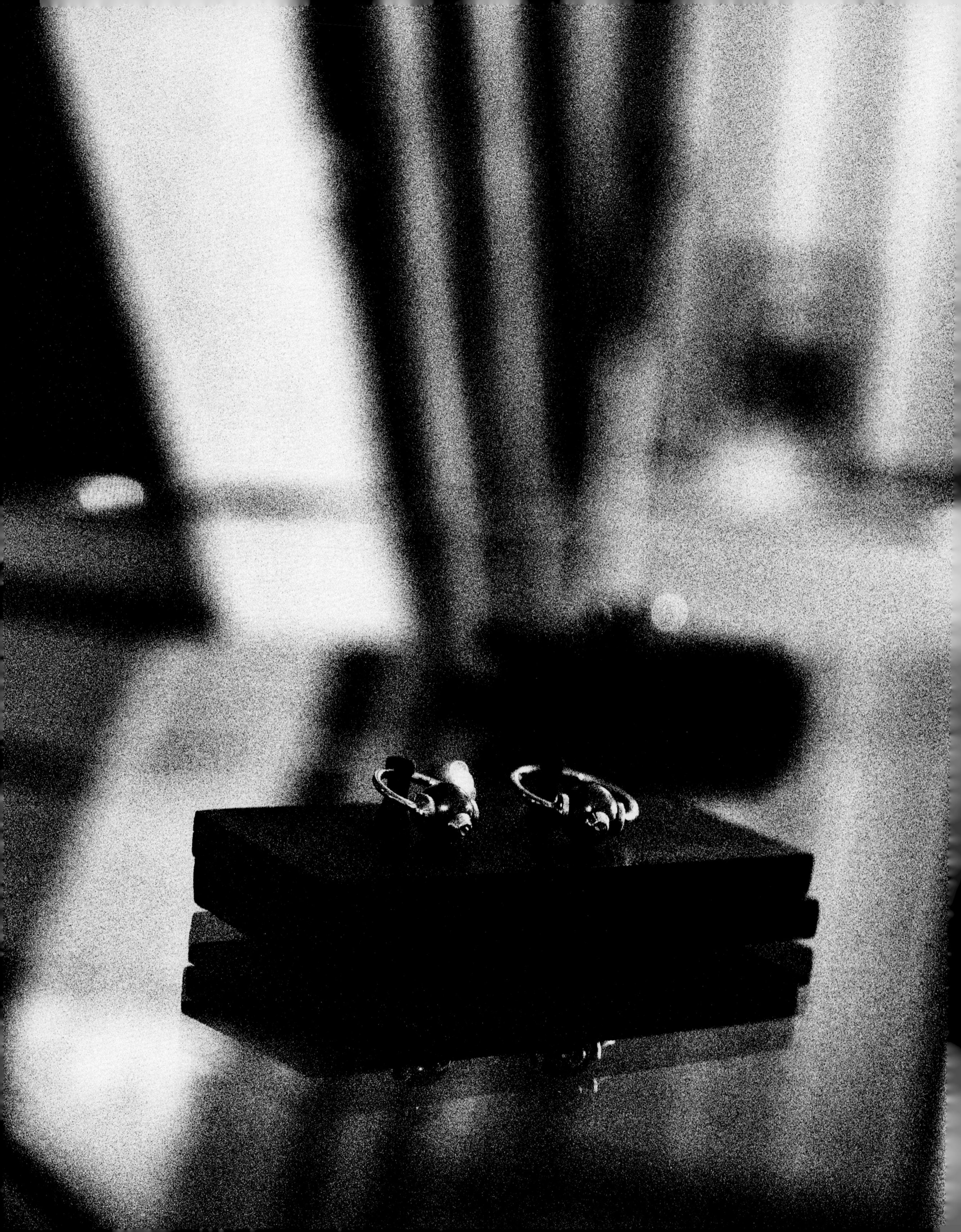

THIS PAGE FROM LEFT: Restraint Ring, 18ct gold, sapphires and diamonds, 2016; Solaris Drop Earrings, 18ct blackened gold, onyx and diamonds, 2012; Unknown Pleasures Ring, 18ct gold, black jade and sapphires, 2016.

FOLLOWING PAGES LEFT: Sketches for Somebody's Sins, 2016.

PAGES 140-141: Moodboards in process for The Perfect Drug, 2024.

' Jewellery should feel like it could last forever. Not just in its materials, but in its meaning. '

the alchemy of adornment < 137

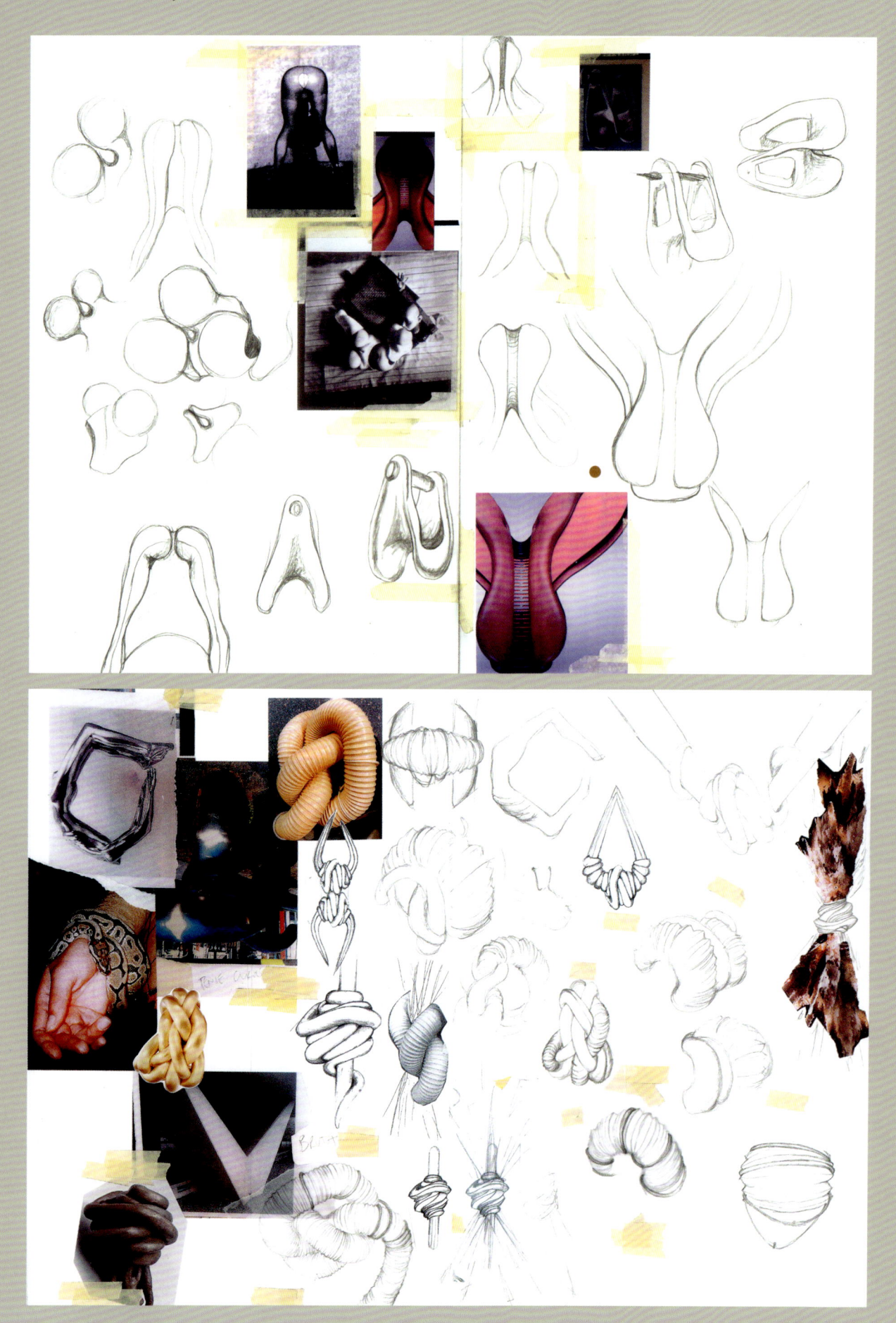

138 > the alchemy of adornment

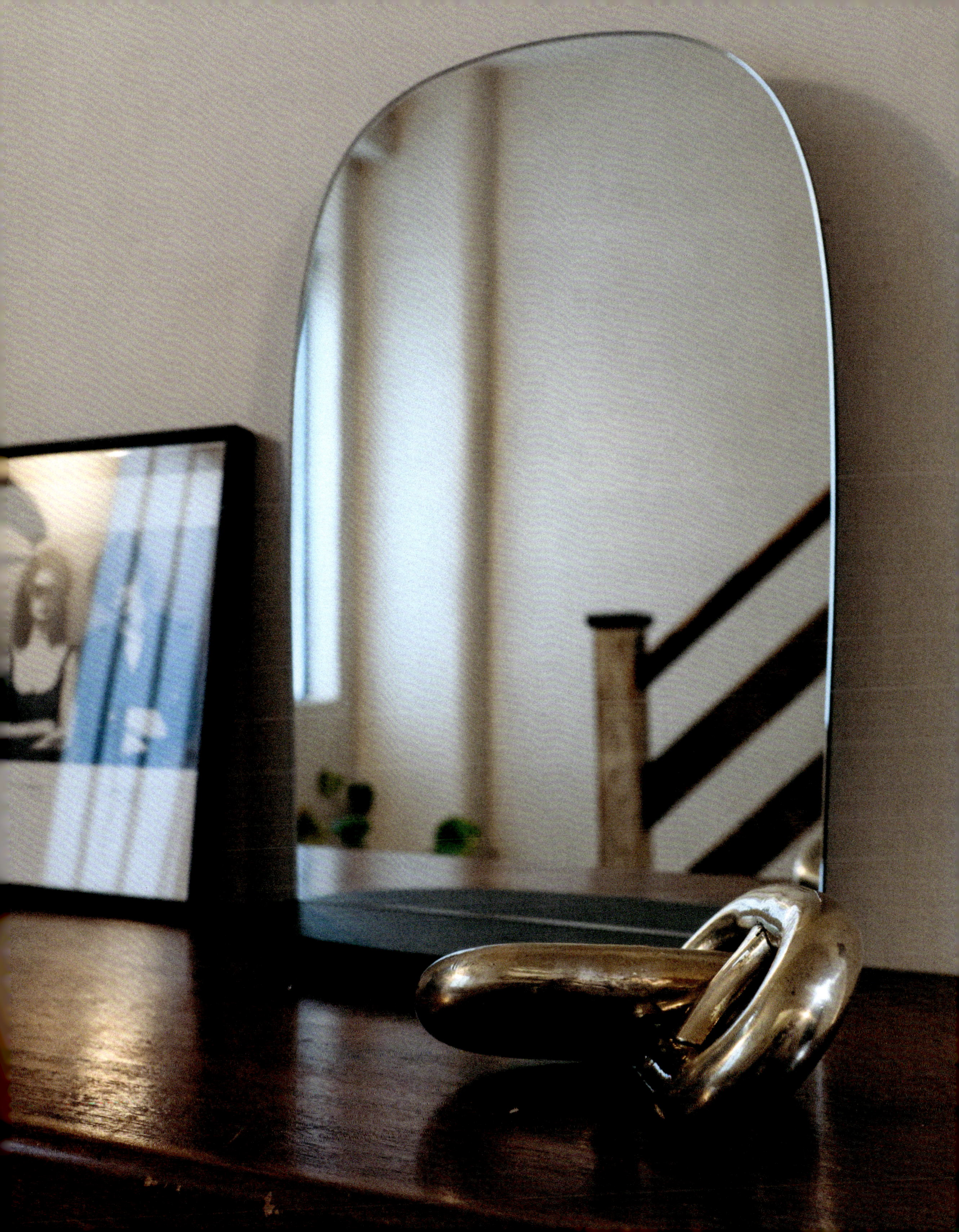

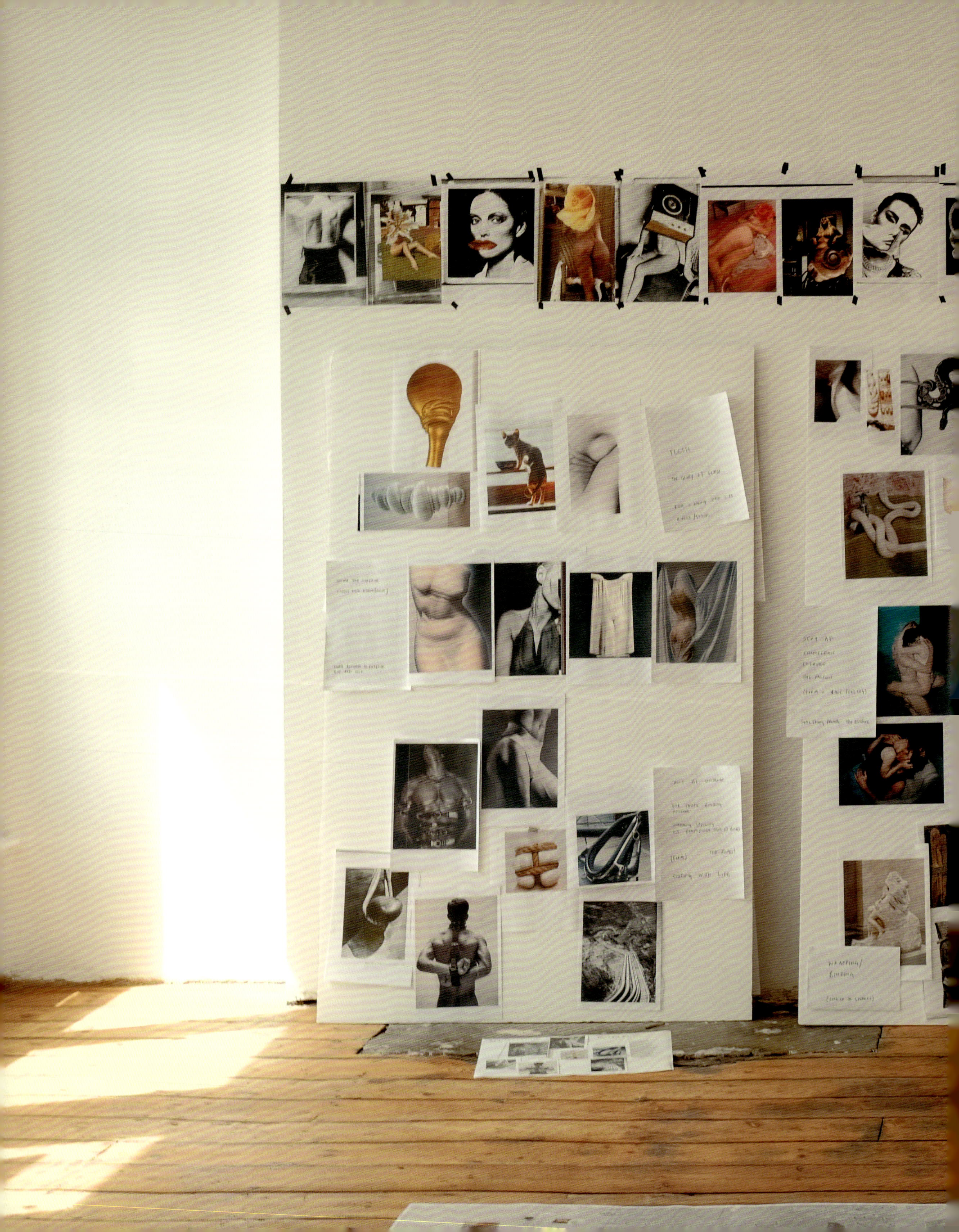

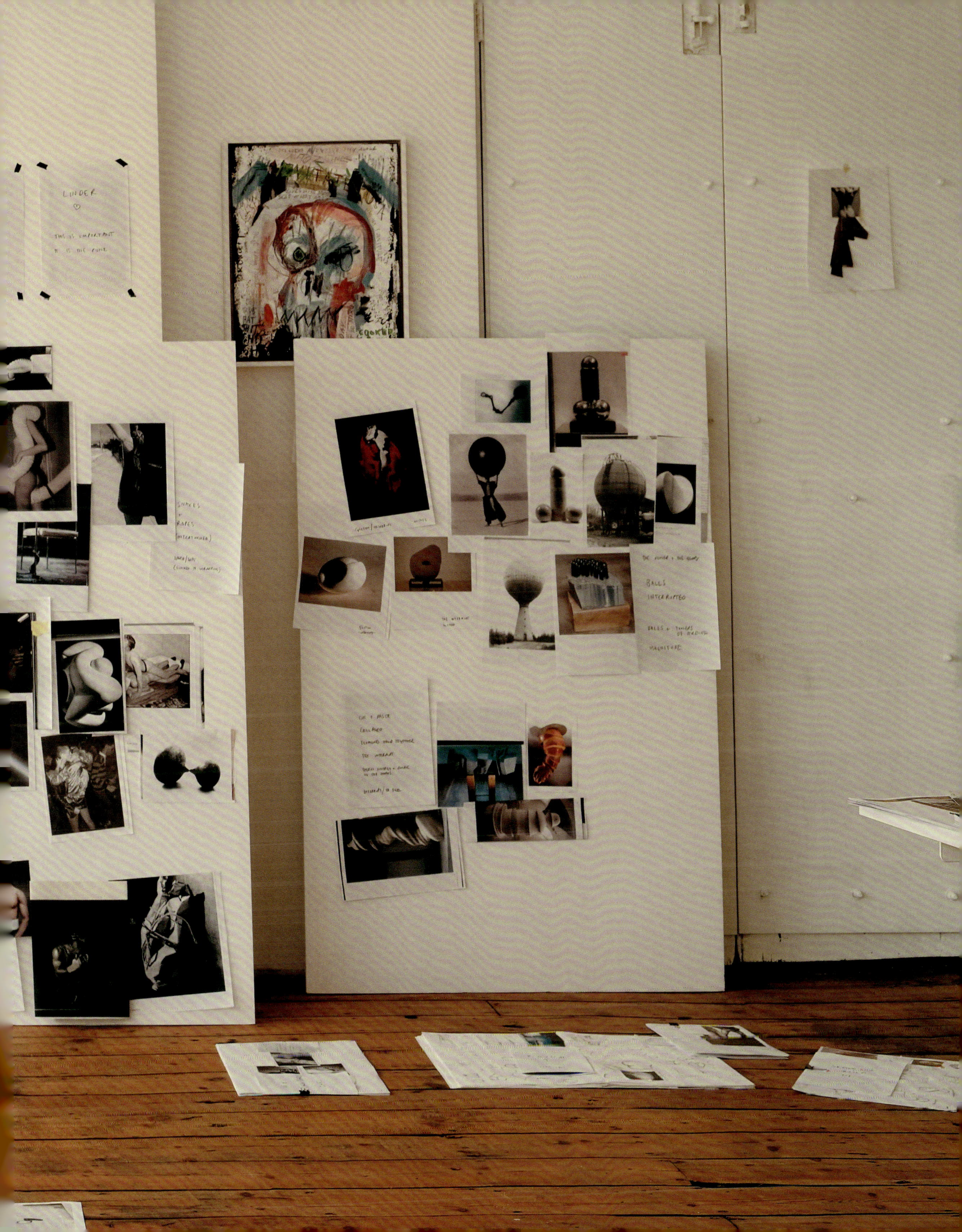

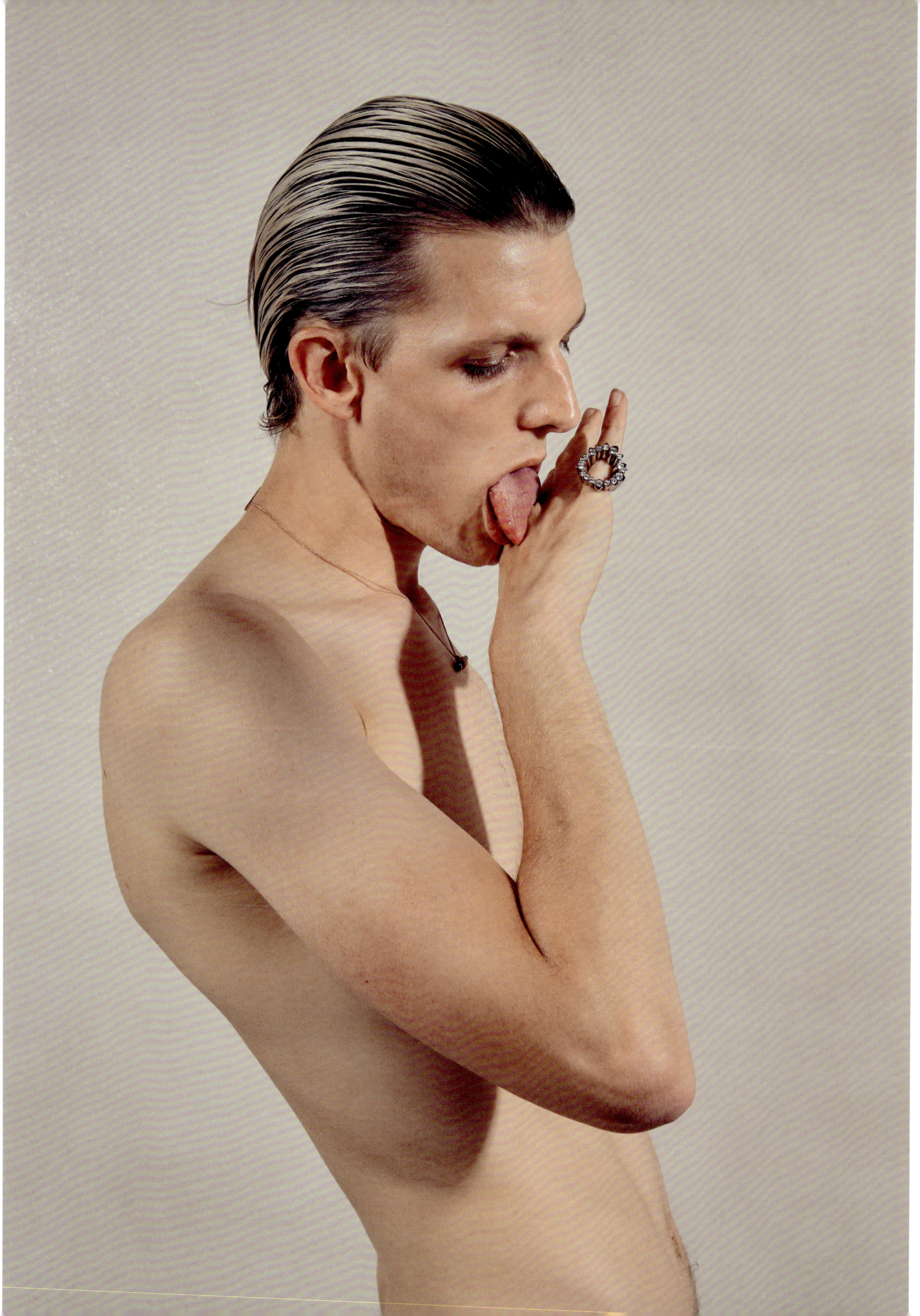

the alchemy of adornment < 143

' Jewellery is an extension of the self.

It's anything but just ornamental. '

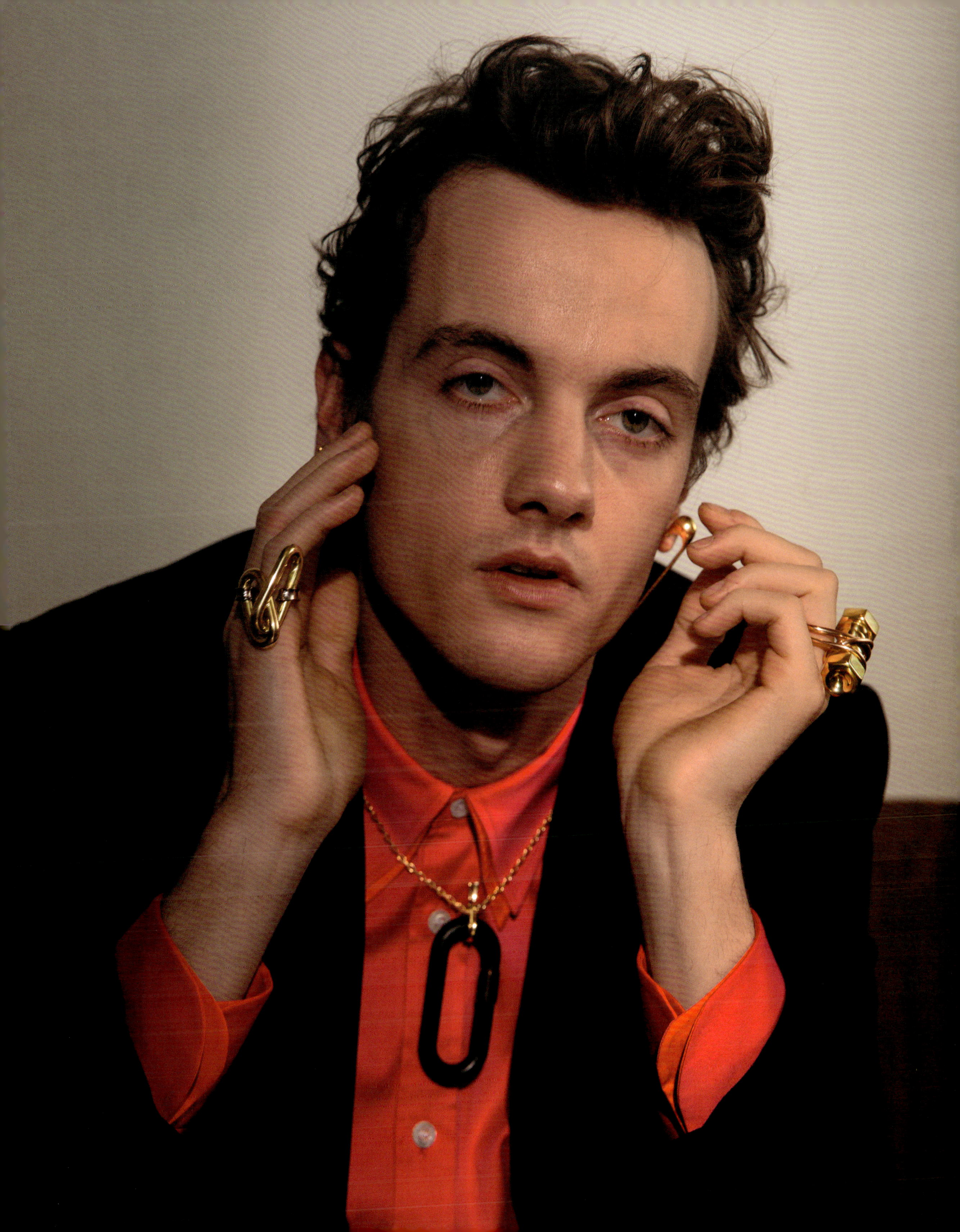

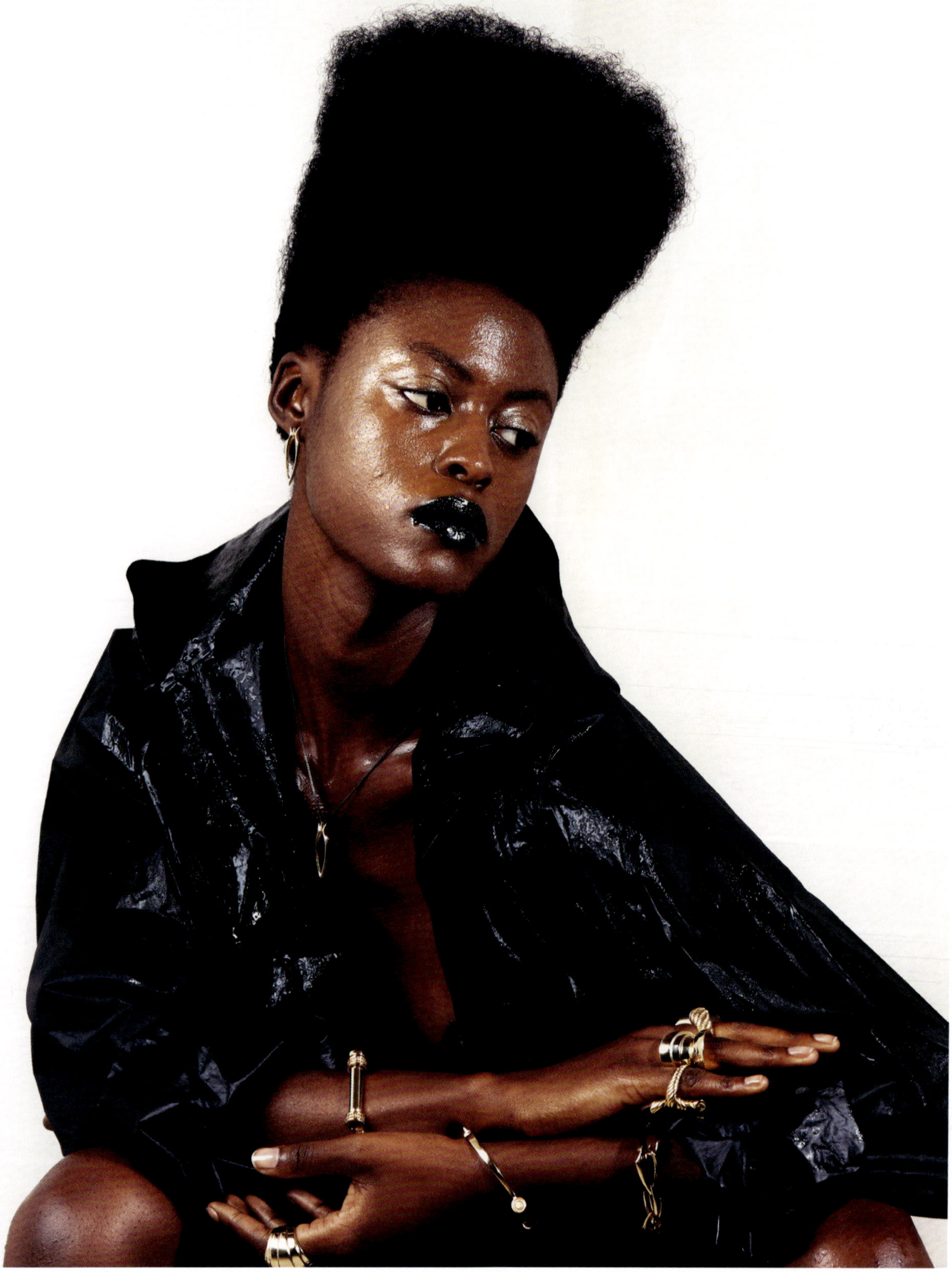

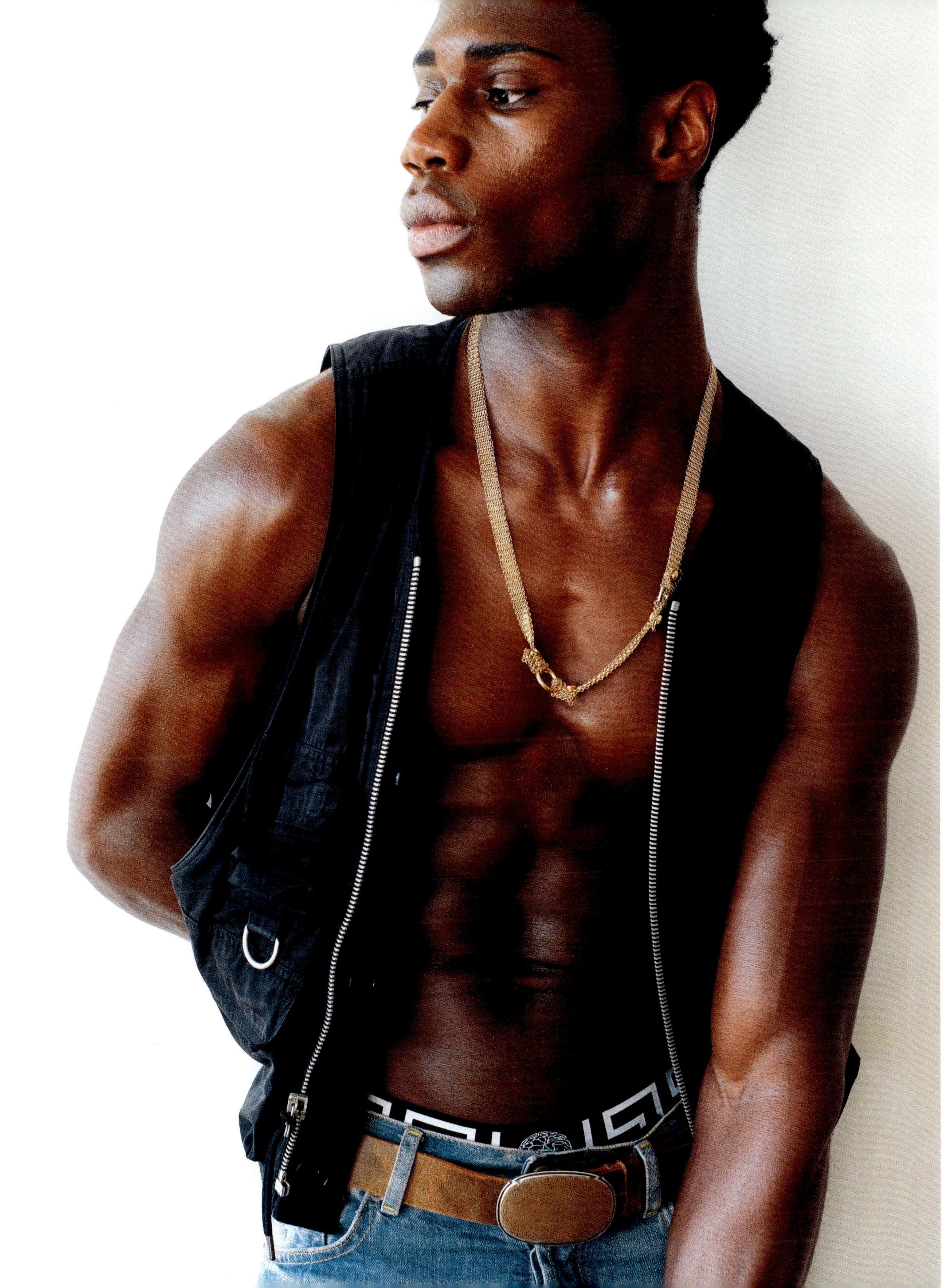

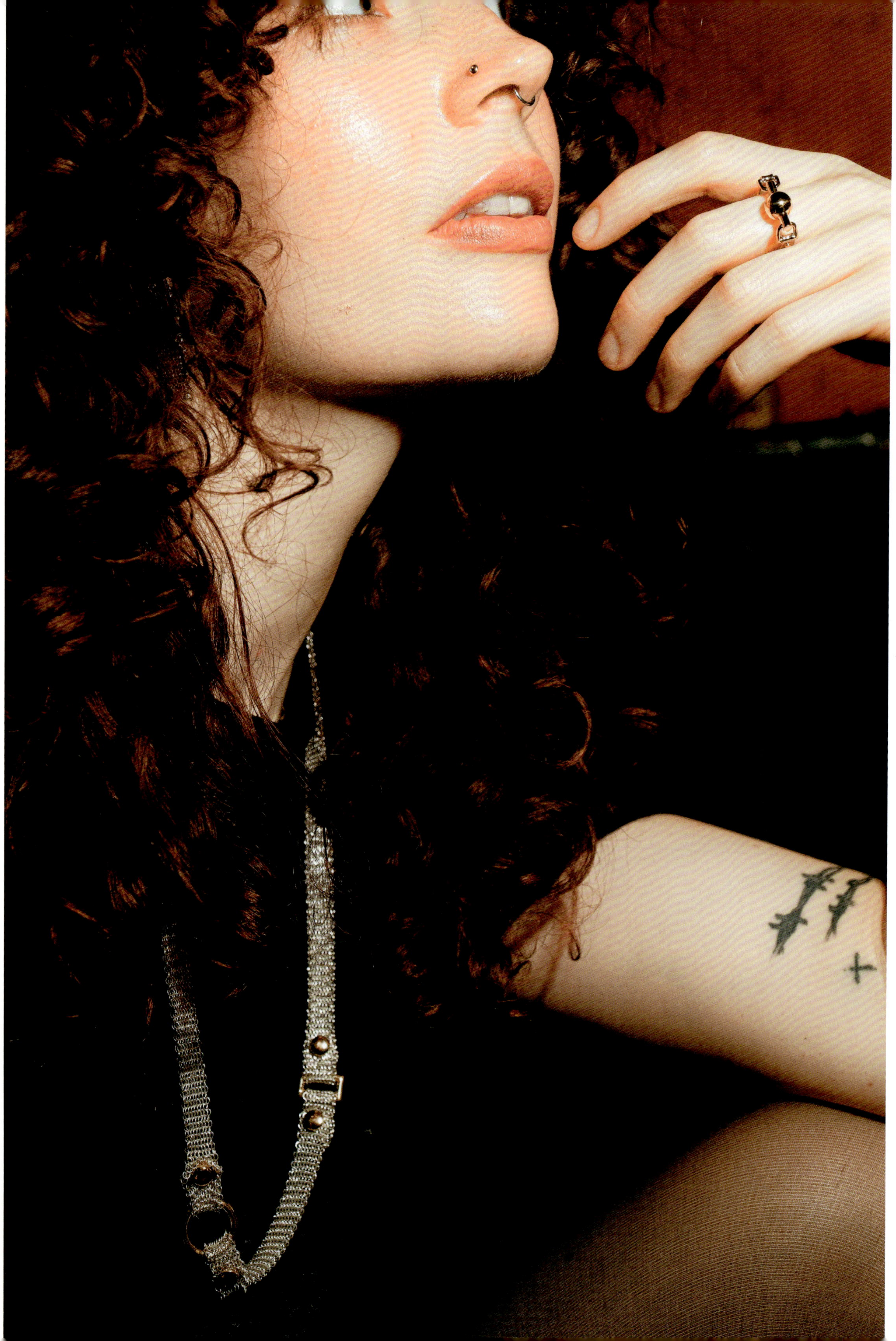

the alchemy of adornment < 149

'From the very beginning I've always said that I want to make sexy jewellery. Jewellery IS sexy.'

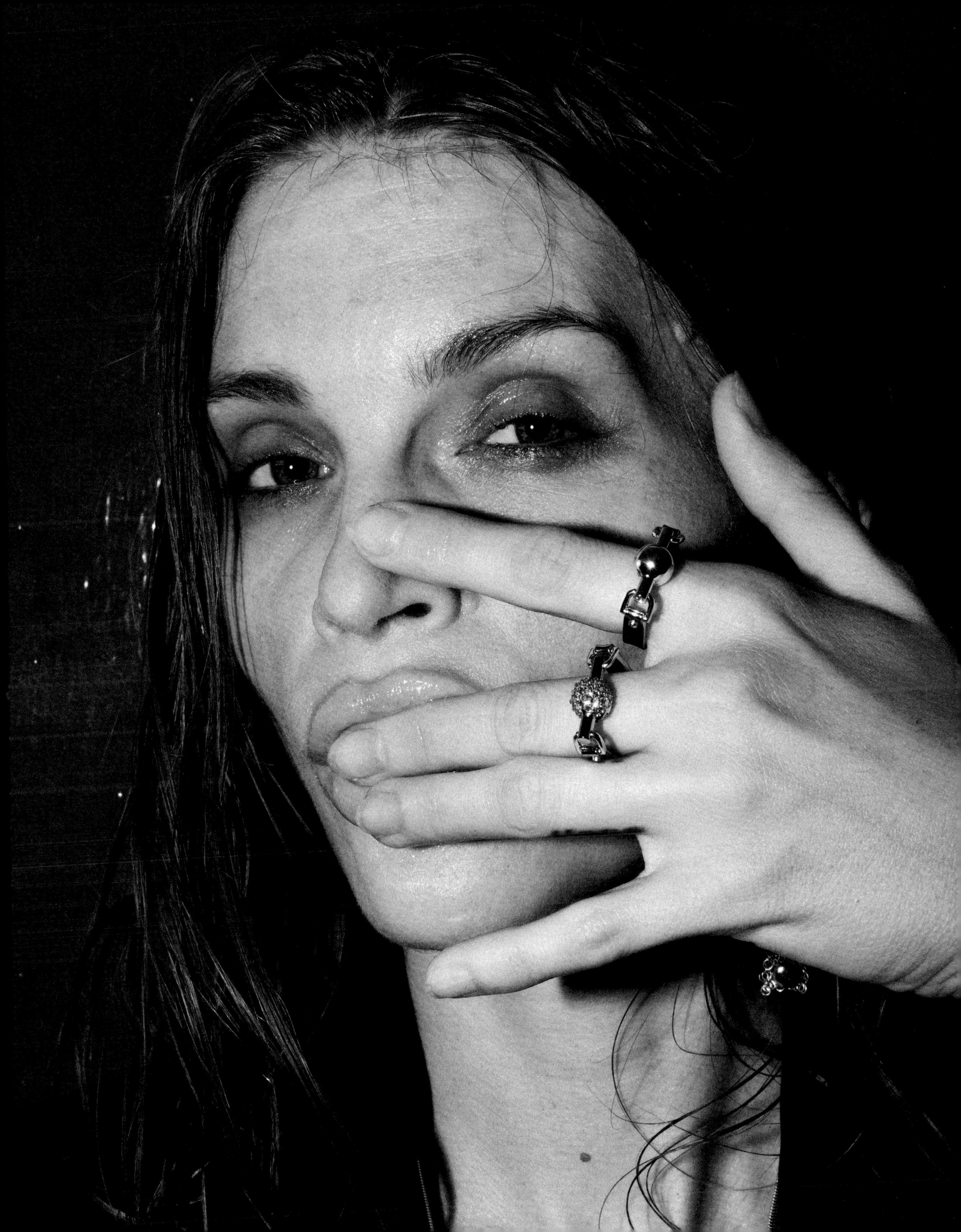

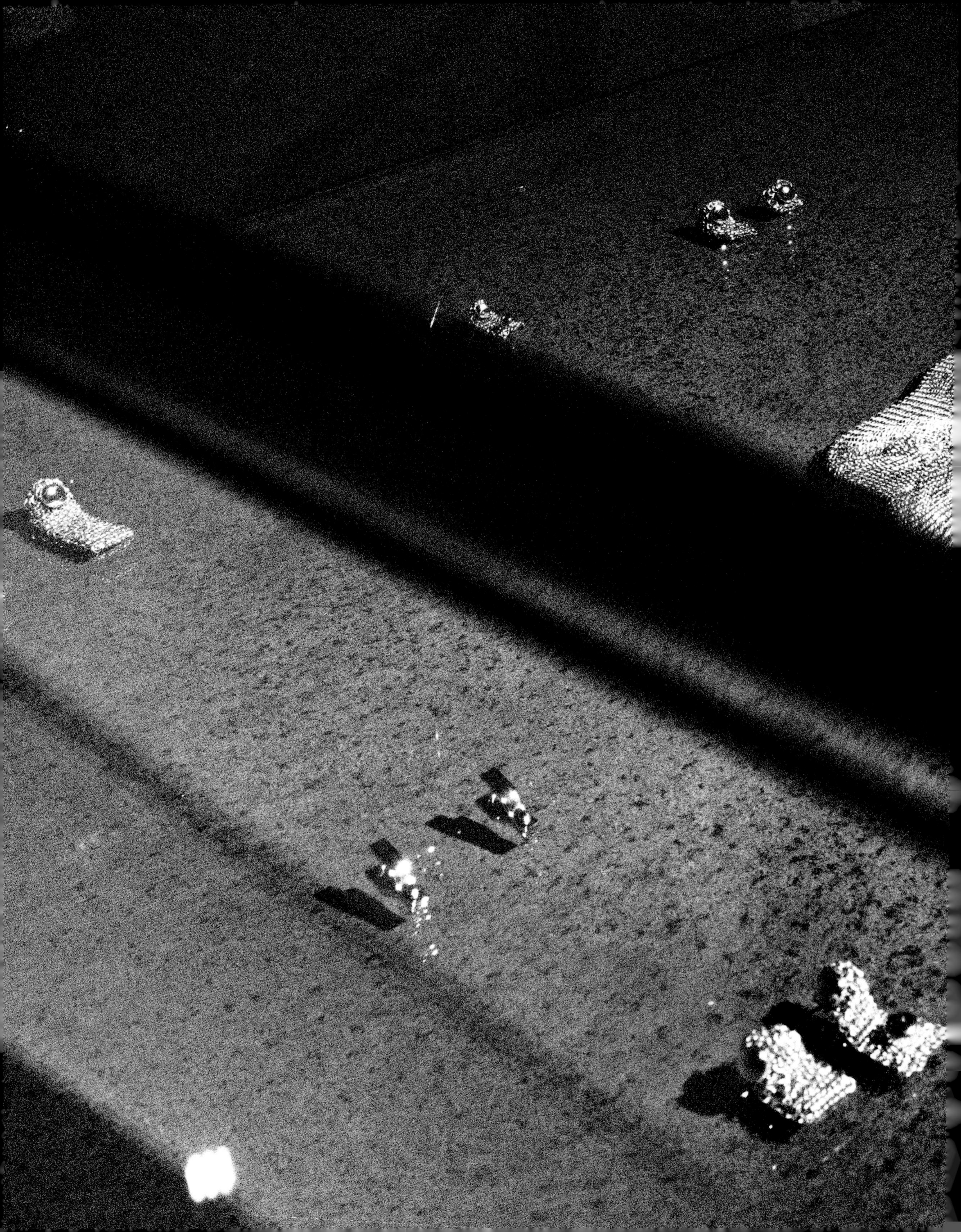

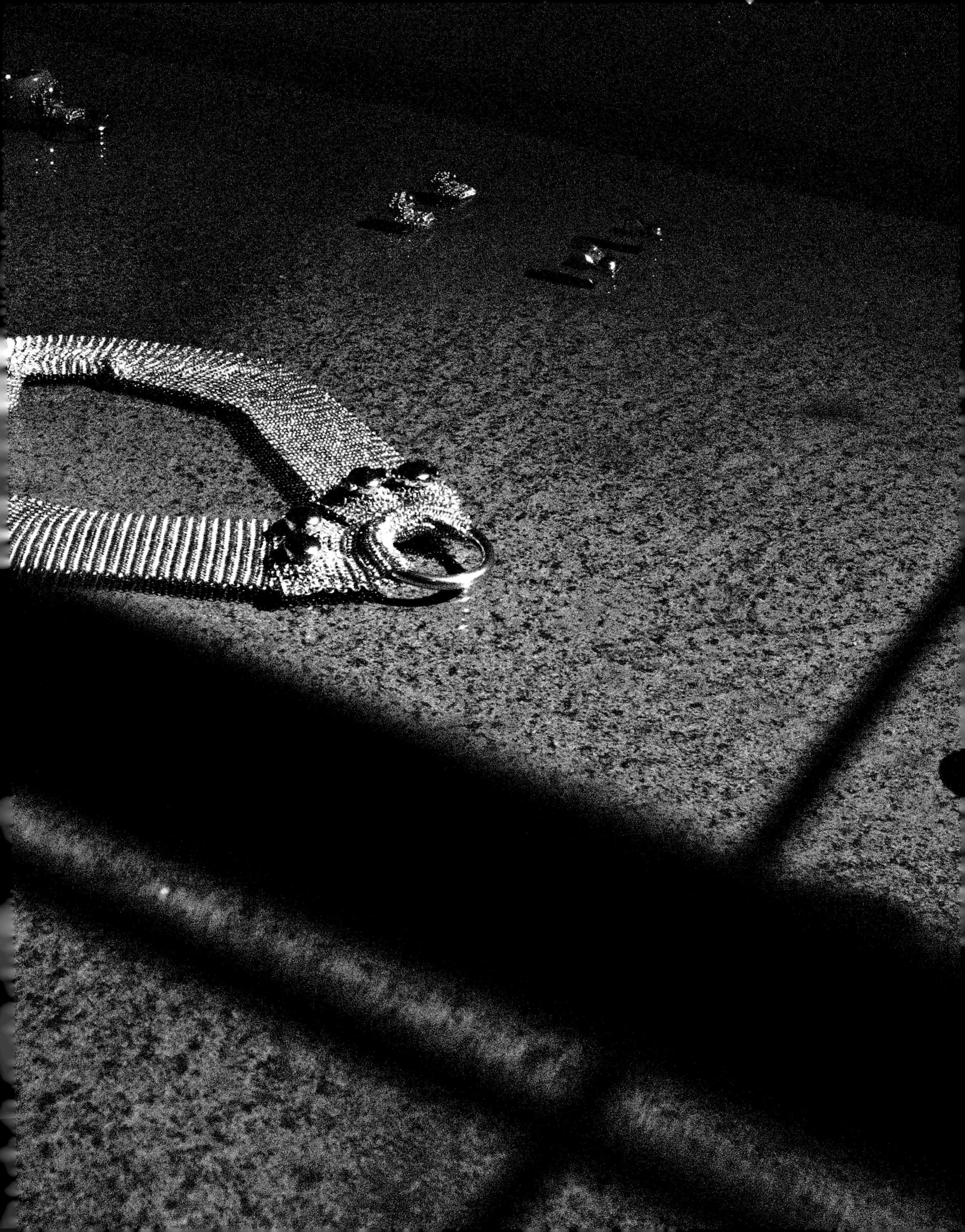

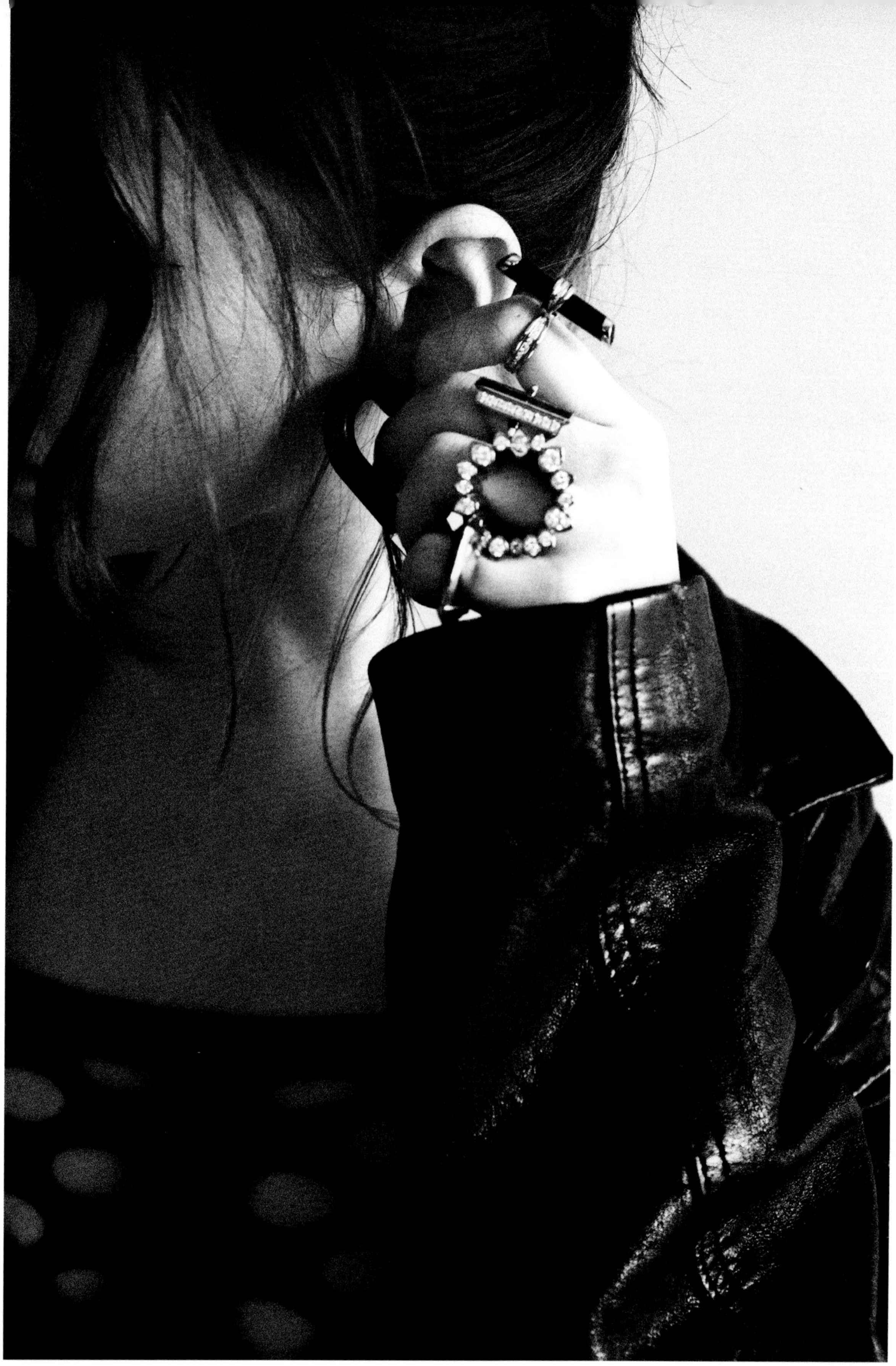

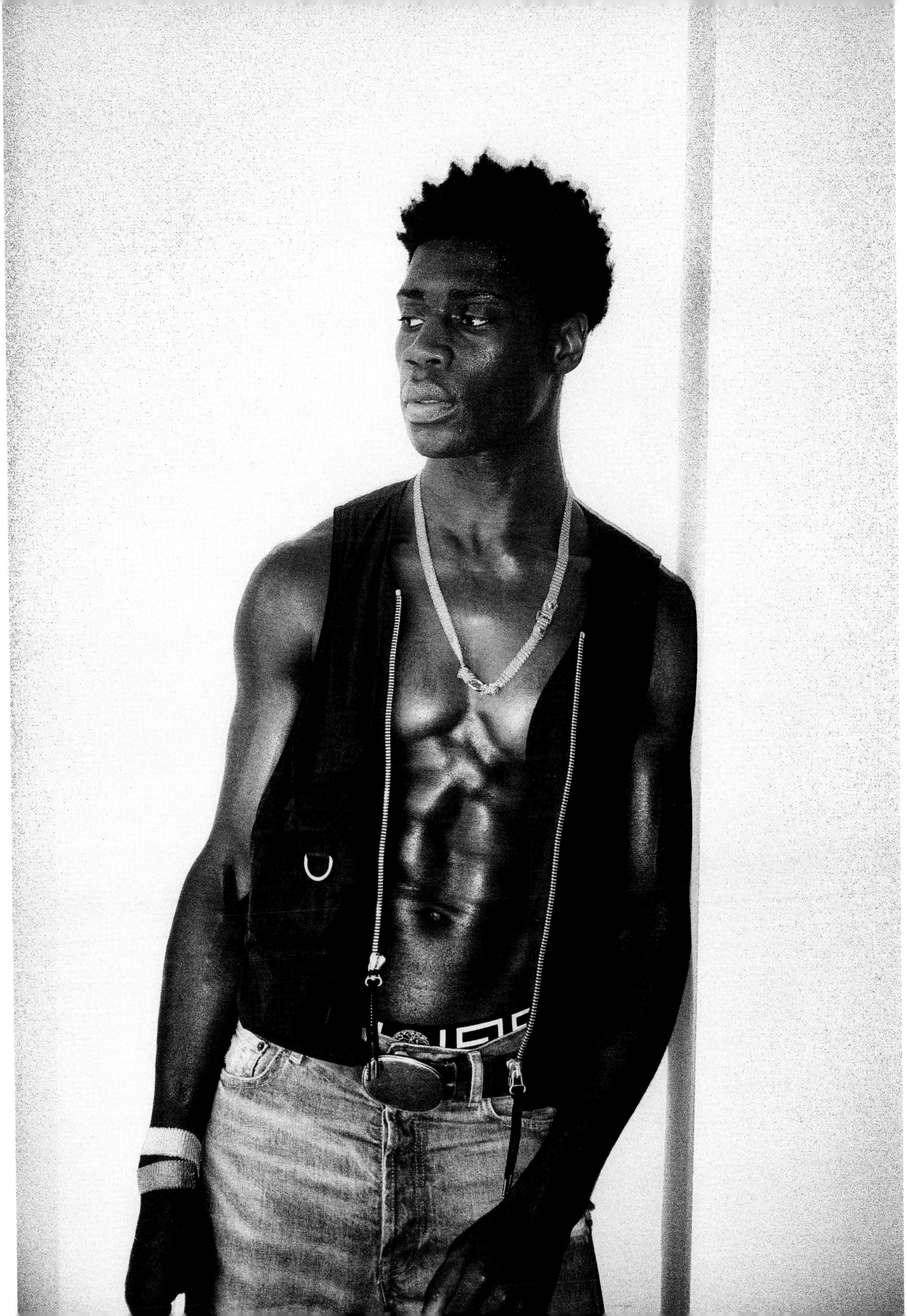

156 > the alchemy of adornment

the alchemy of adornment < 157

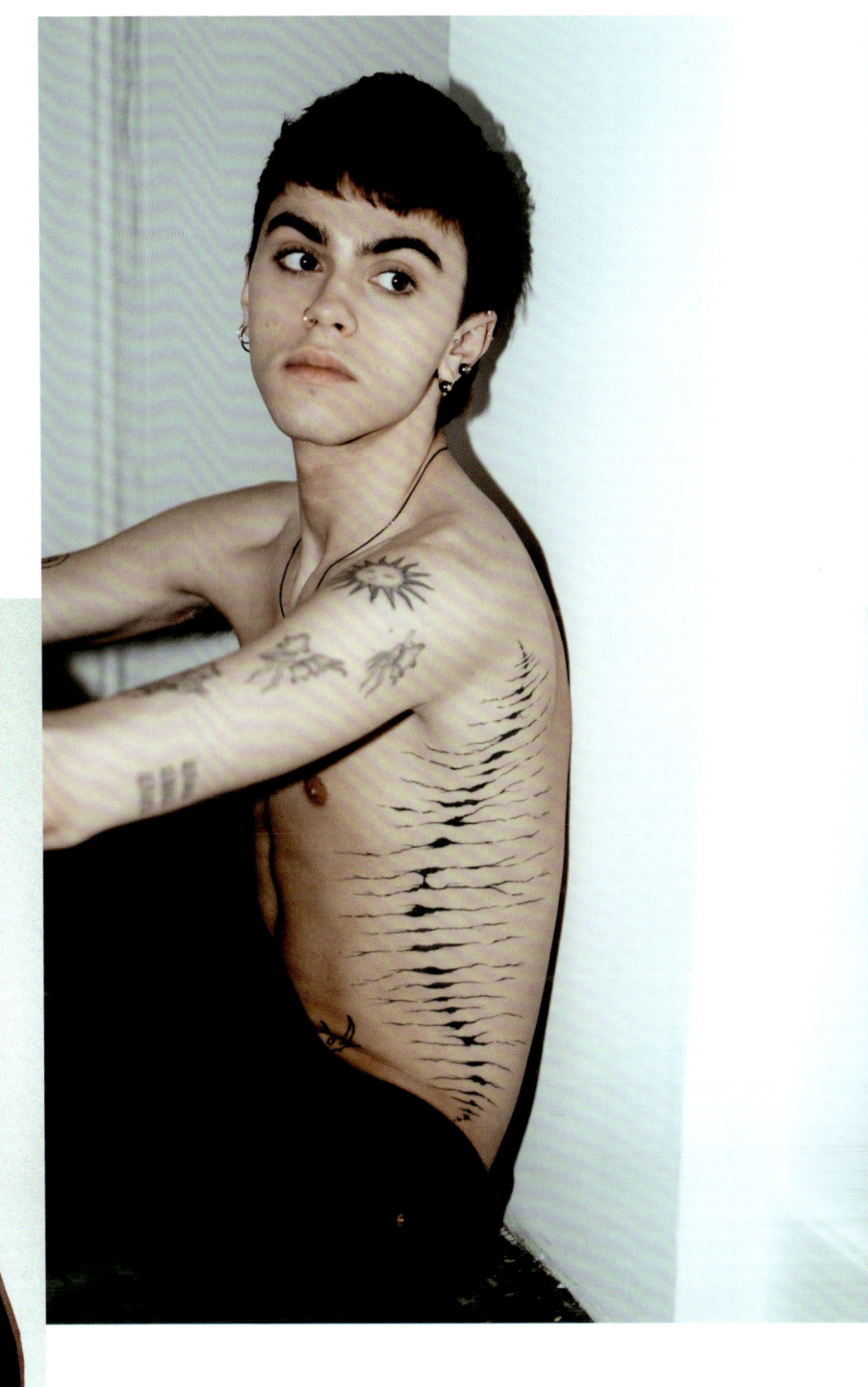

158 > the alchemy of adornment

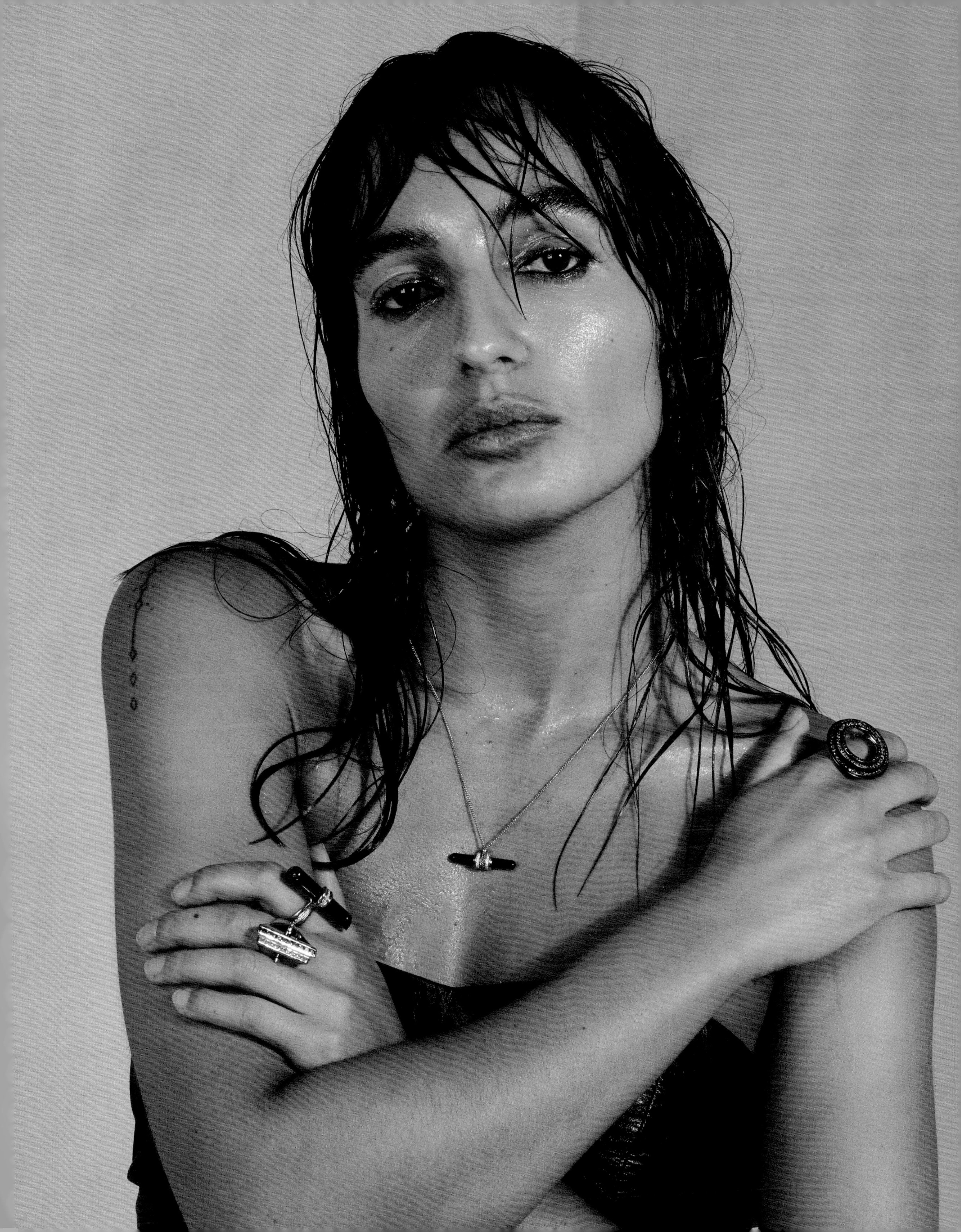

160 > the alchemy of adornment

' I didn't know that I was not supposed to do that with luxury, because it was never ingrained in me. '

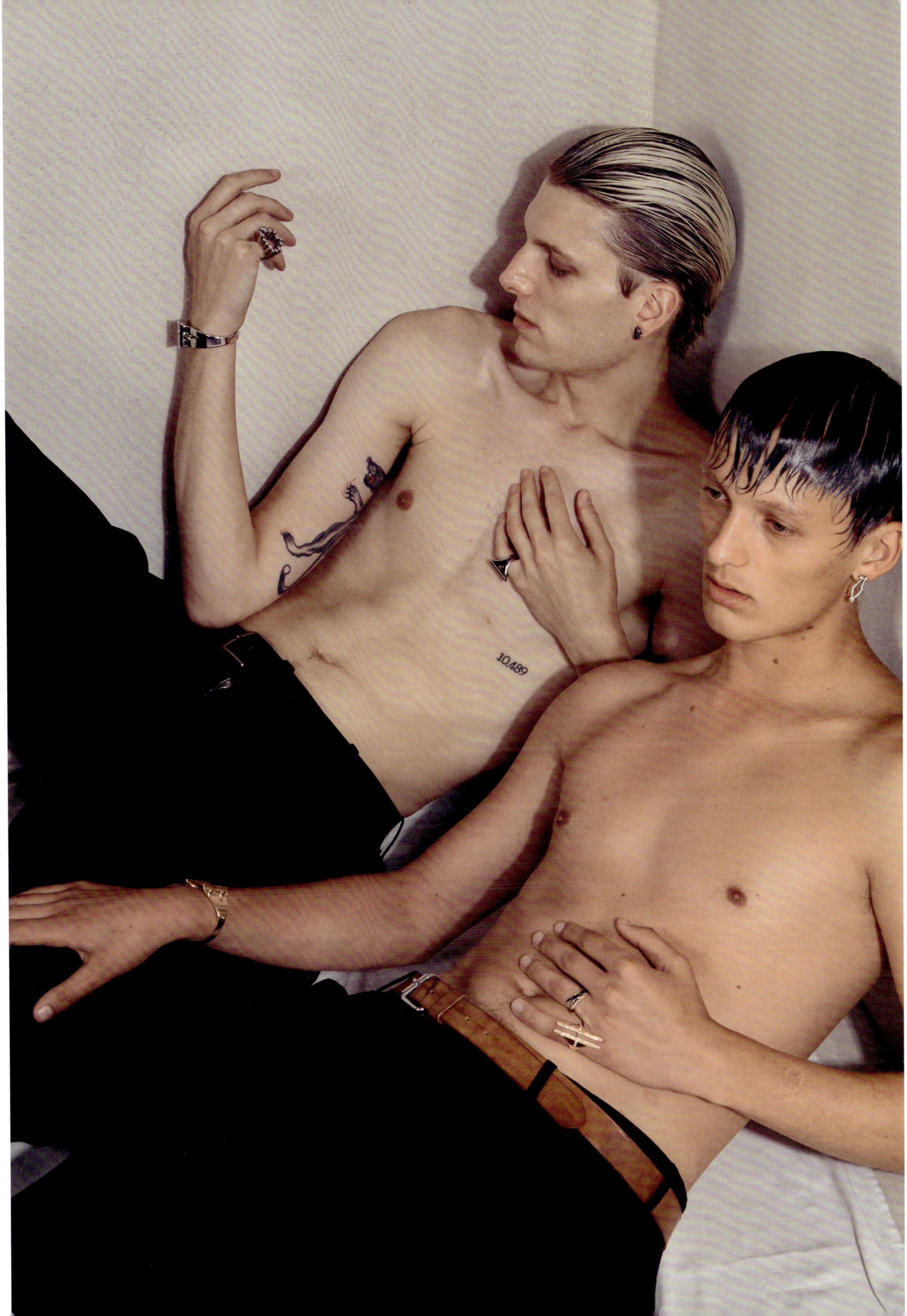
10,489

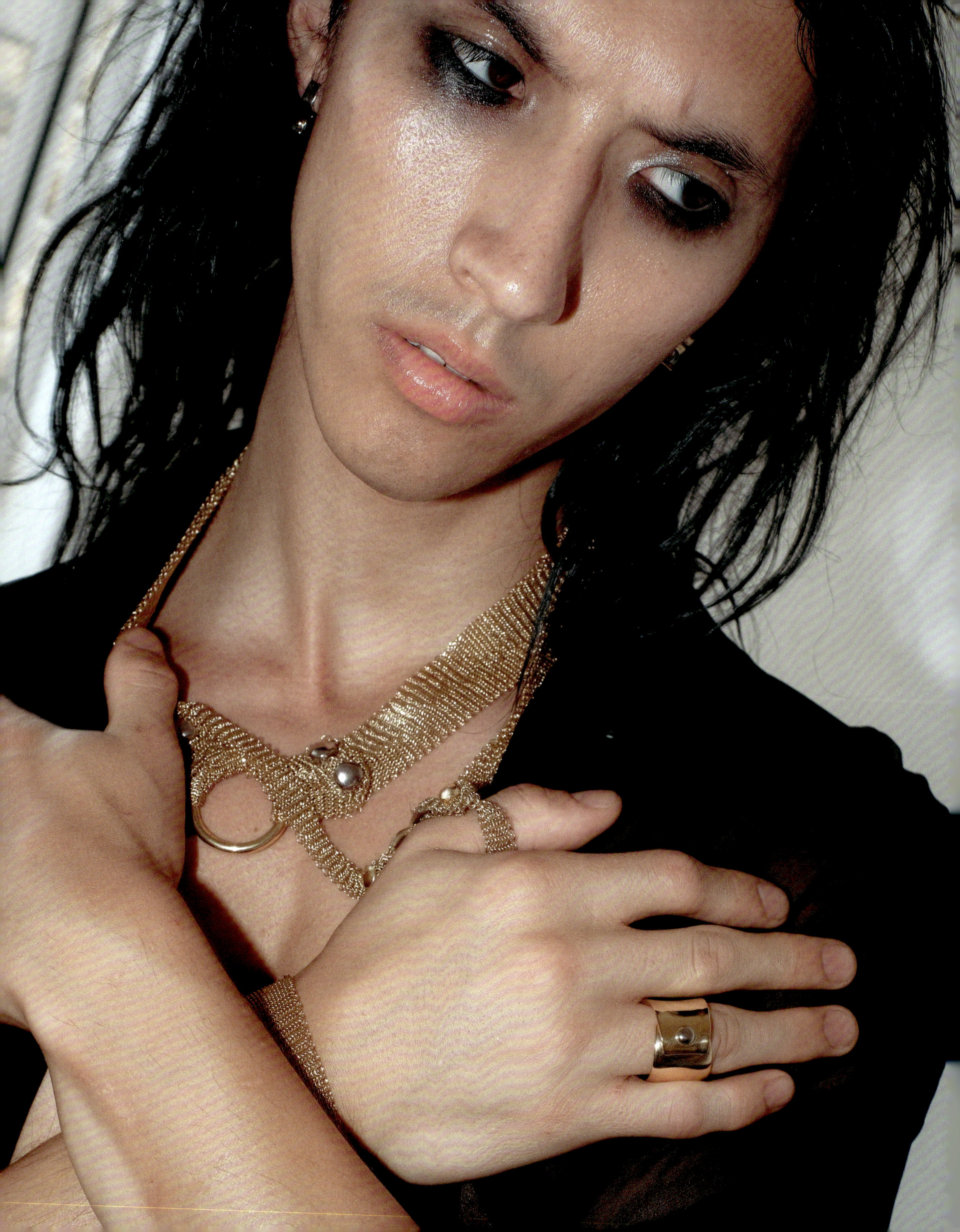

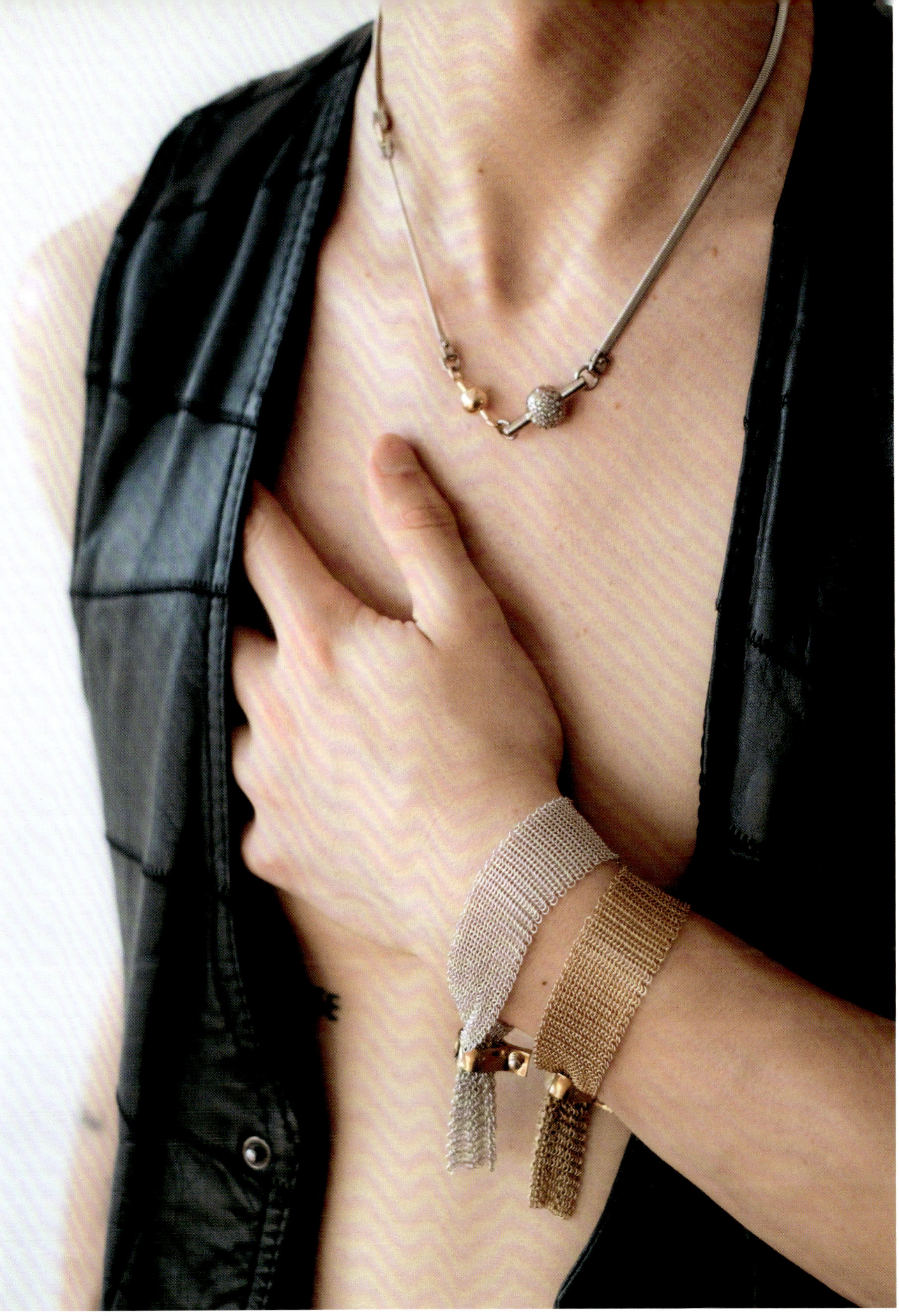

"Jewellery should not merely be worn. It should be felt."

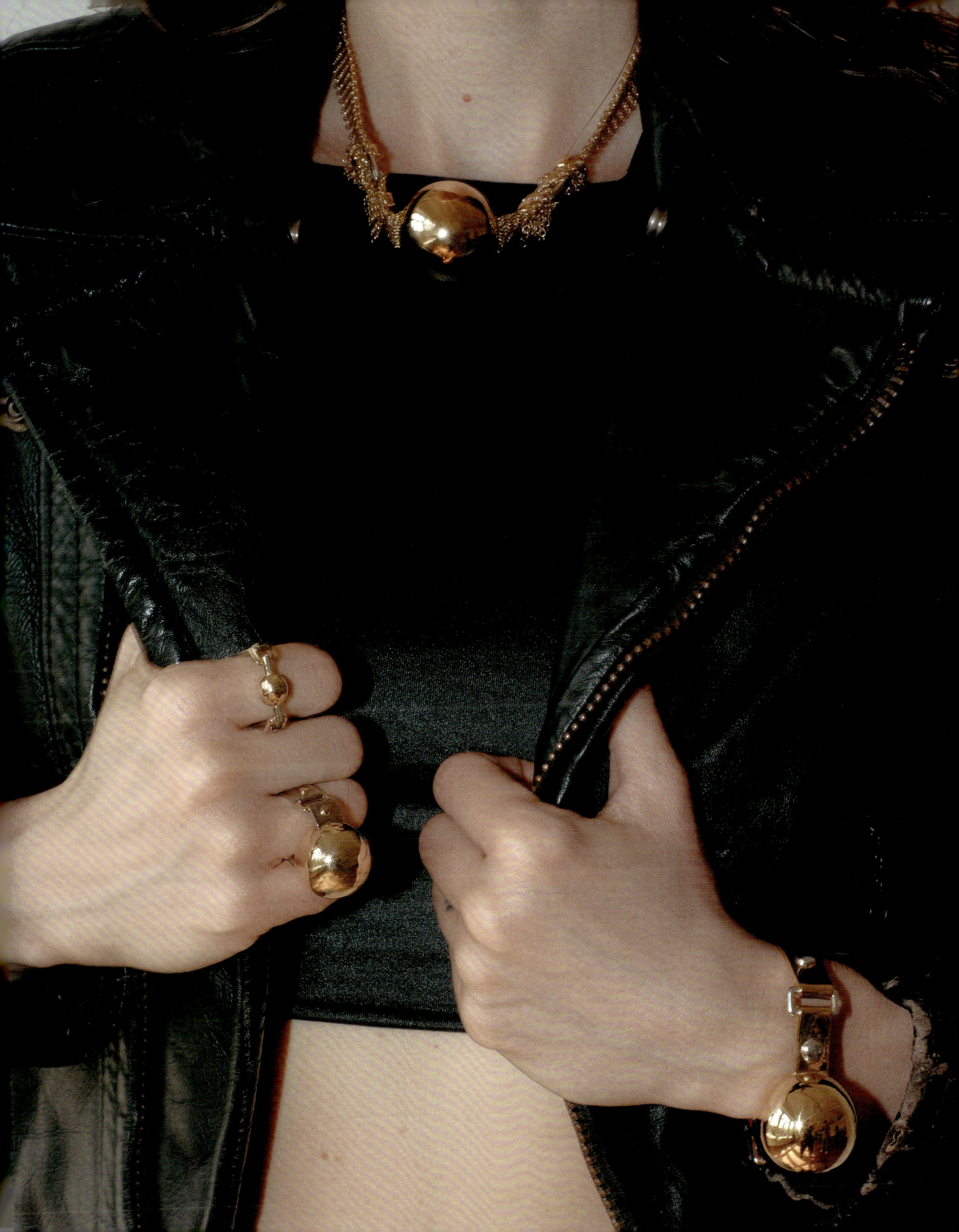

166 > the alchemy of adornment

the alchemy of adornment < 167

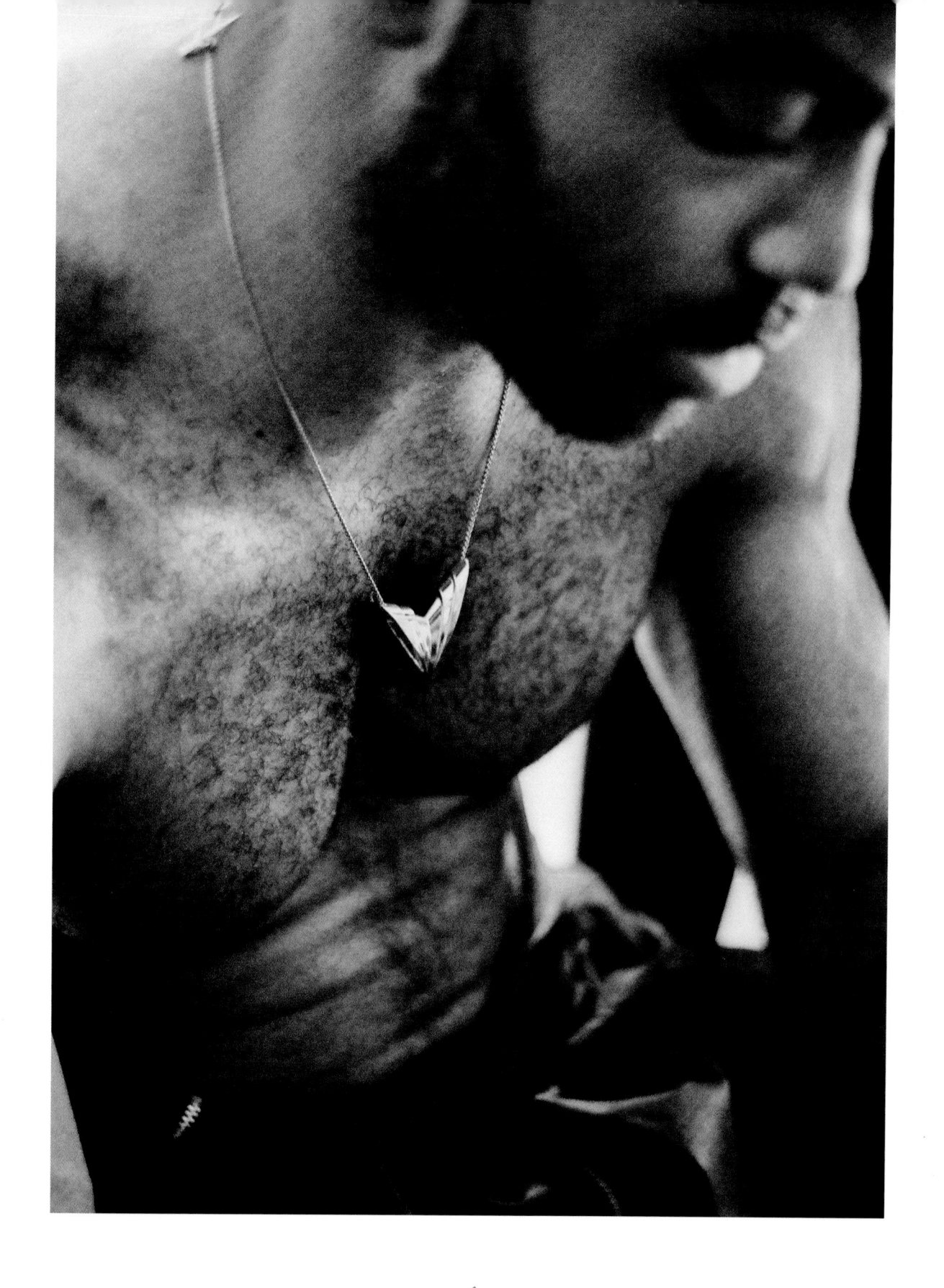

❛ I want this work to make my heart beat faster. To make *your* heart beat faster. ❜

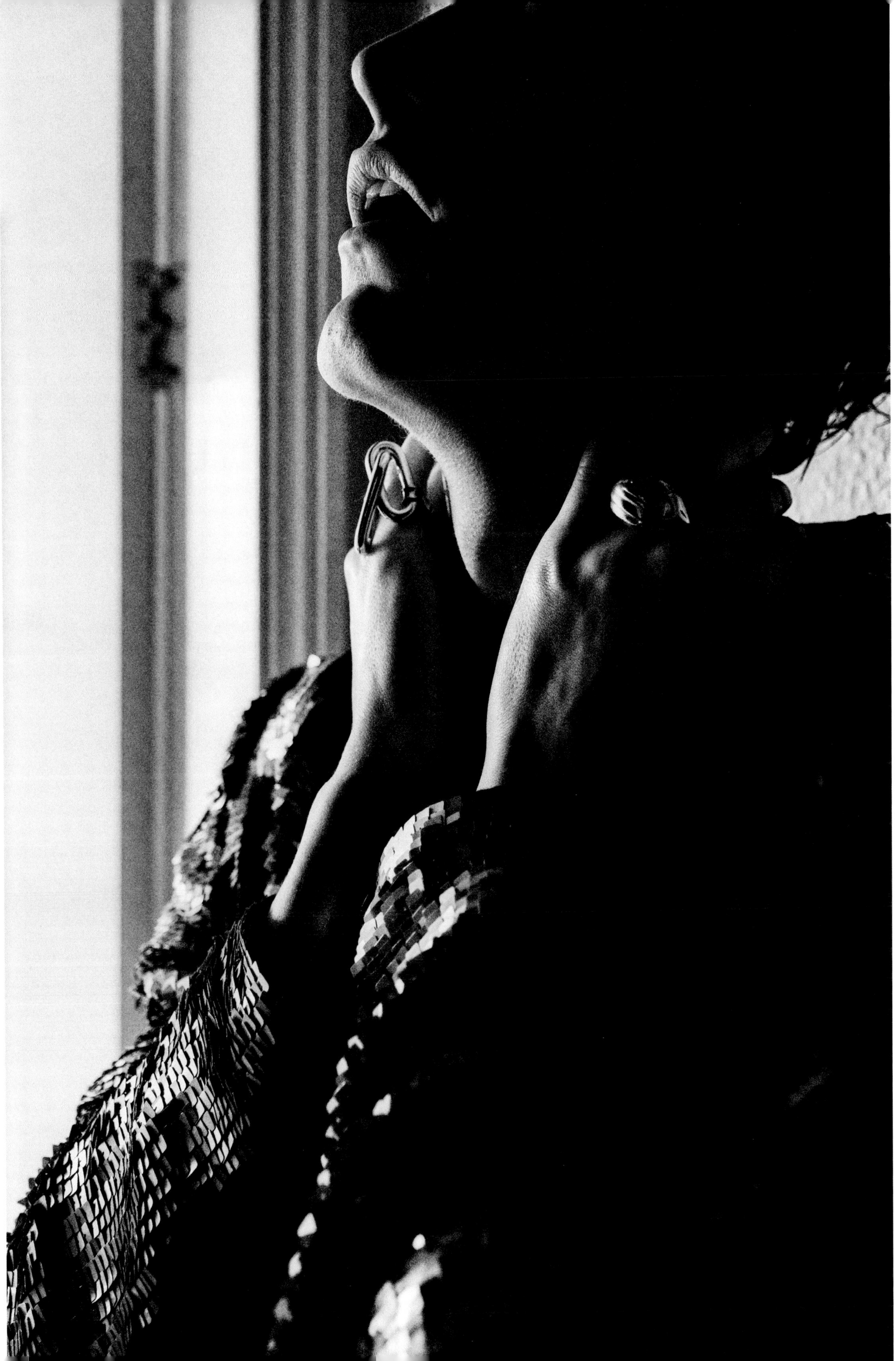

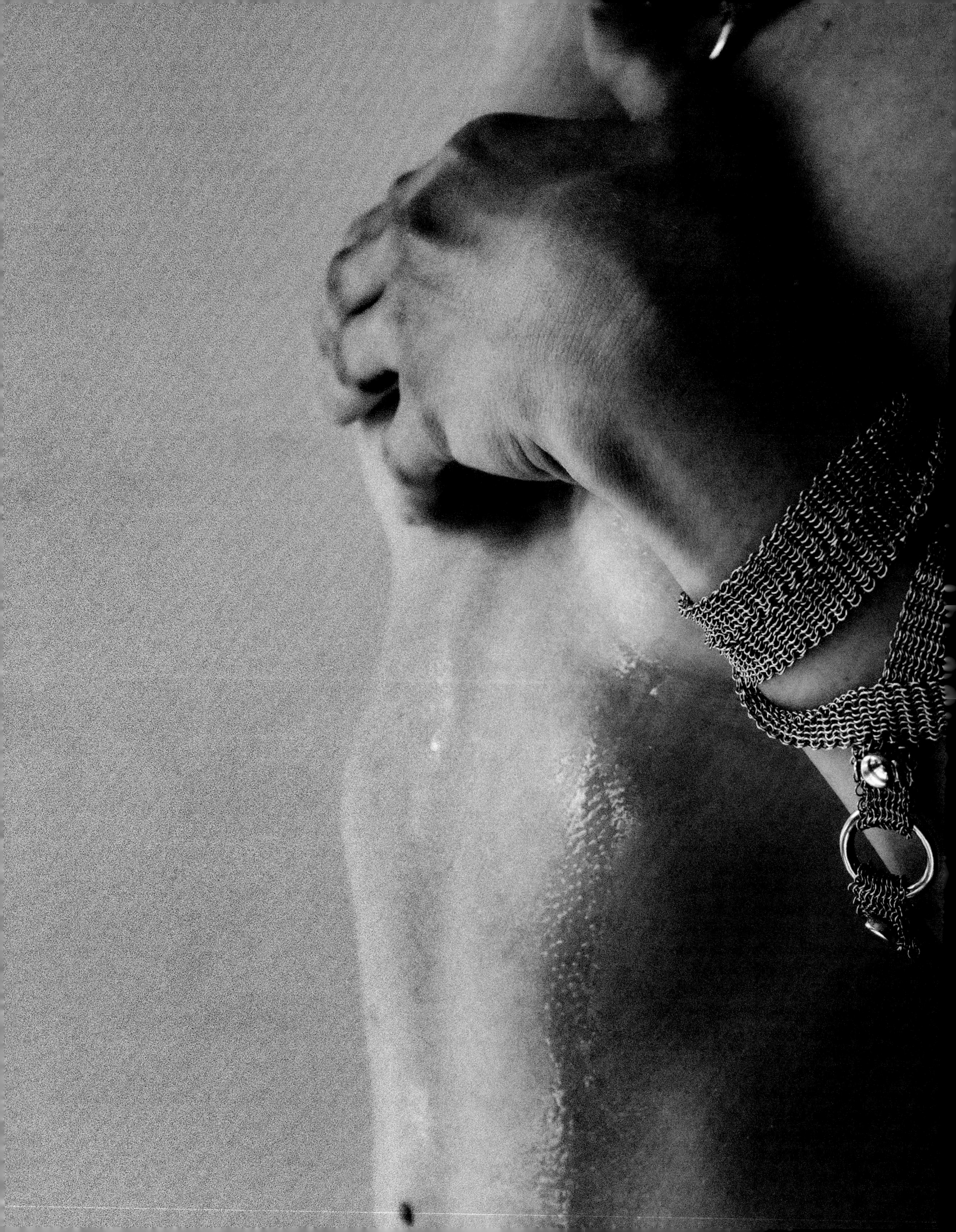

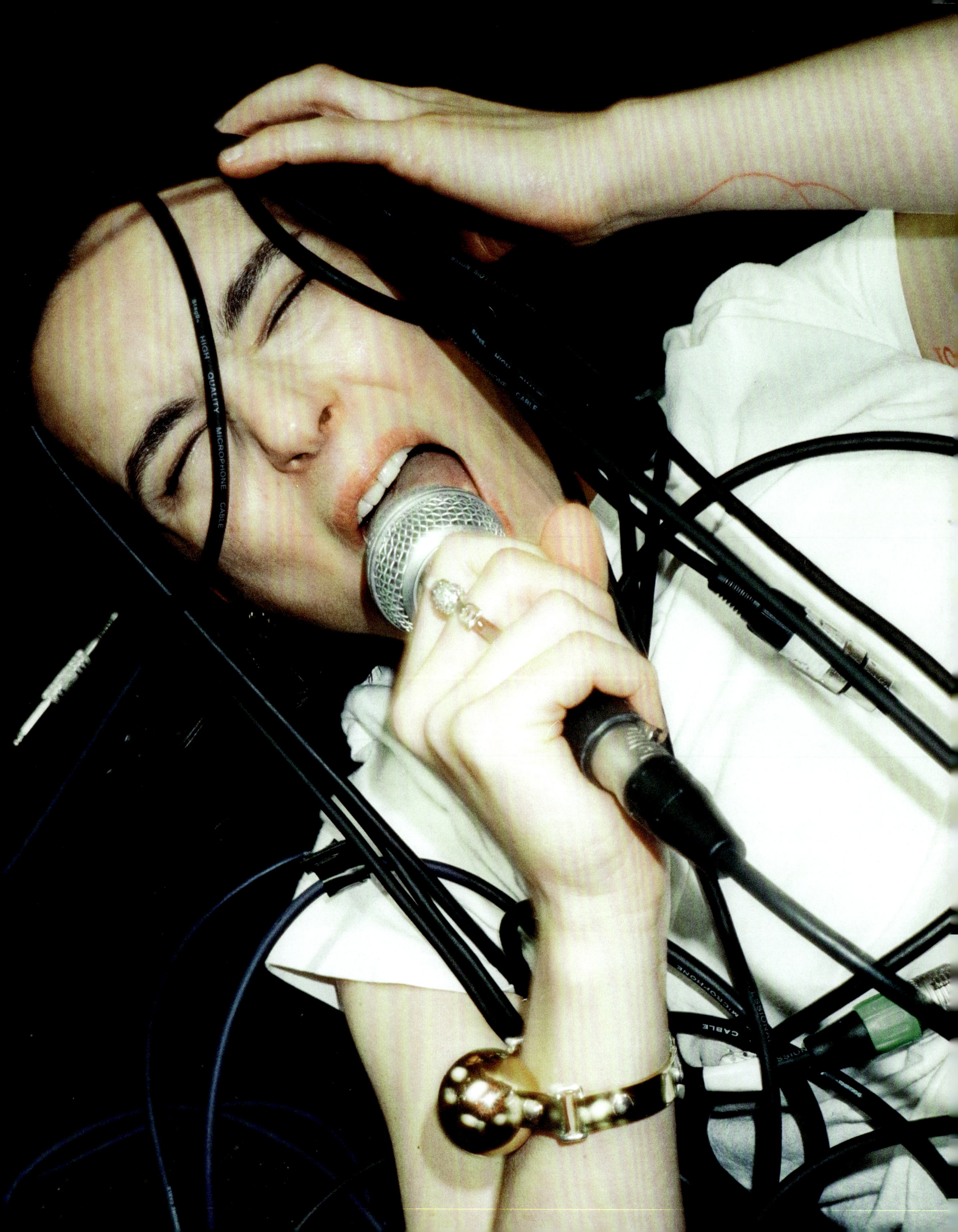
HIGH QUALITY MICROPHONE CABLE

DEFIANT
ELEGANCE

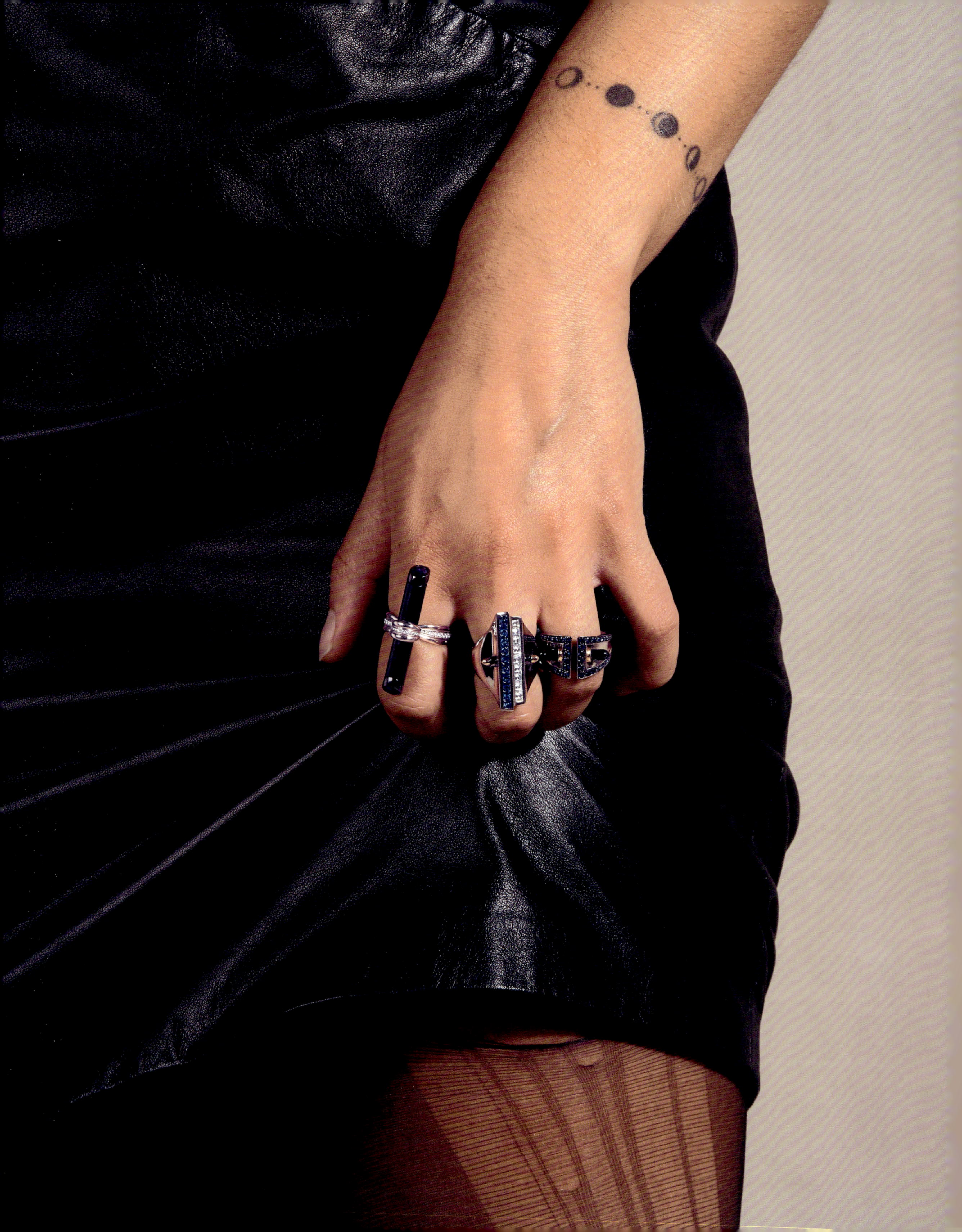

Rebellion is a tricky mistress. It flirts on the fringe of culture, daring to disrupt, only to be tamed, smoothed, commodified and trickled down for a new audience. As this book was taking shape, punk currents had circled back to the runway. What might have been shocking or at least raised eyebrows two generations ago now resurfaced with knowing winks and a wry smile. For anyone who remembered the original, the resurgence paled by comparison. It only feels fresh to those born later.

But every so often, a creative comes along who can hold fast to the essence of rebellion, refusing to let it be diluted while also drawing in ever-concentric circles of new admirers. Hannah's truth is that rebellion resonates through visual cues backed by an entire aesthetic language, its vocabulary writ in gold, silver, pearls and precious stones – a statement steeped in the frisson of defiance.

Since her student days, Hannah's work has stood out for its refusal to conform. Though her talent won her the prestigious Cartier Award internship in Paris – and her mentors would gladly have kept her there – a graduate presentation titled It's Only Rock 'n' Roll set down a refrain that would evolve while holding fast for the next two decades. Like true creators – a Belperron for modern times – Hannah believes that her work is more than an accessory or a status statement: it is an expression of individuality.

defiant elegance < 175

176 > defiant elegance

Why should that be limited to gender, or cis-normative aesthetics? Where's the mystery in conspicuous displays of wealth or power? Why couldn't traditional high-jewellery techniques be applied to jewels that speak simultaneously of craftsmanship and disruption, of inner depths and freedom – from the constraints of gender, of society, of expectations? Judge me if you will, her jewels seem to say, there is more to this story.

Her musical fluency lets Hannah take raw energy to the bench where, with her jeweller's eye and flair for craftsmanship, she bends it to her will. Wresting high jewellery-making from the staid ways of the Place Vendôme, she sets it down in east London, stripping it of haughtiness and transforming it into something alive, vibrant, immediate. Inspired by the underground and the Barbican, a complex she would eventually call home, she elevated elements of counterculture – bolts, spines and spikes, shackles and gangster links – into something precious and defiant.

ABOVE FROM LEFT: Gentleman Gangster Lined Link Bracelet, 18ct gold, 2009; Bound Earrings, 18ct gold, black jade and sapphires, 2016; Restraint Cuff, 18ct gold, diamonds and sapphires, 2016.

Protection and provocation, revelry and rebellion, hard lines and soft curves produced coils clutching rubies or sapphires, to slip through pierced lobes, safety pins anchored in malachite and gemstones unapologetically set point-up, a nod to punk uniforms. Her ideas and attitude that would be picked up and copied, yet never equalled, from London to Paris, New York and Tokyo.

In Hannah's hands, the burn of all-nighters, the energy of the rebel yell finds power in restraint. Her 20th-anniversary collection, The Perfect Drug – an antidote for a broken heart, a declaration of independence and empowerment – is its most intimate expression yet. Emotional and extreme, it speaks of despair and euphoria, survival and release. Born in a mosh pit, it draws on fetishism, surrealism and punk influences, resulting in jewels that are at once recognisable. A voluptuous ball of carved obsidian is lashed audaciously to the finger with a gold strap and contrasting precious studs.

defiant elegance

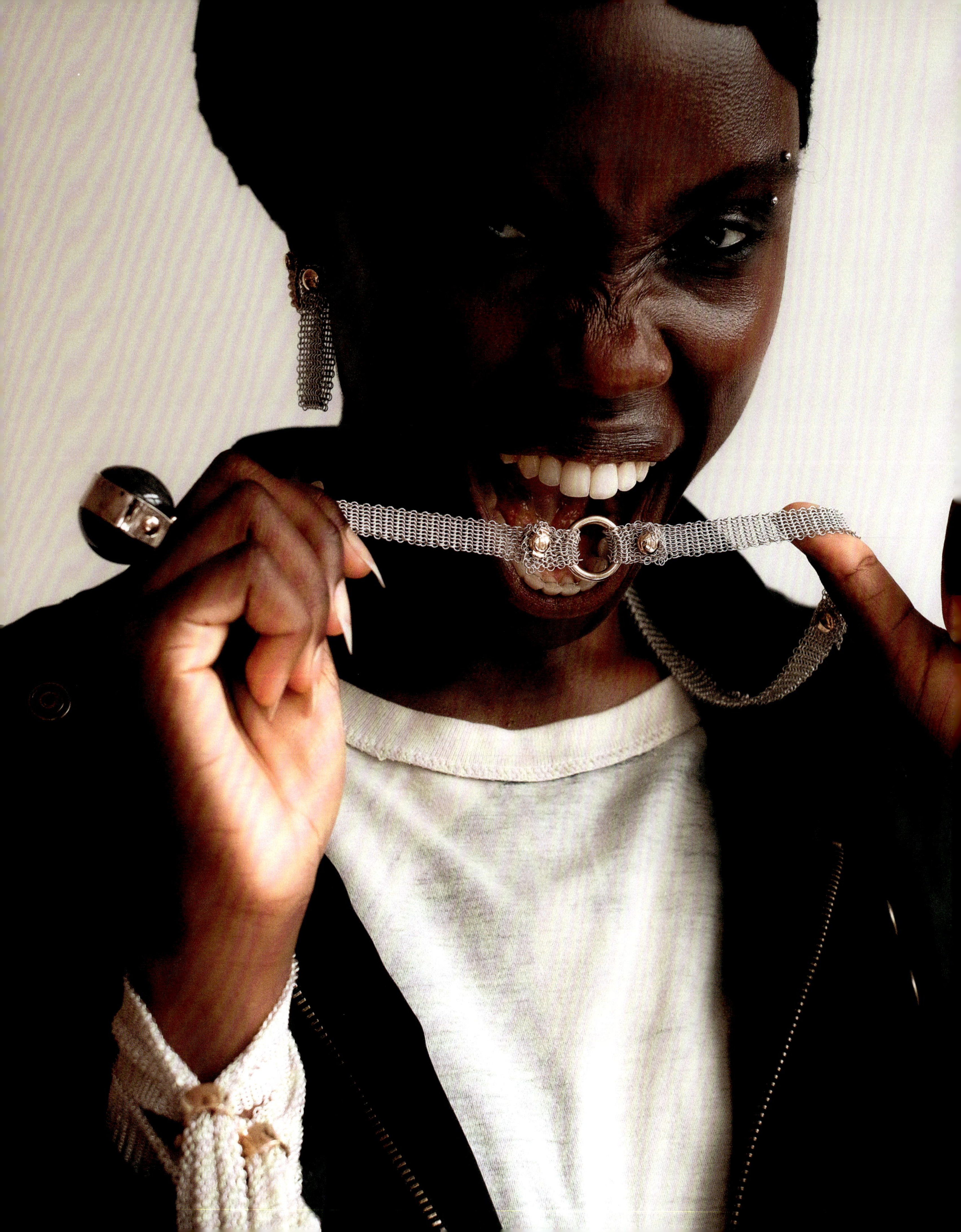

Sketches for The Perfect Drug, 2024, All Access Two-Tone Bracelet, 18ct gold and sterling silver chainmail.

A festival wristband becomes liquid mesh, a statement of sensuality imbued with a restless, rebellious spirit. A wide, supple harness chain is anchored with engineered studs and an industrial ring. This is conspiratorial, defiant luxury. If you know, you know. For its wearers, every Hannah Martin piece is a reminder that where there is vulnerability, and even danger, there is beauty. A suggestion that, in a world increasingly designed to keep the masses digitally numb, we are made for connection.

Or, as Hannah puts it, that 'we are fucking alive.'

defiant elegance < 179

180 > defiant elegance

The jewellery landscape is changing fast, but those who know Hannah's work see no limit to what she can achieve. 'She has already proven that she is not afraid to take risks', Simon Fraser observes. 'She has built something entirely her own. And in an industry that often rewards conformity, that's remarkable.'

As she fashions jewels, Hannah continues to shape conversations around craftsmanship, individuality and the very nature of adornment. 'What she is doing now is not just for today. It will have a lasting impact. She is creating a legacy', notes Simon.

After a moment's reflection, he adds, 'She came in with raw talent and a fierce sense of self. Now, she has honed that into something truly extraordinary. And the best part? She's just getting started.'

The Perfect Drug, 2024.

ABOVE FROM LEFT: Harnessed Earrings (Long), 18ct gold; The Full Spectrum Bracelet, 18ct gold and ebony; The Full Spectrum Ring, 18ct gold and agate.

Opposite: The Perfect Drug Choker, 18ct gold.

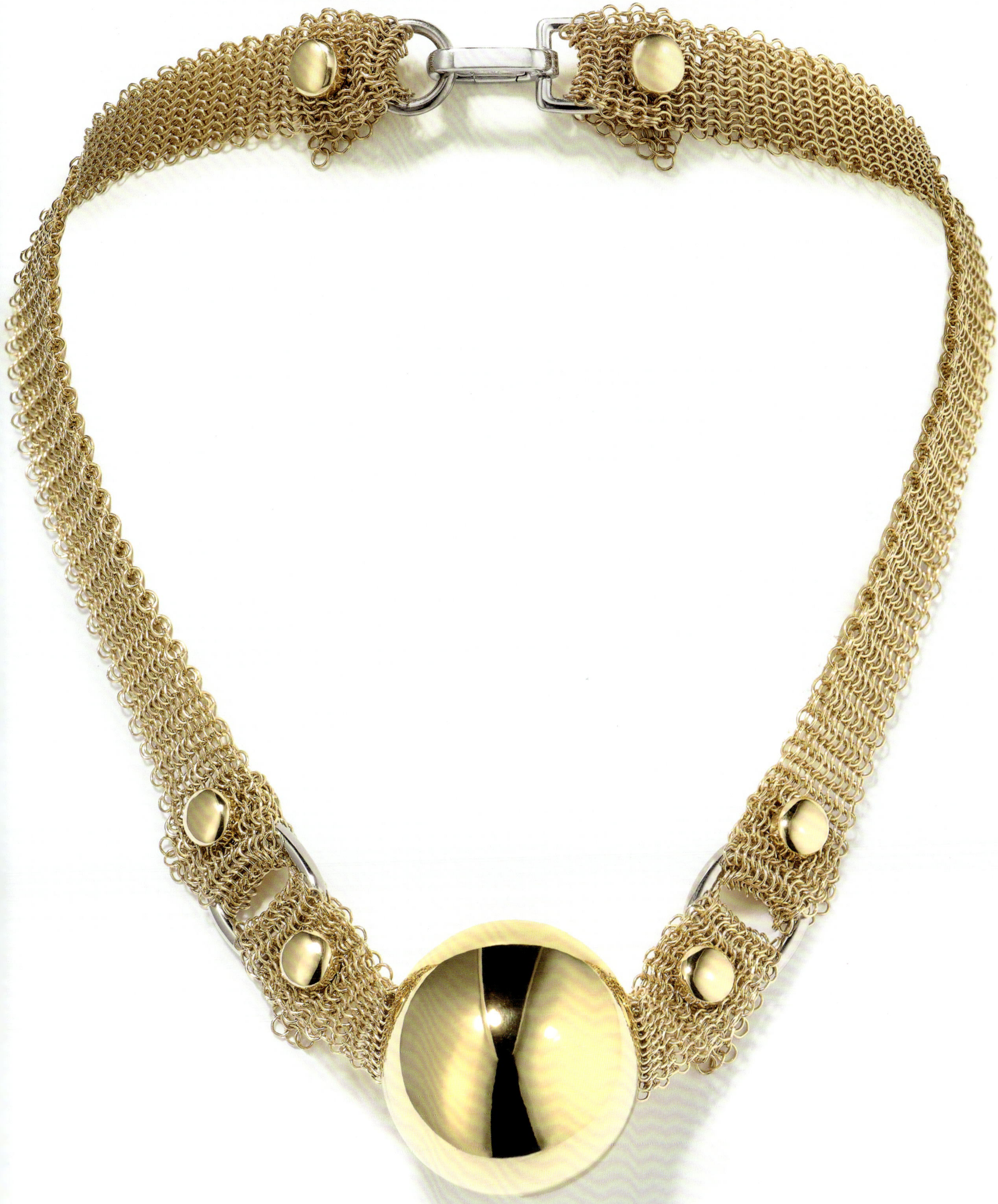

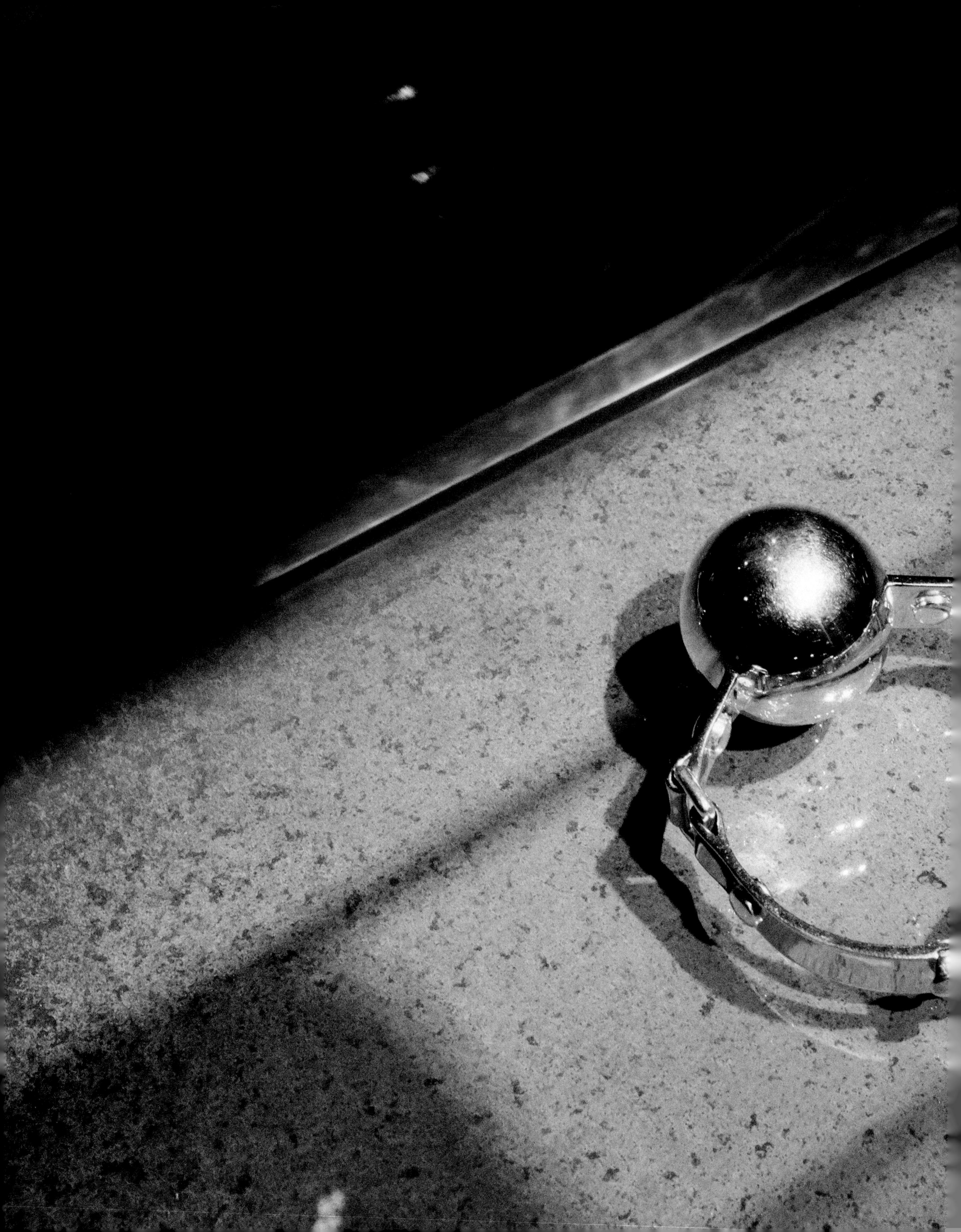

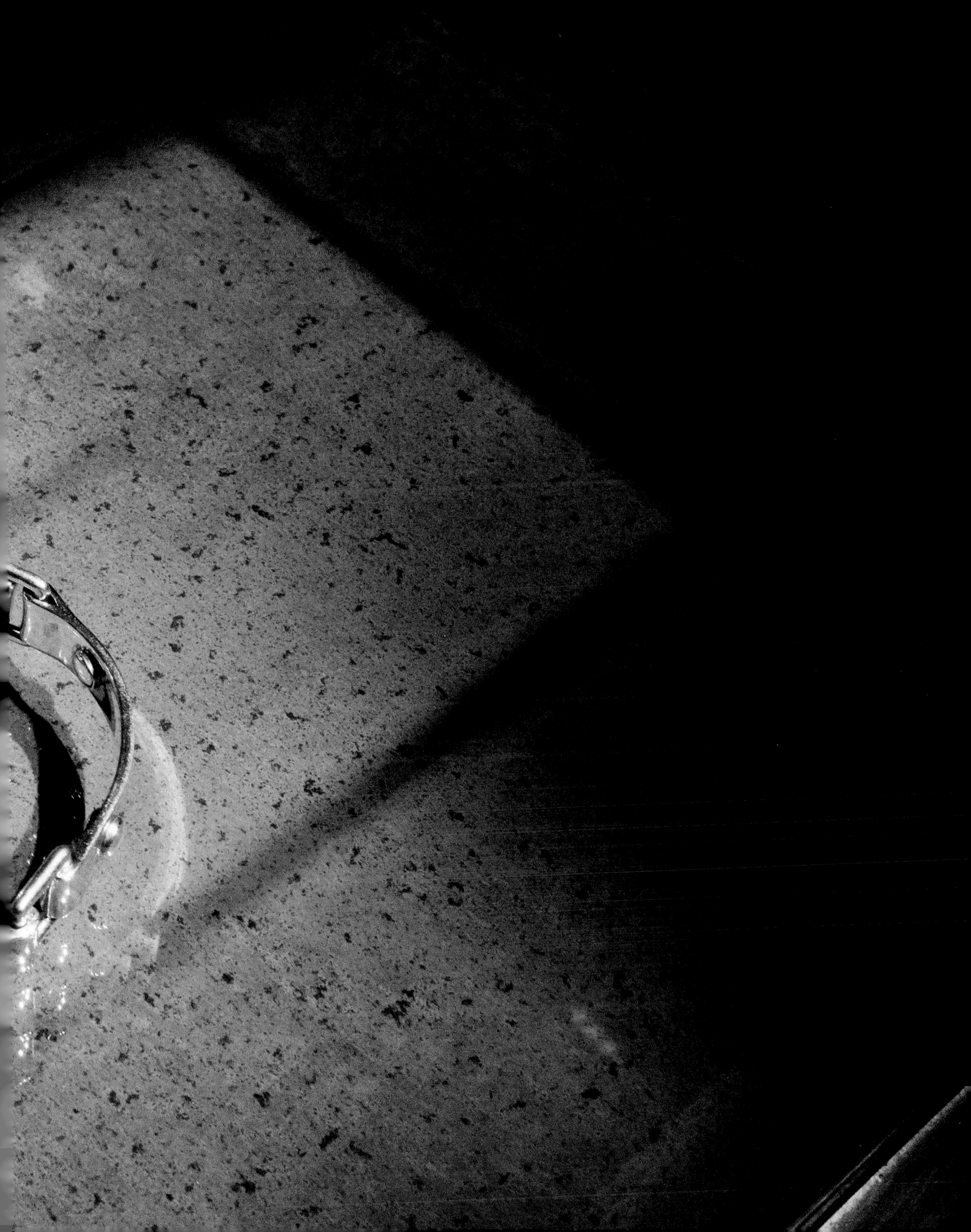

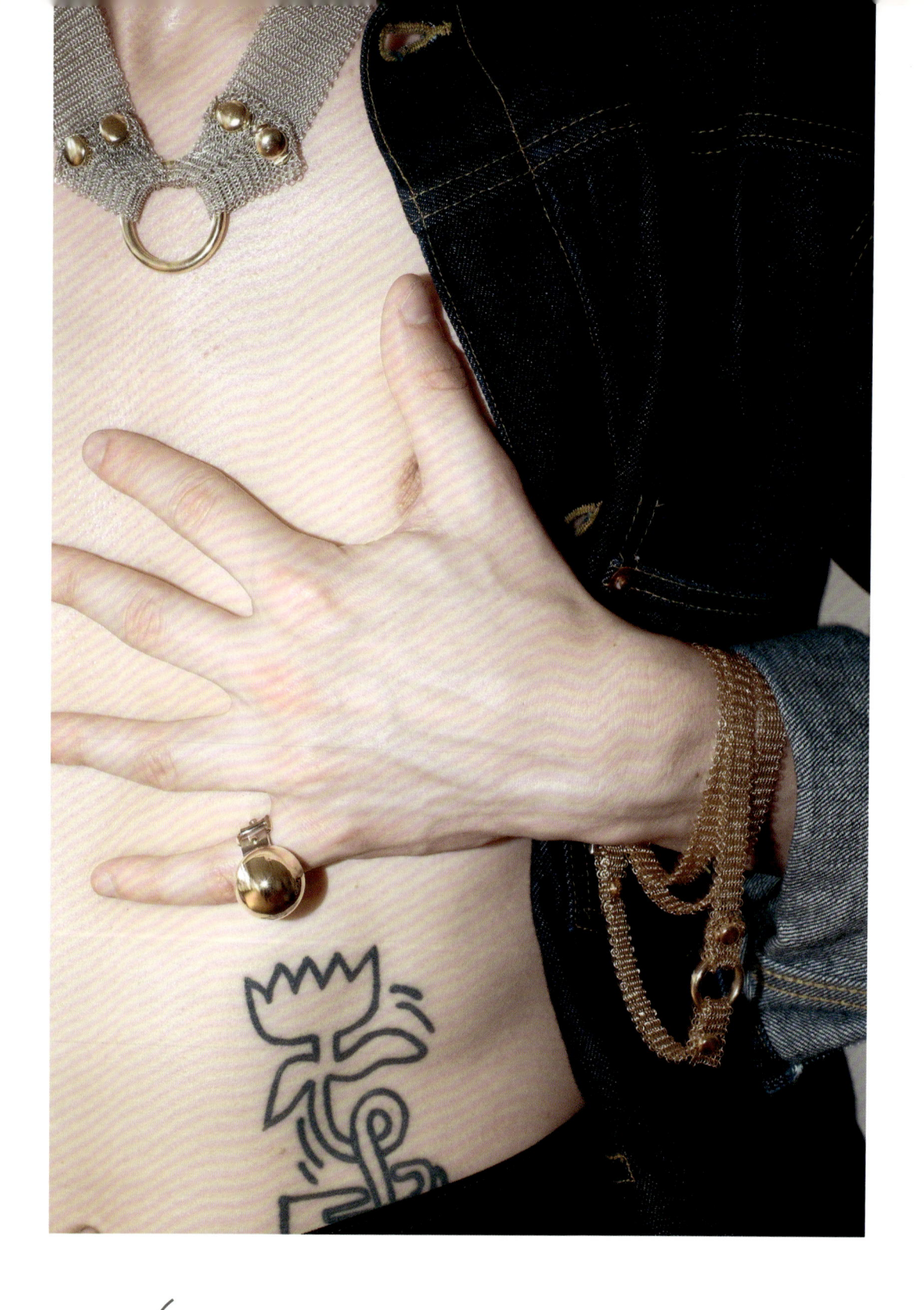

'Luxury was definitively NOT part of my world growing up. No one in my family had jewellery. There are no heirlooms passed down from previous generations. I didn't even know these precious things existed. I am free to play because I lack the reverence for it that others have coming from a different background.'

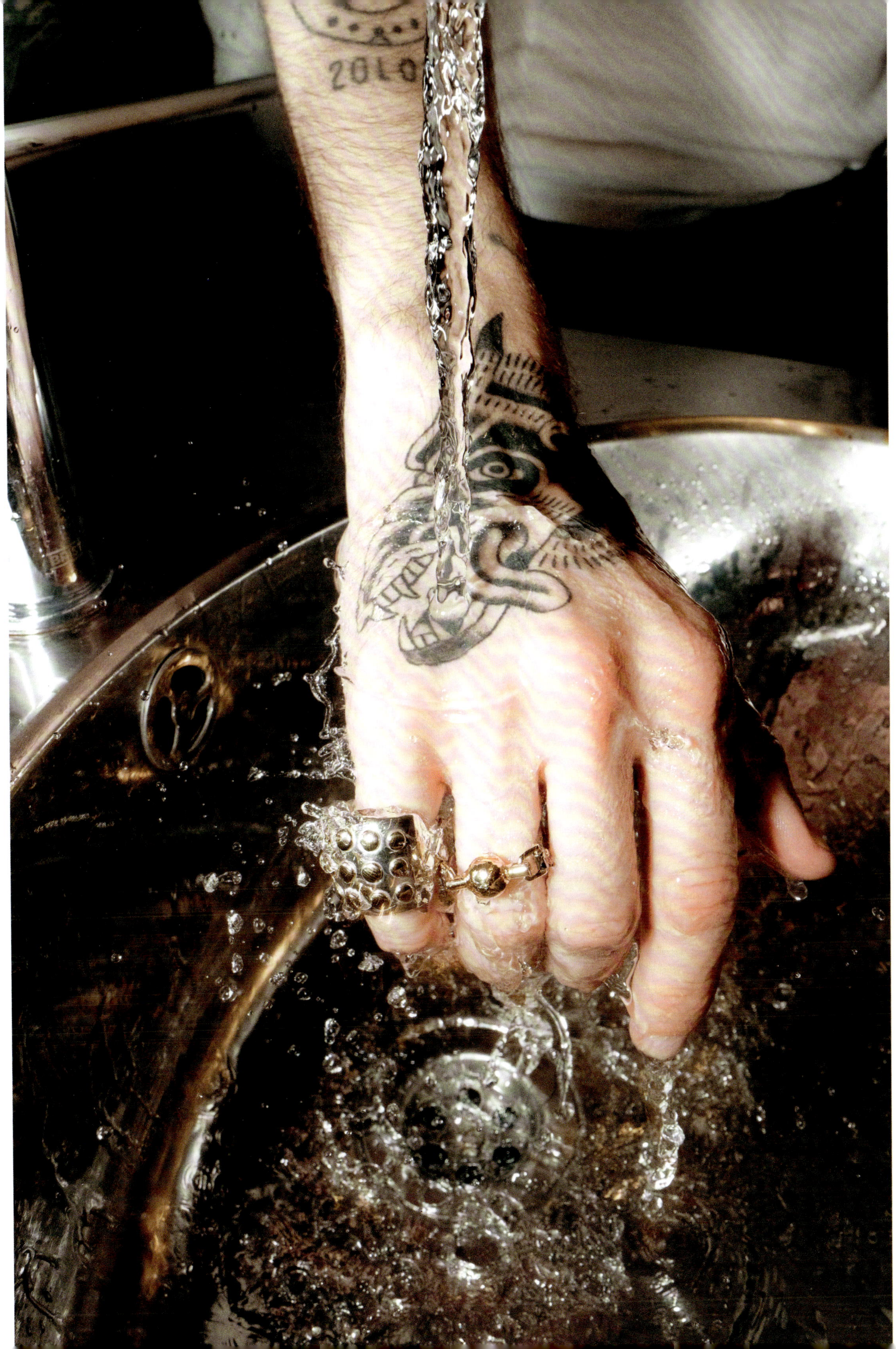

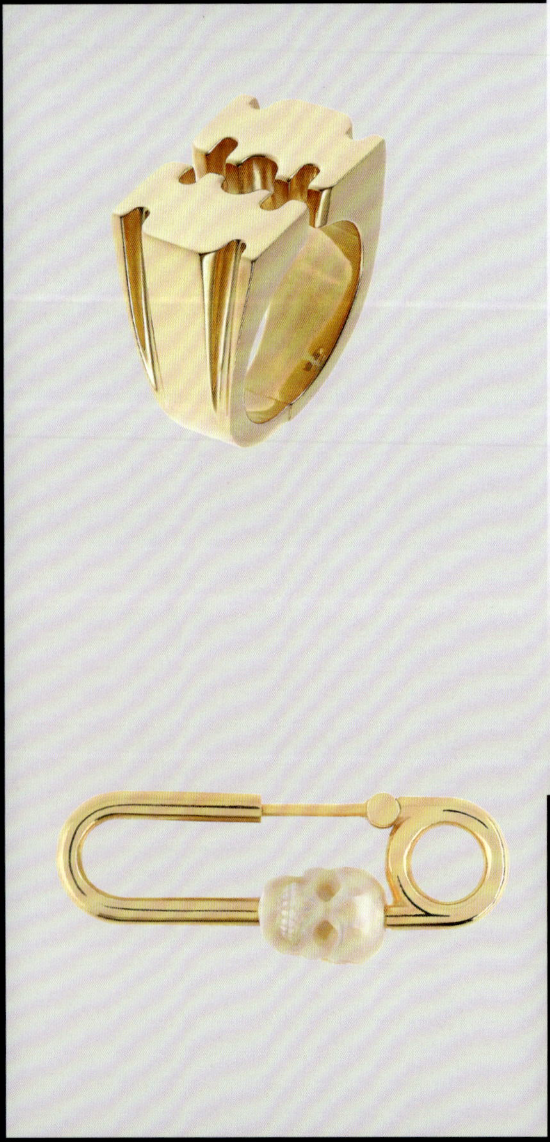

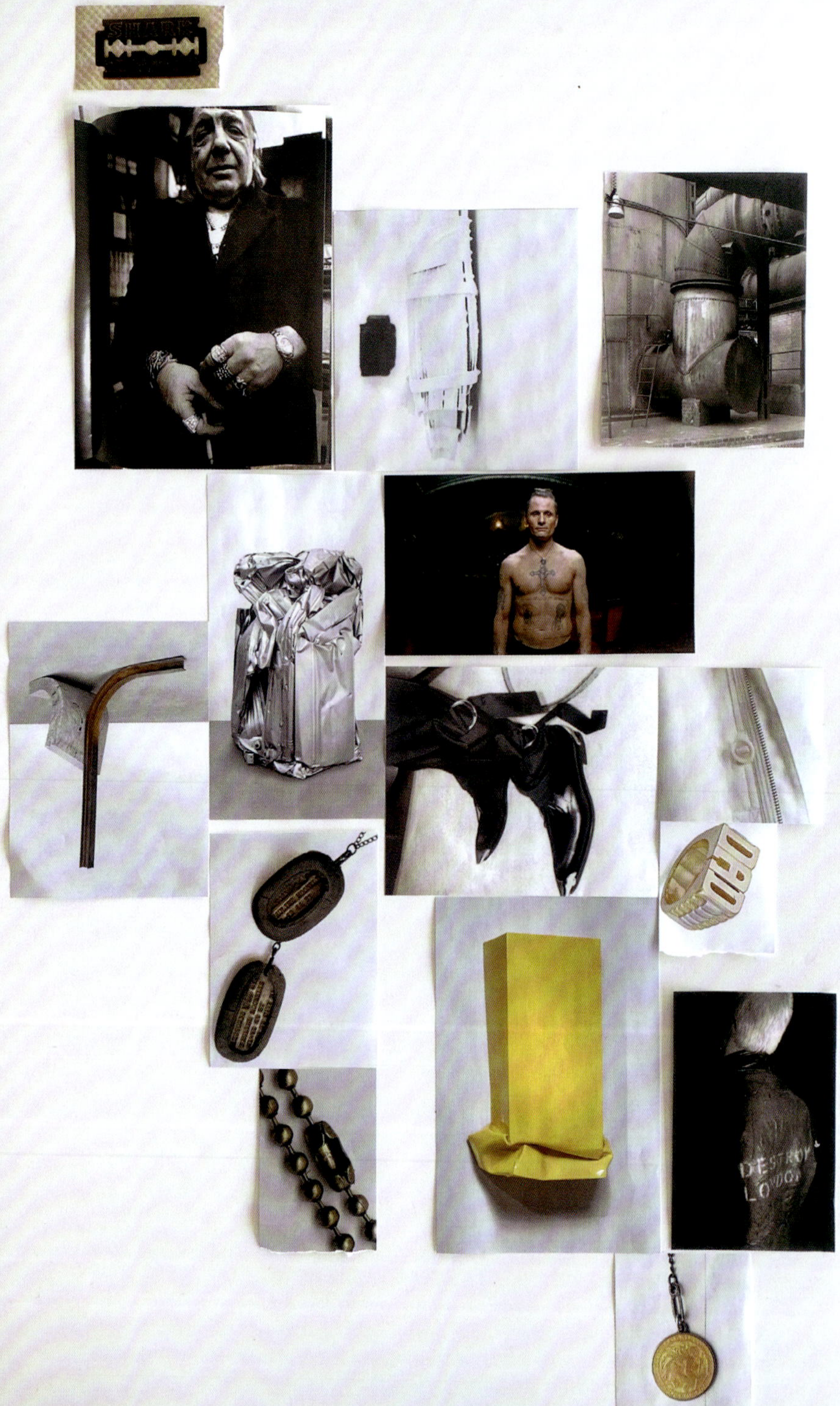
DESTROY

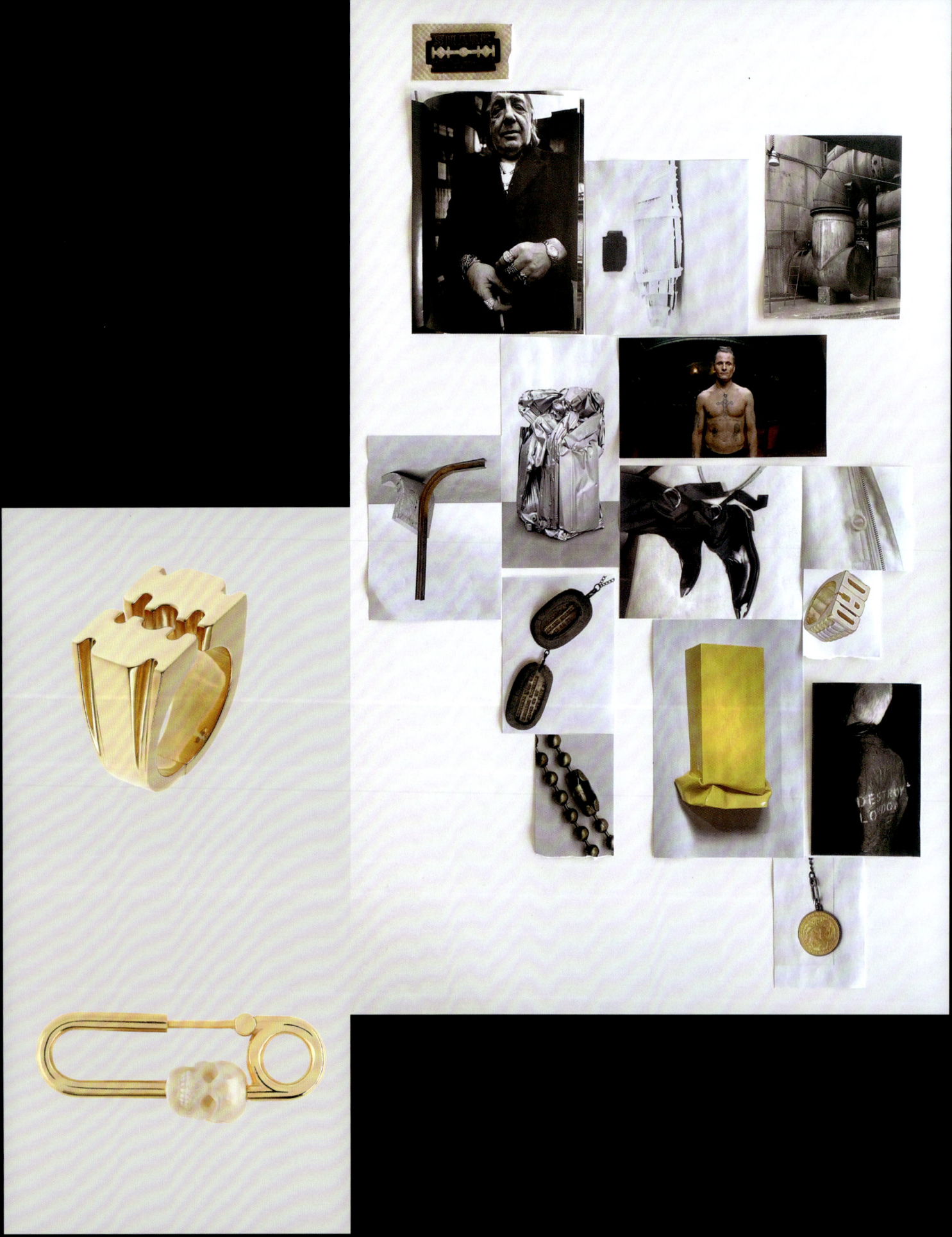

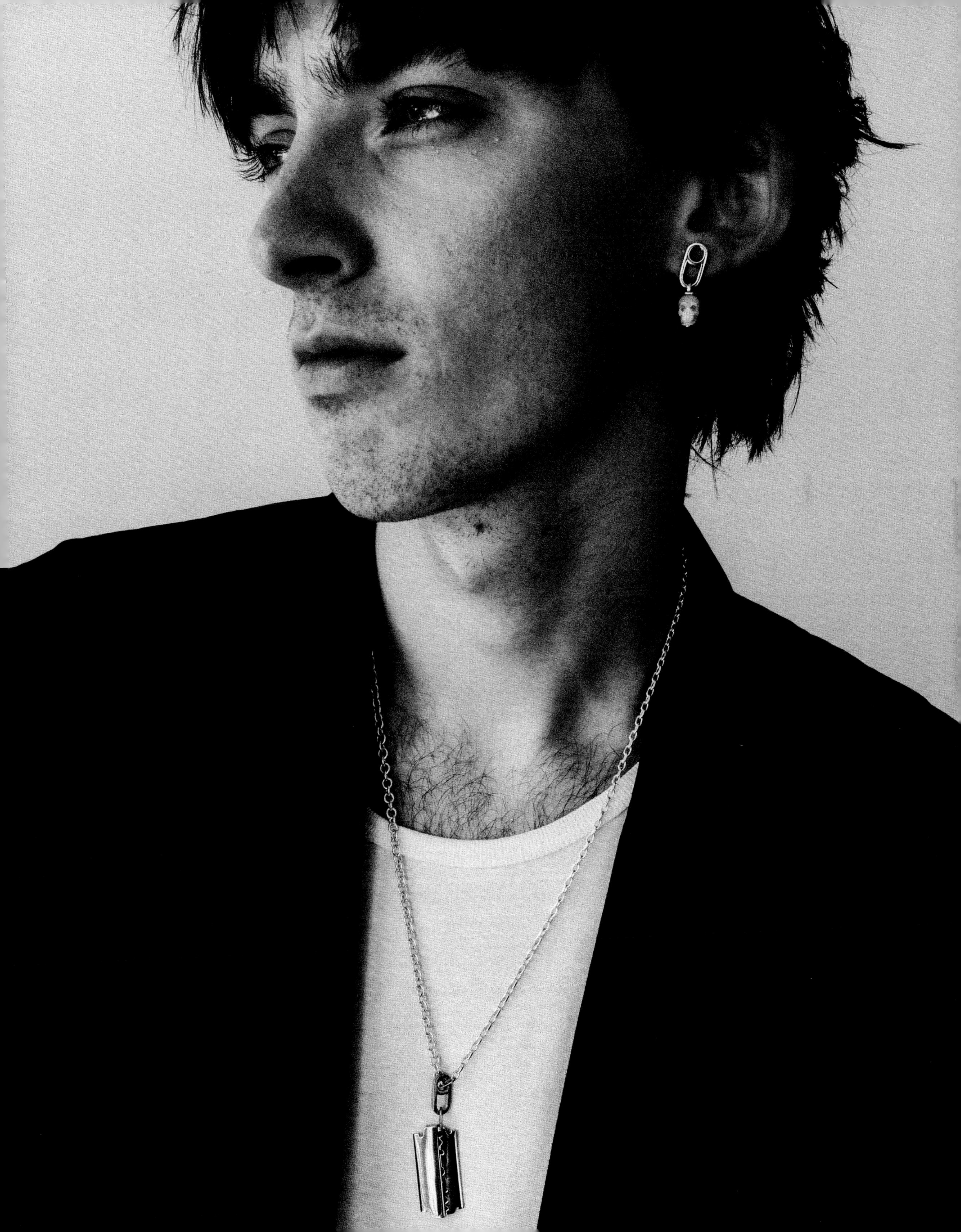

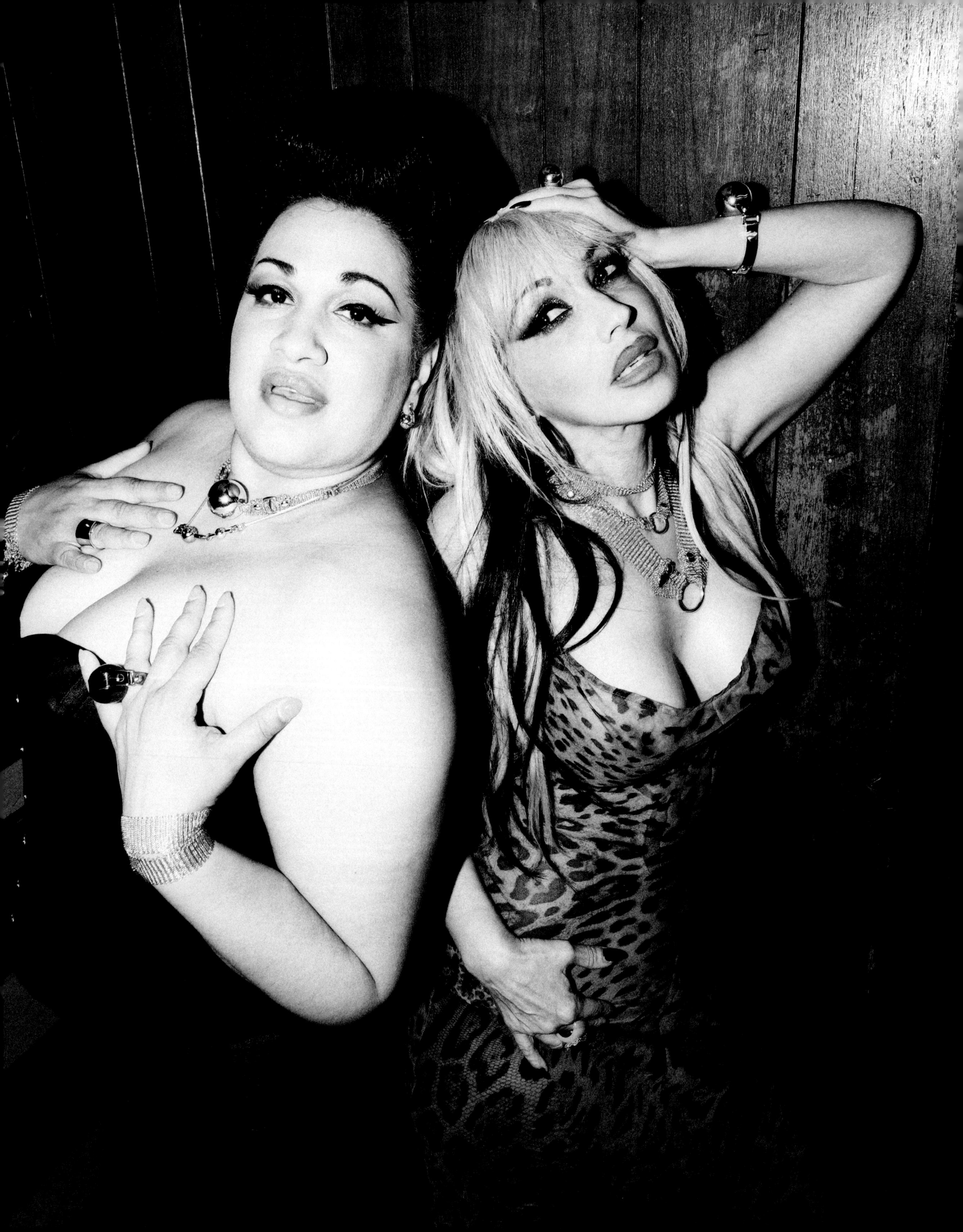

Previous pages: A Vanitas, 2023.

This page: Hannah Martin Pierced, 2022.

Opposite: BISHI and Rita D'Albert shot by Stewart Baxter at The 100 Club, London, 2024.

Following pages left: Polly Fey shot by Stewart Baxter at The 100 Club, London, 2024.

Following pages right: Nigel Mogg and Rita D'Albert shot by Stewart Baxter at The 100 Club, London, 2024.

defiant elegance < 189

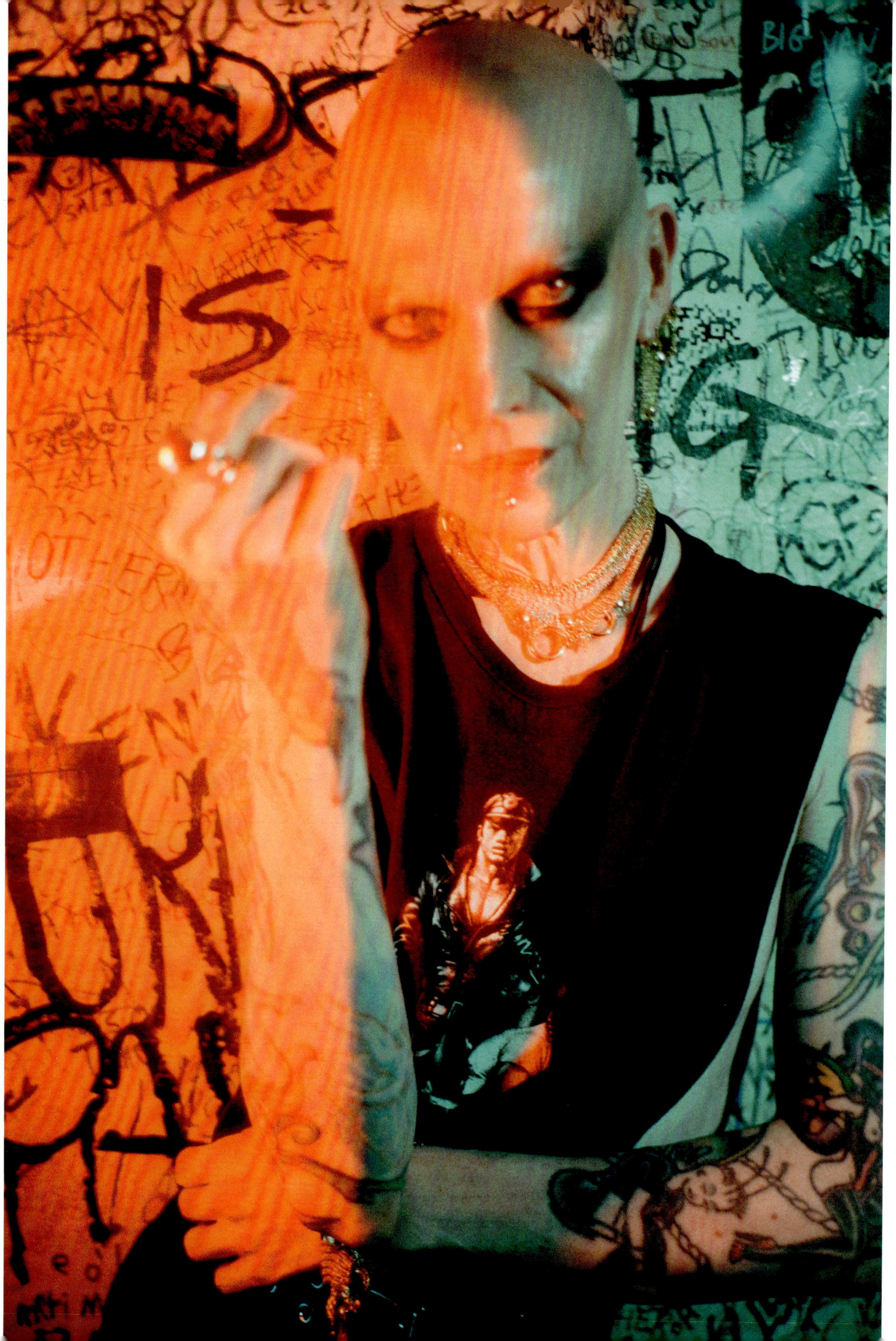
IS

defiant elegance < 191

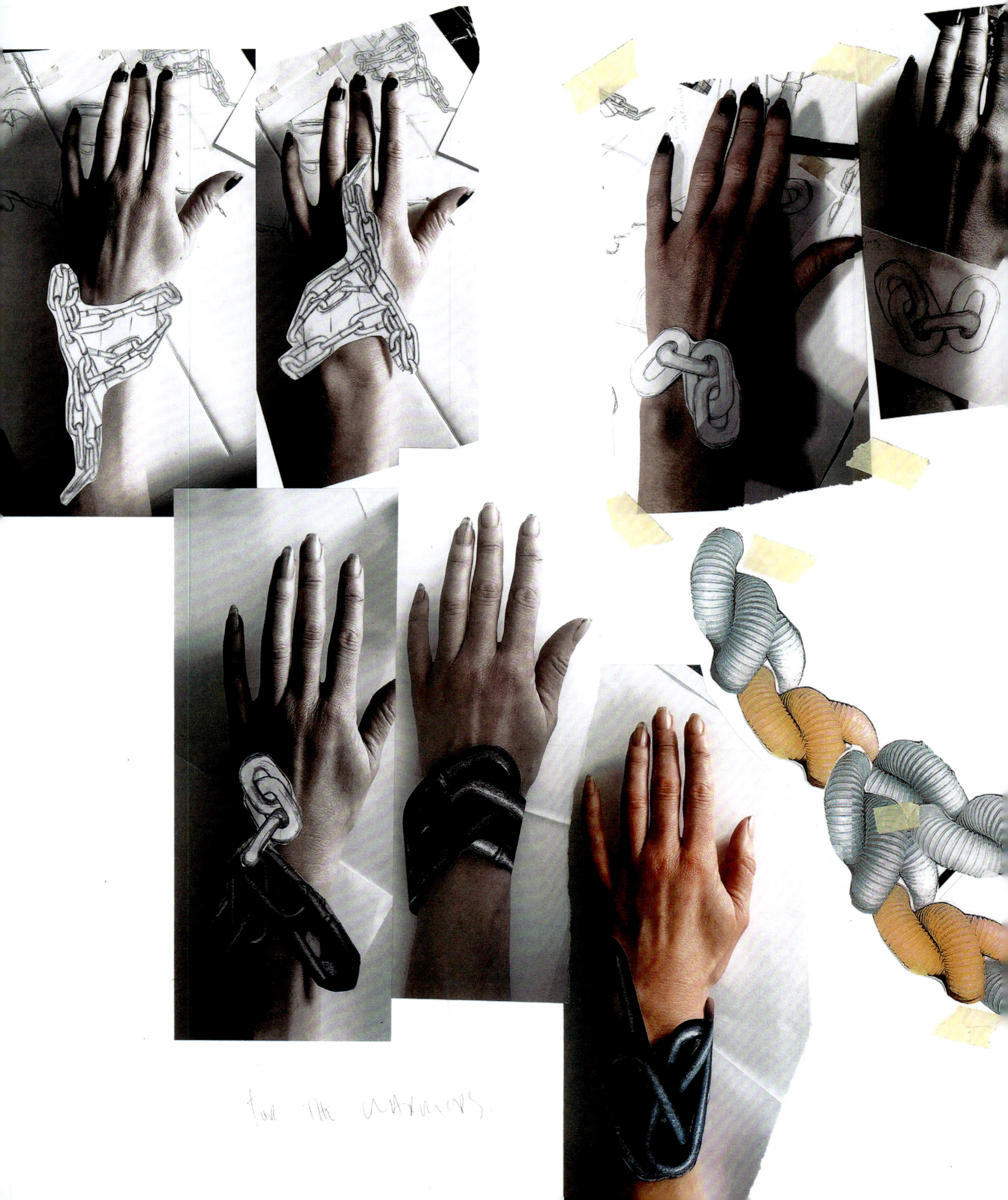
FOR THE WARRIORS.

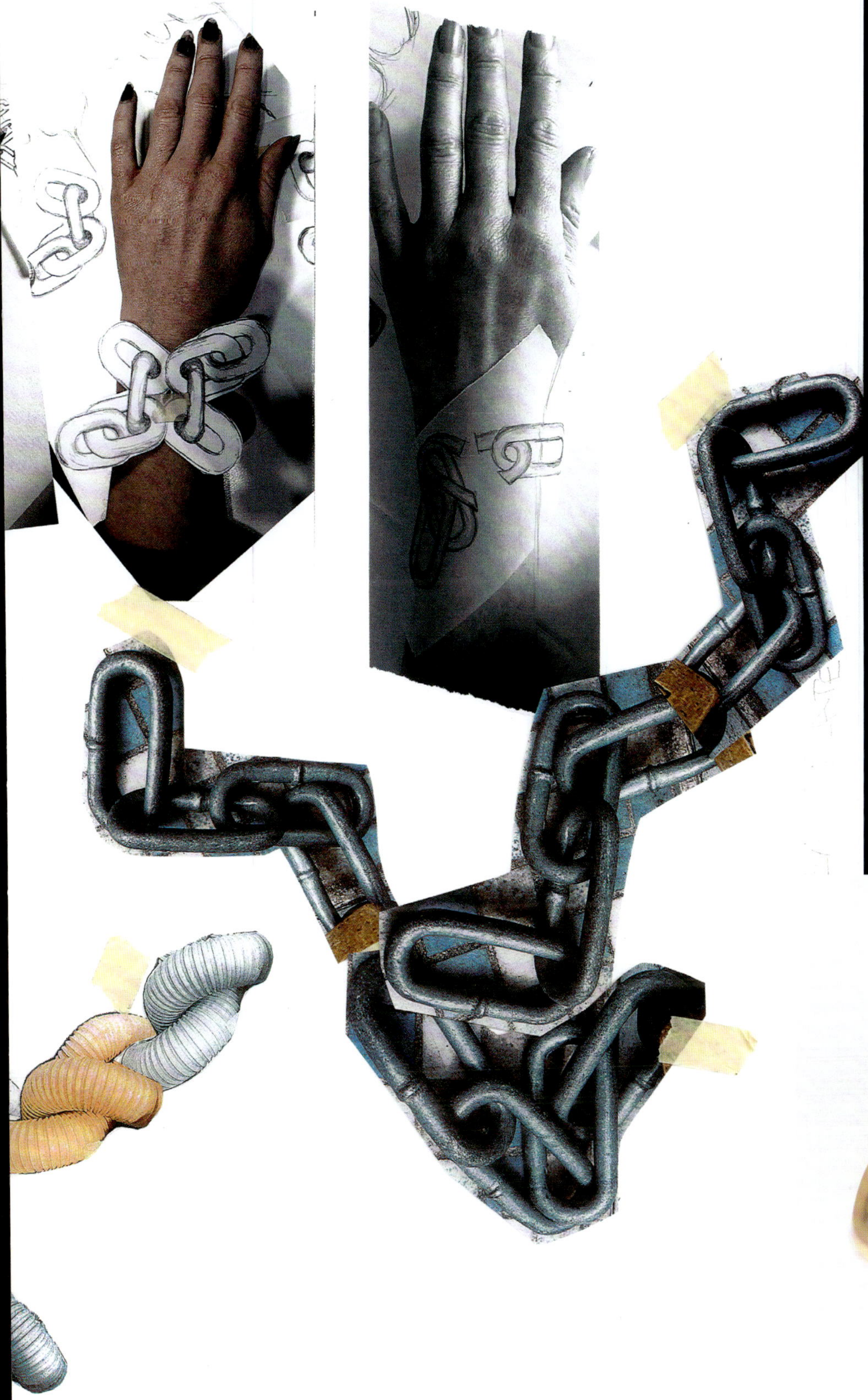

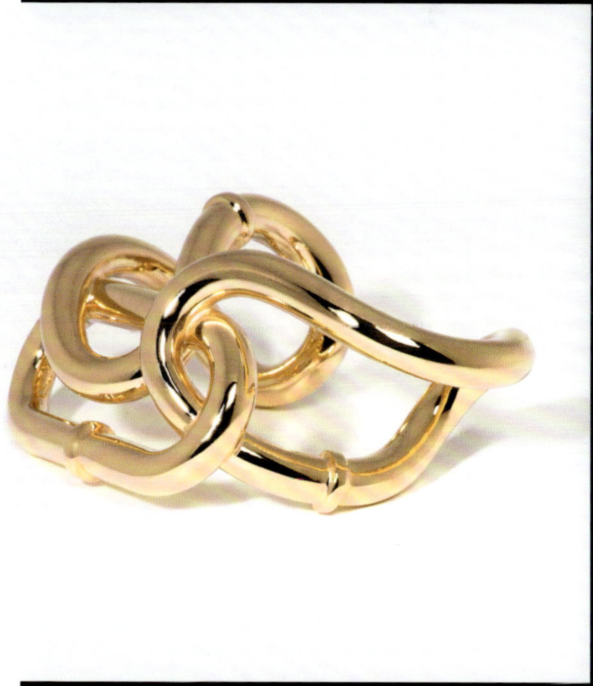

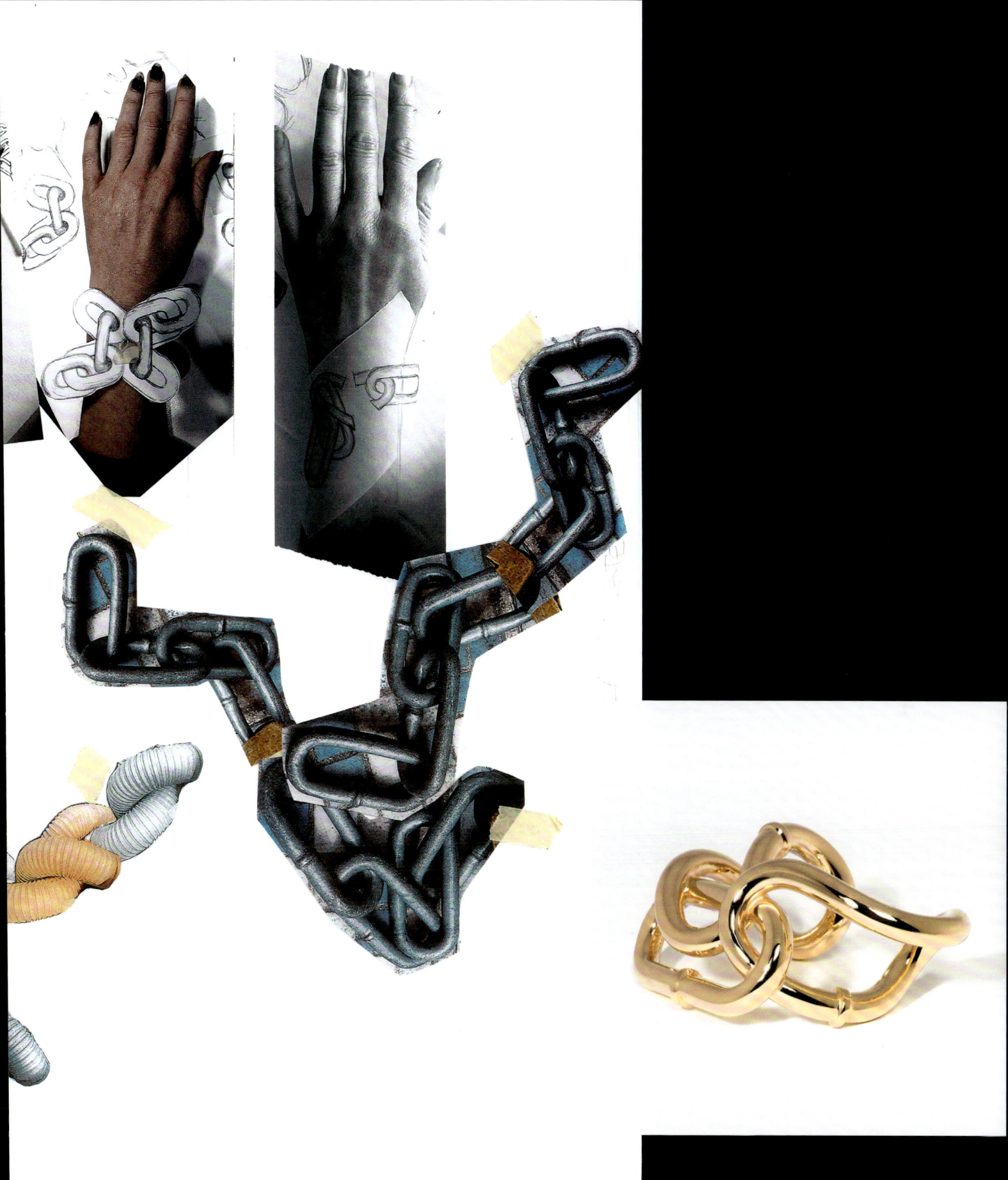

194 > defiant elegance

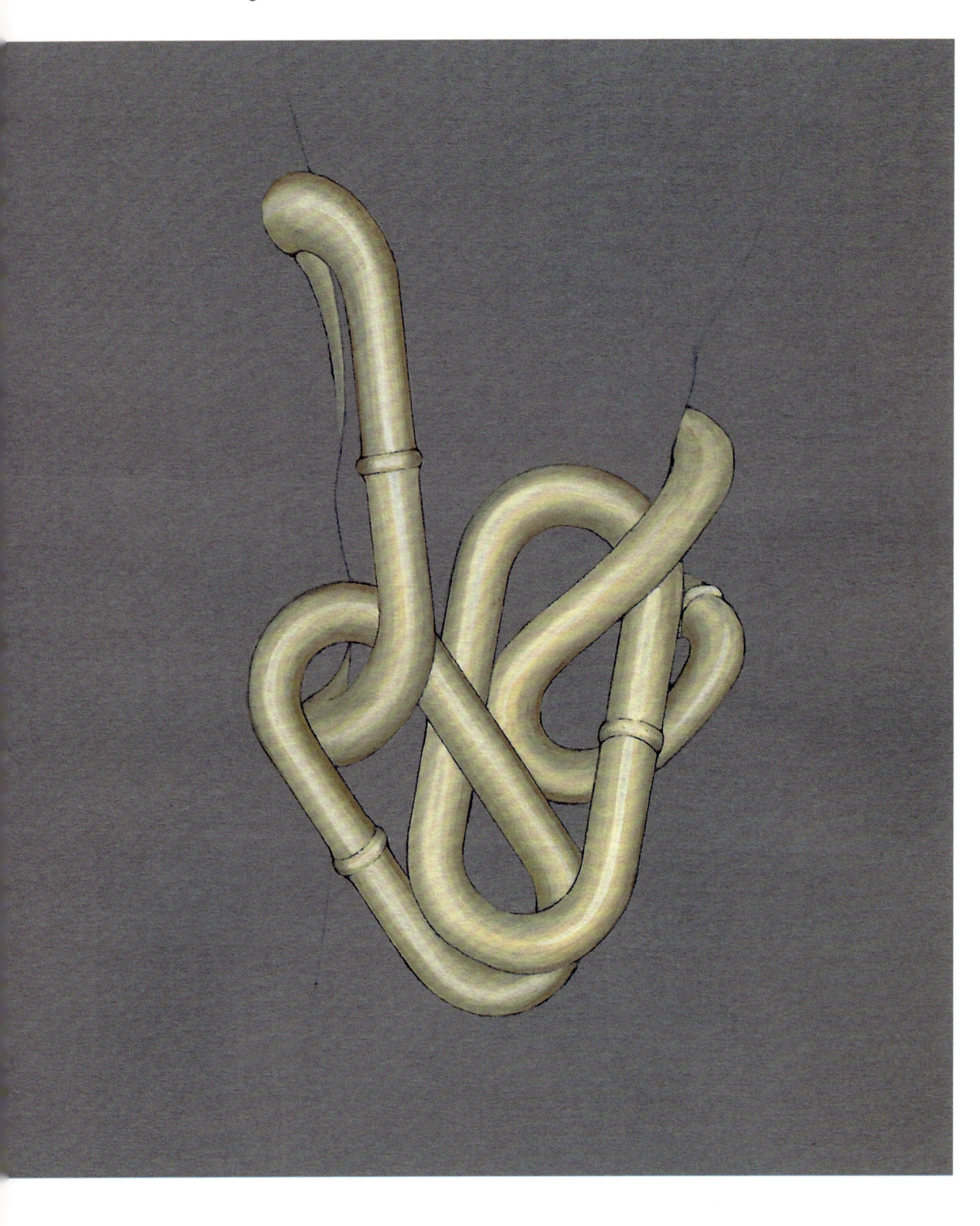

Pages 192-197: A cuff in process – sketching, models, gouache and campaign. The Unchained Warrior Threesome and Foursome Cuffs, 2020.

❝ I like to think that my work is an antidote to our world of surface, to a system of being that encourages us to be numb. It is an act of defiance. ❞

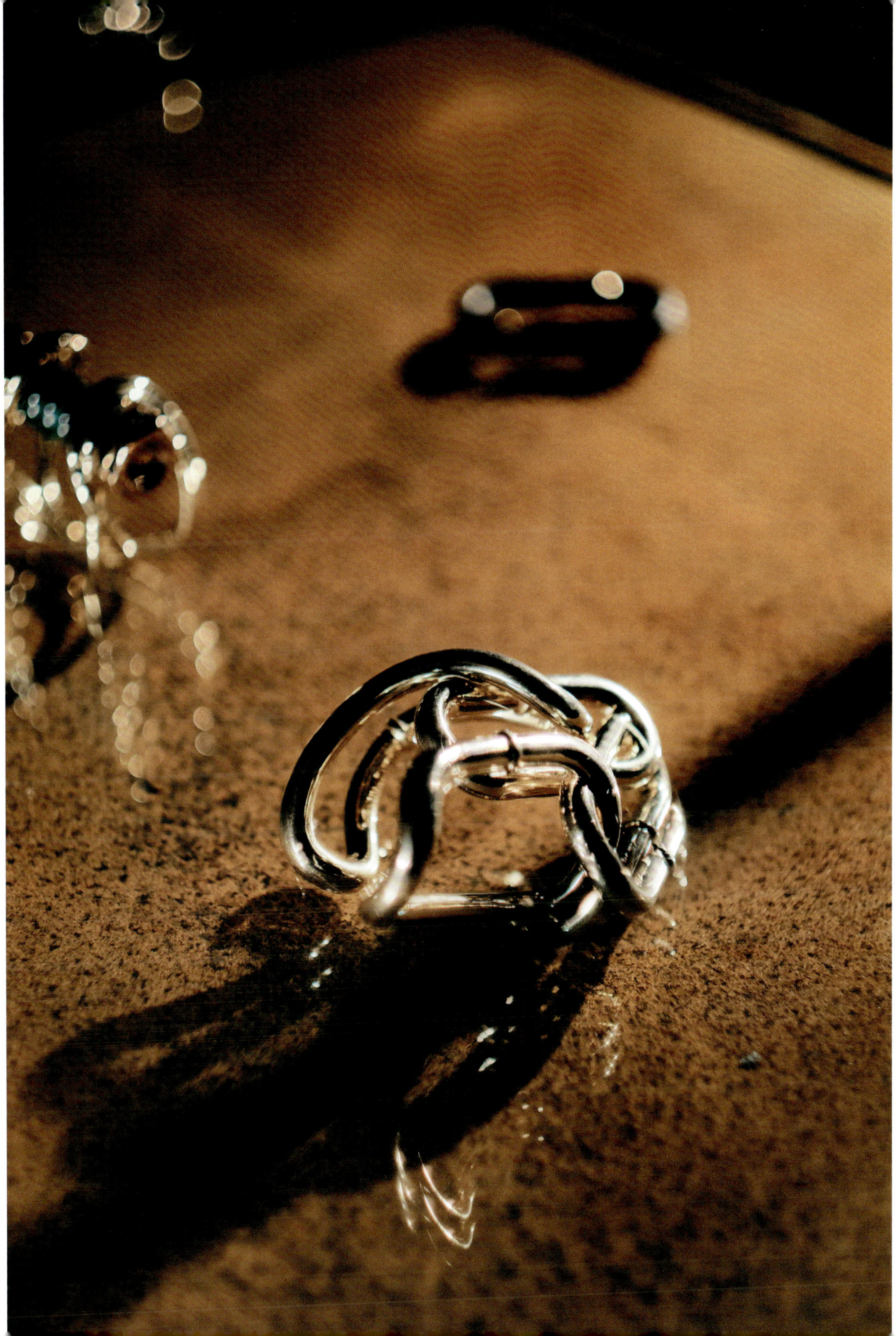

SMASH IT

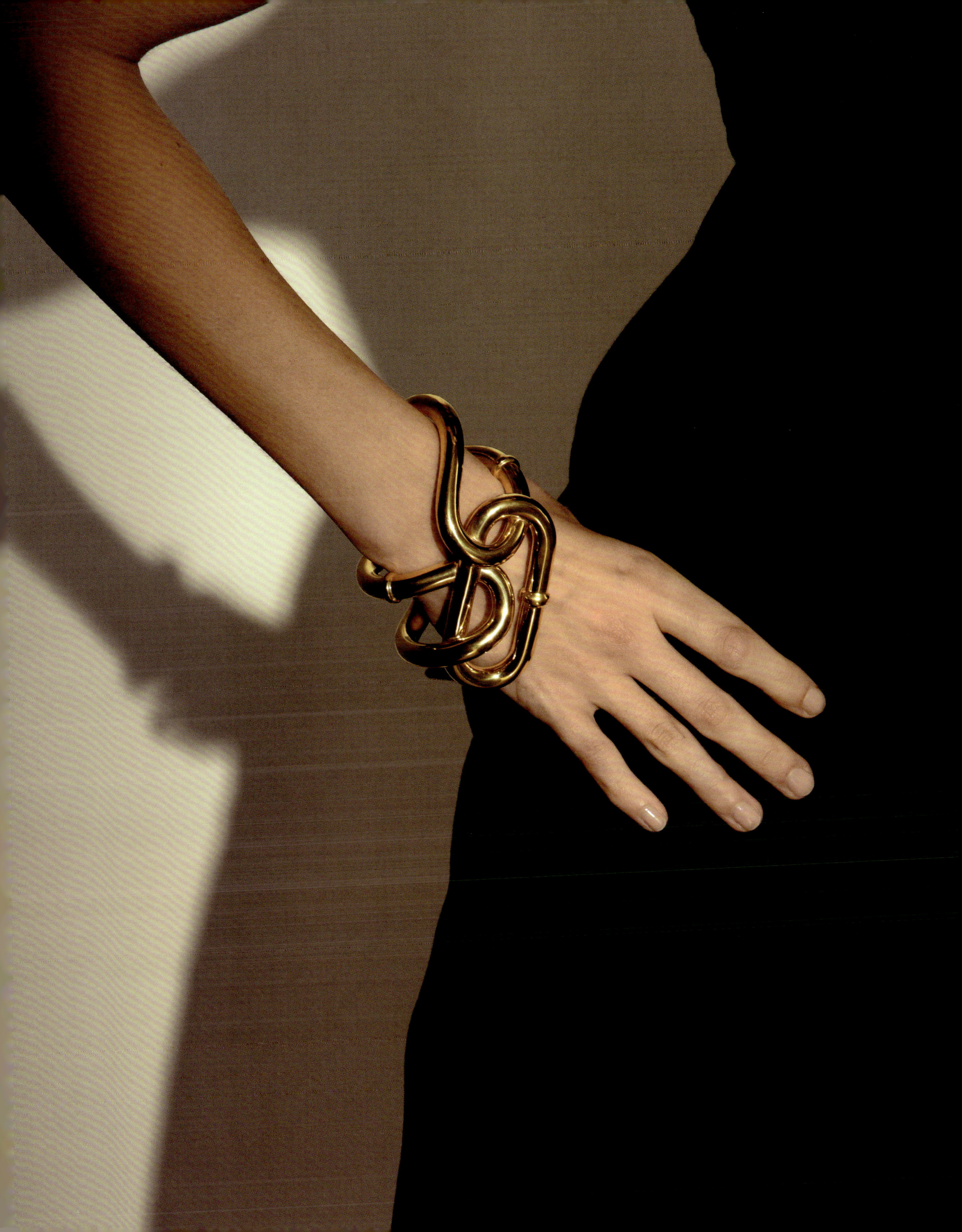

198 > defiant elegance

Pages 198-205: A New Act of Rebellion, 2020.

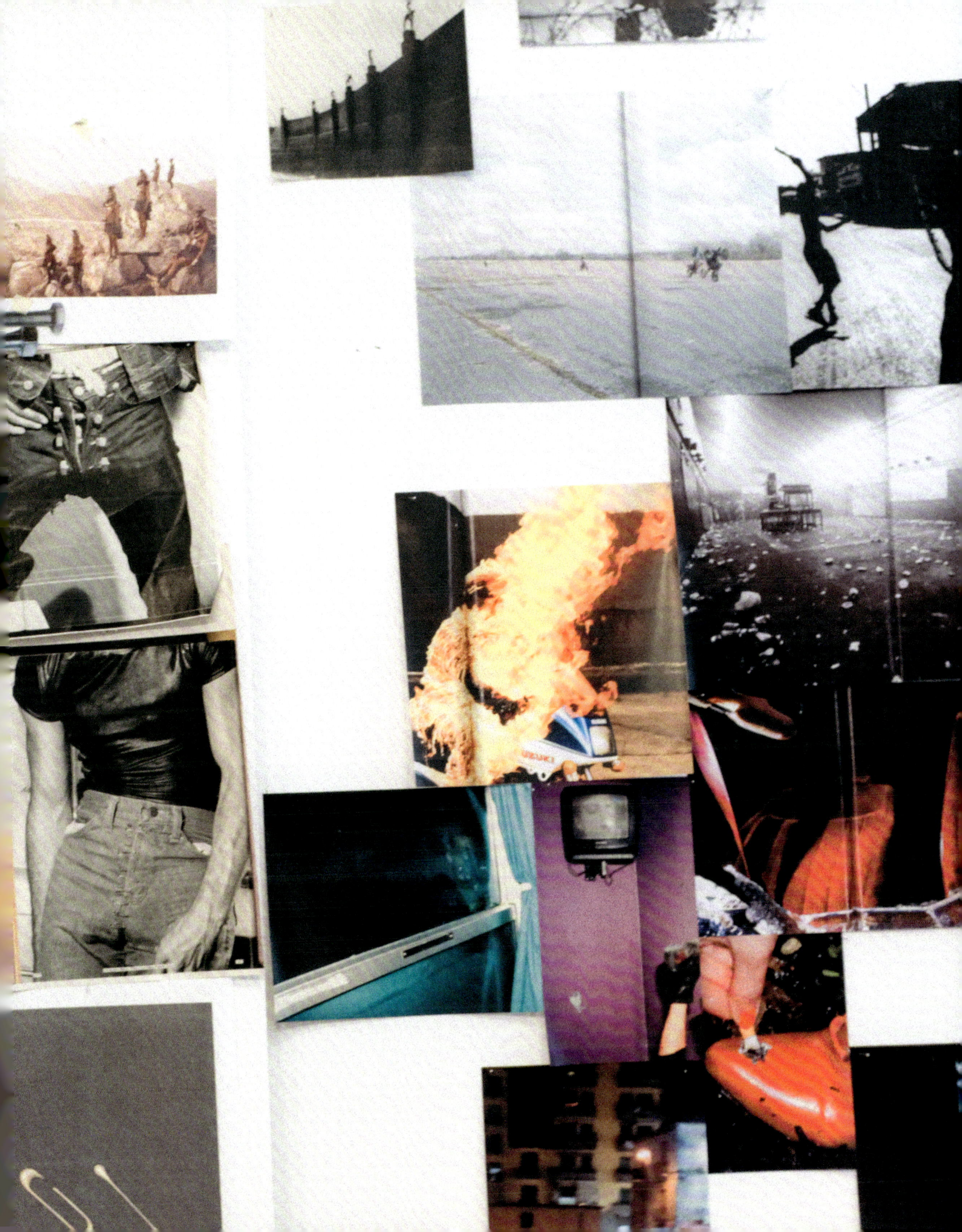

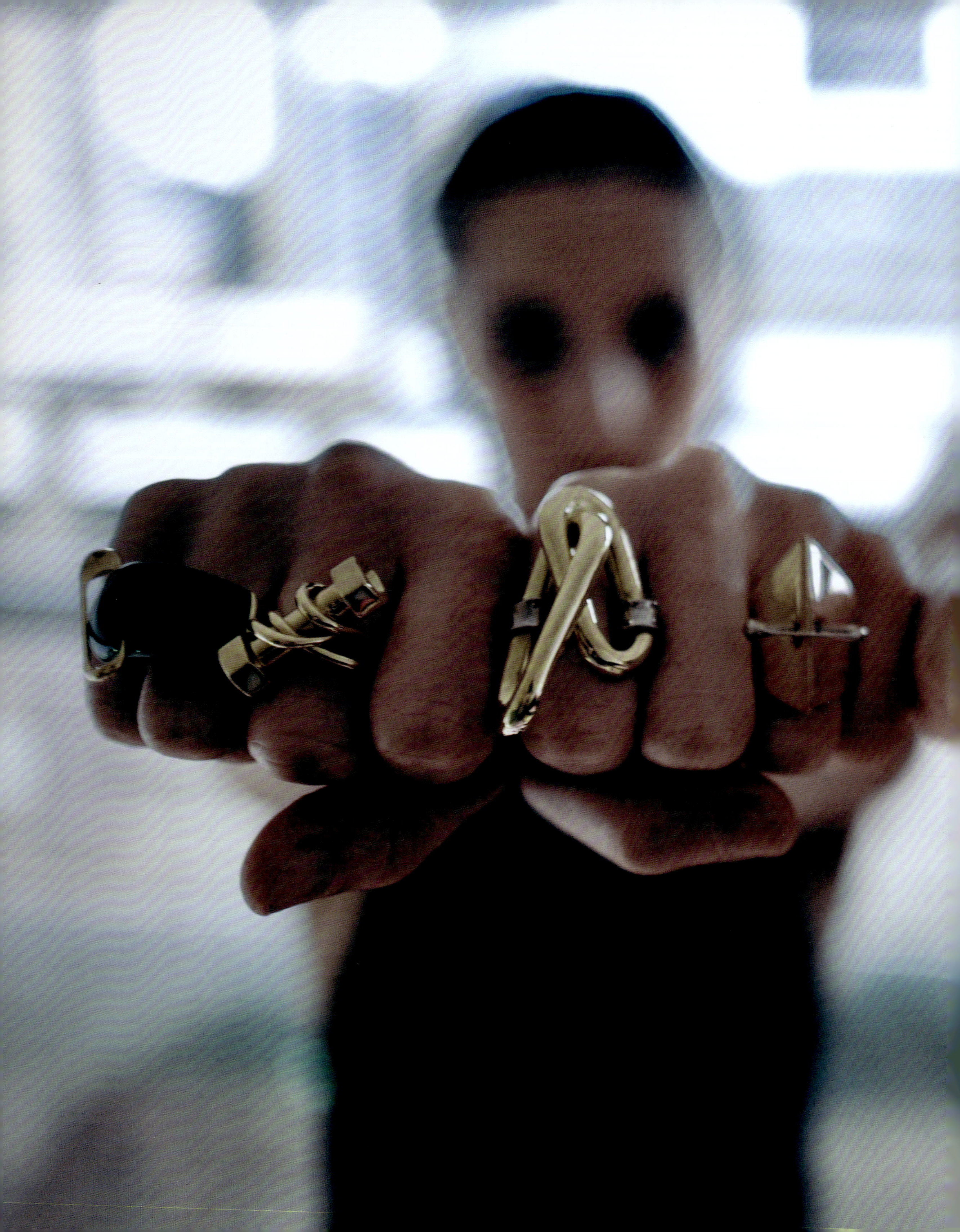

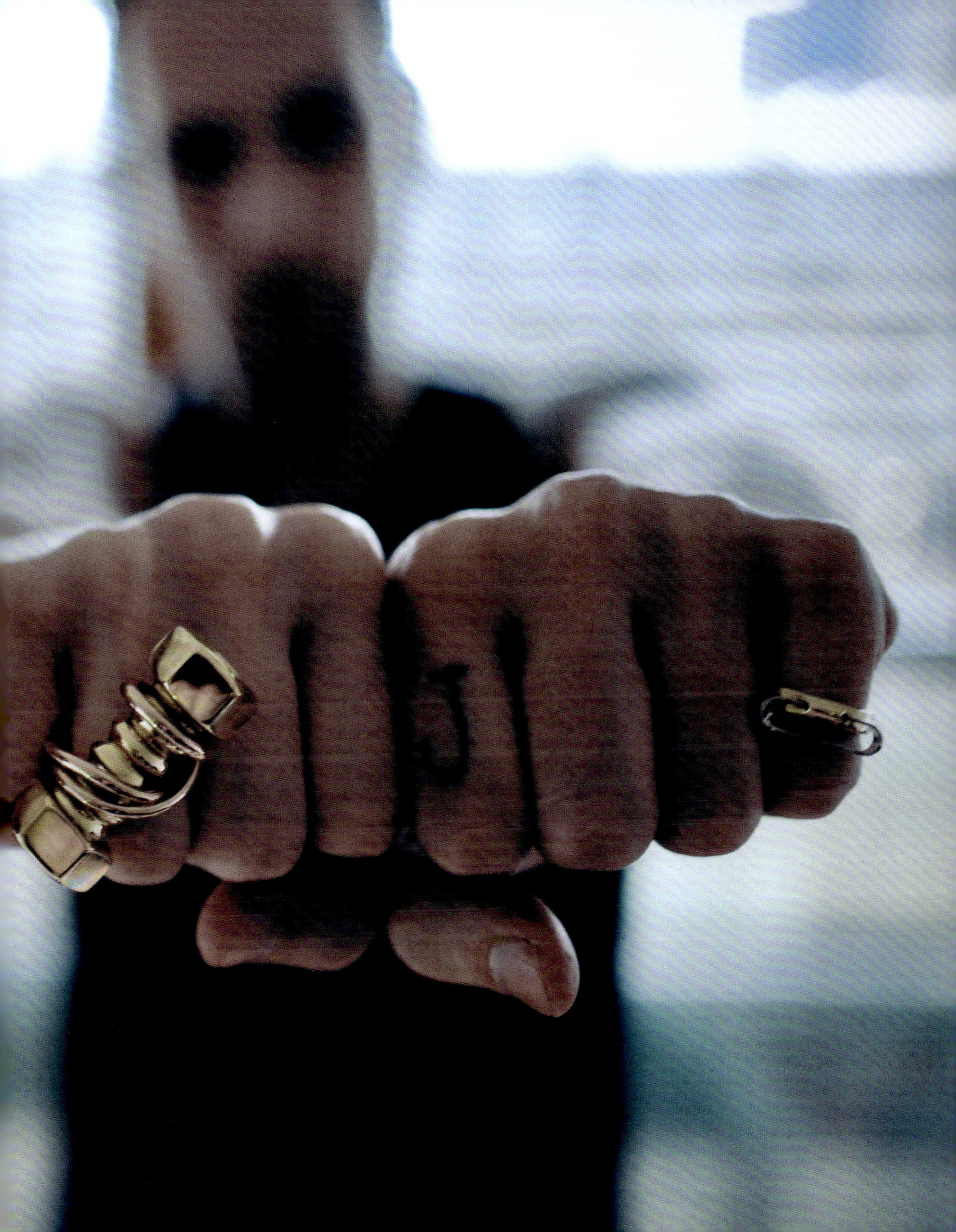

202 > defiant elegance

"Given my background, the very fact that I do what I do is an act of rebellion in a way."

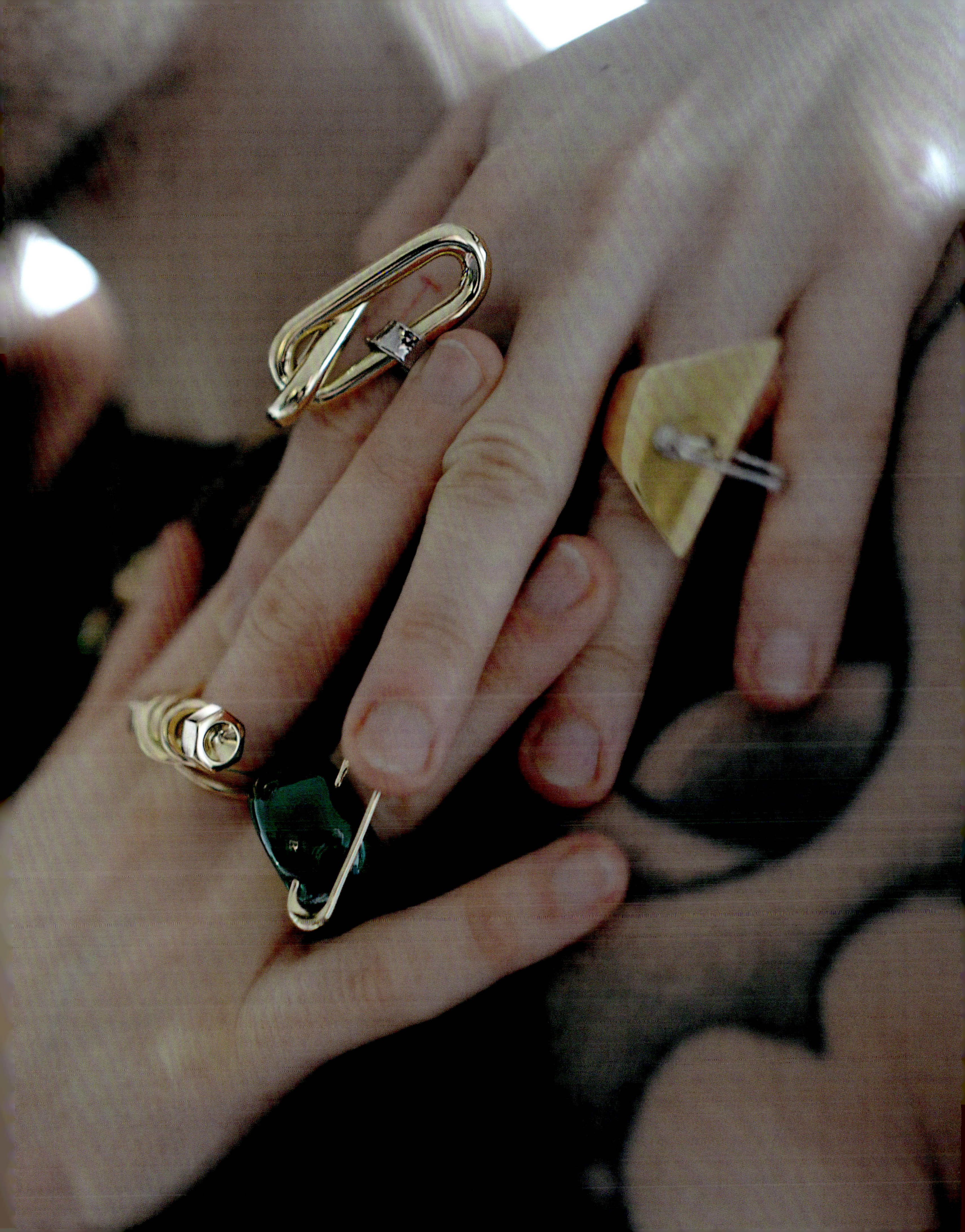

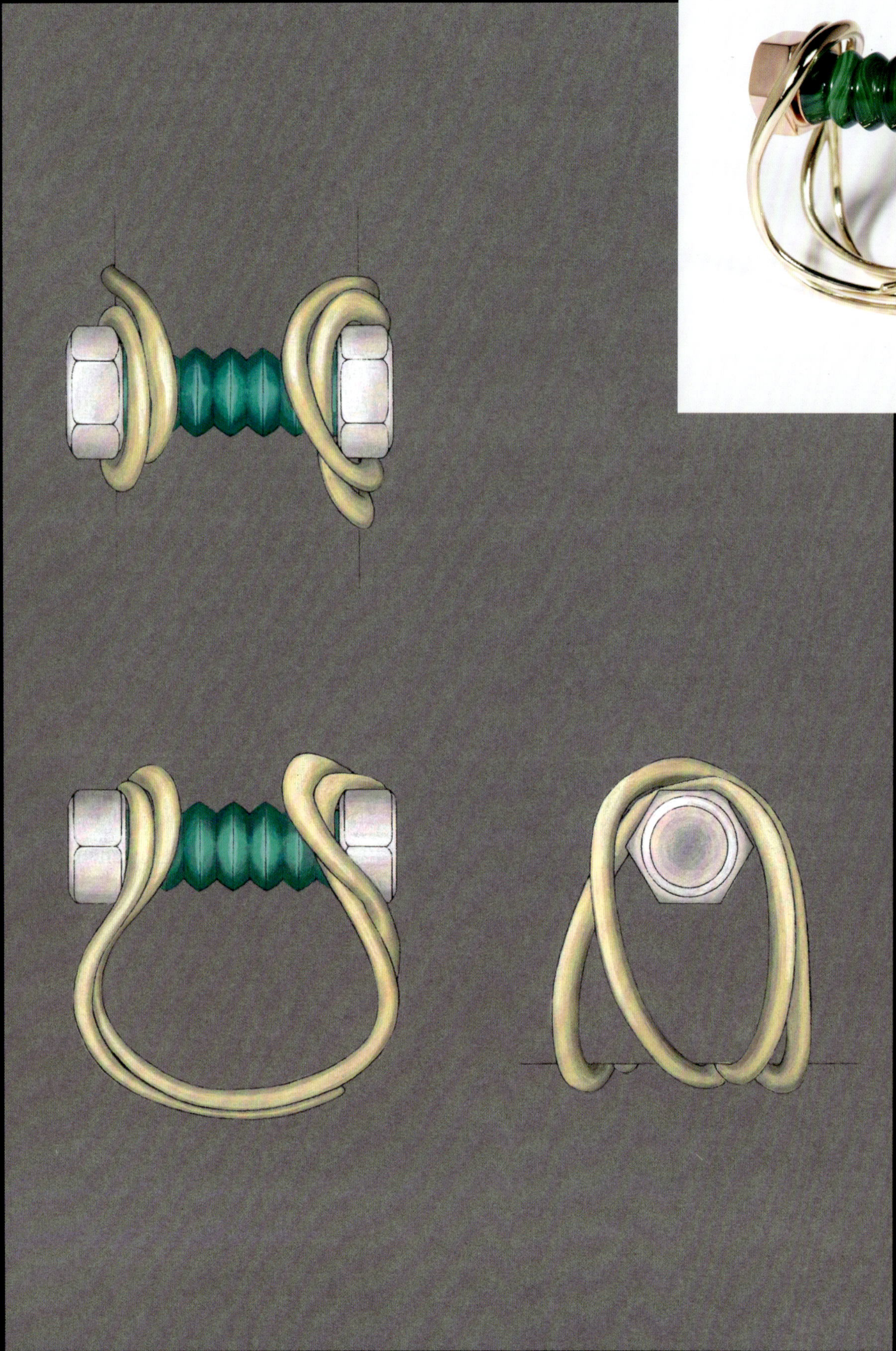

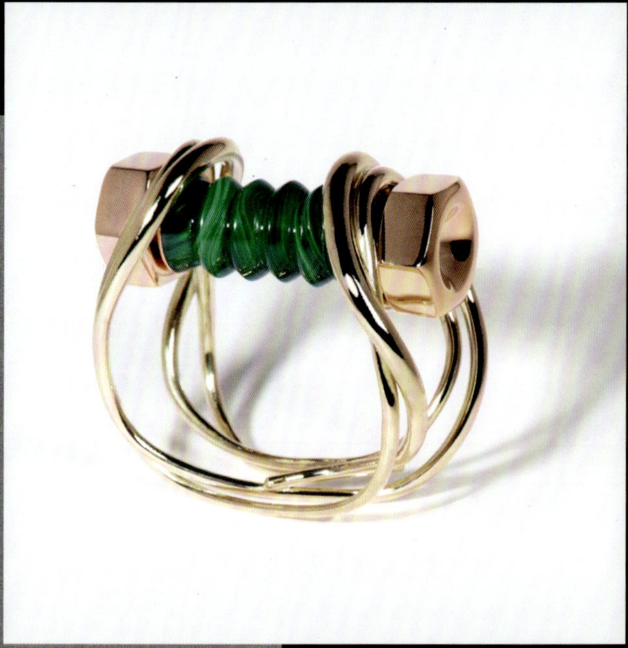

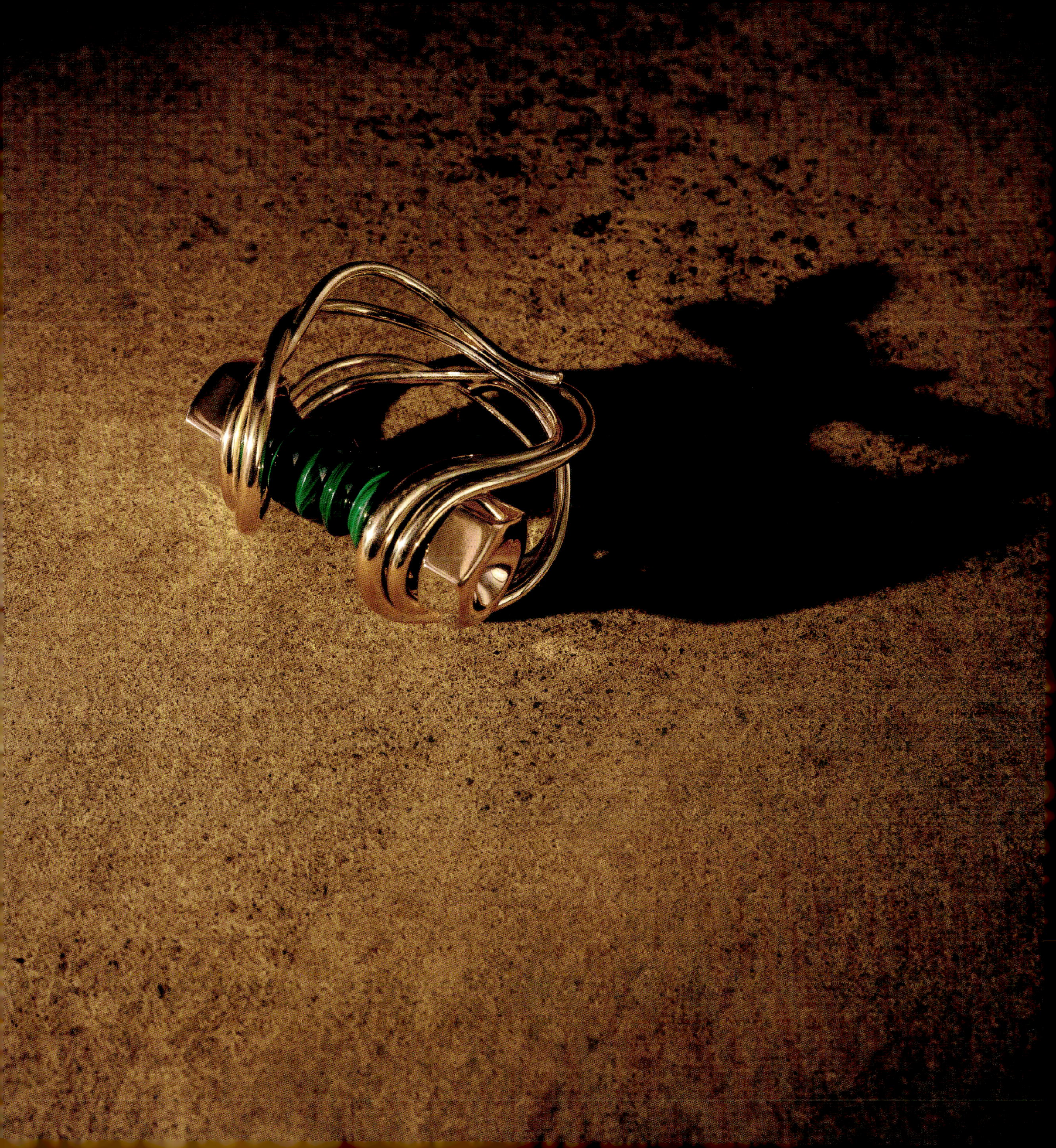

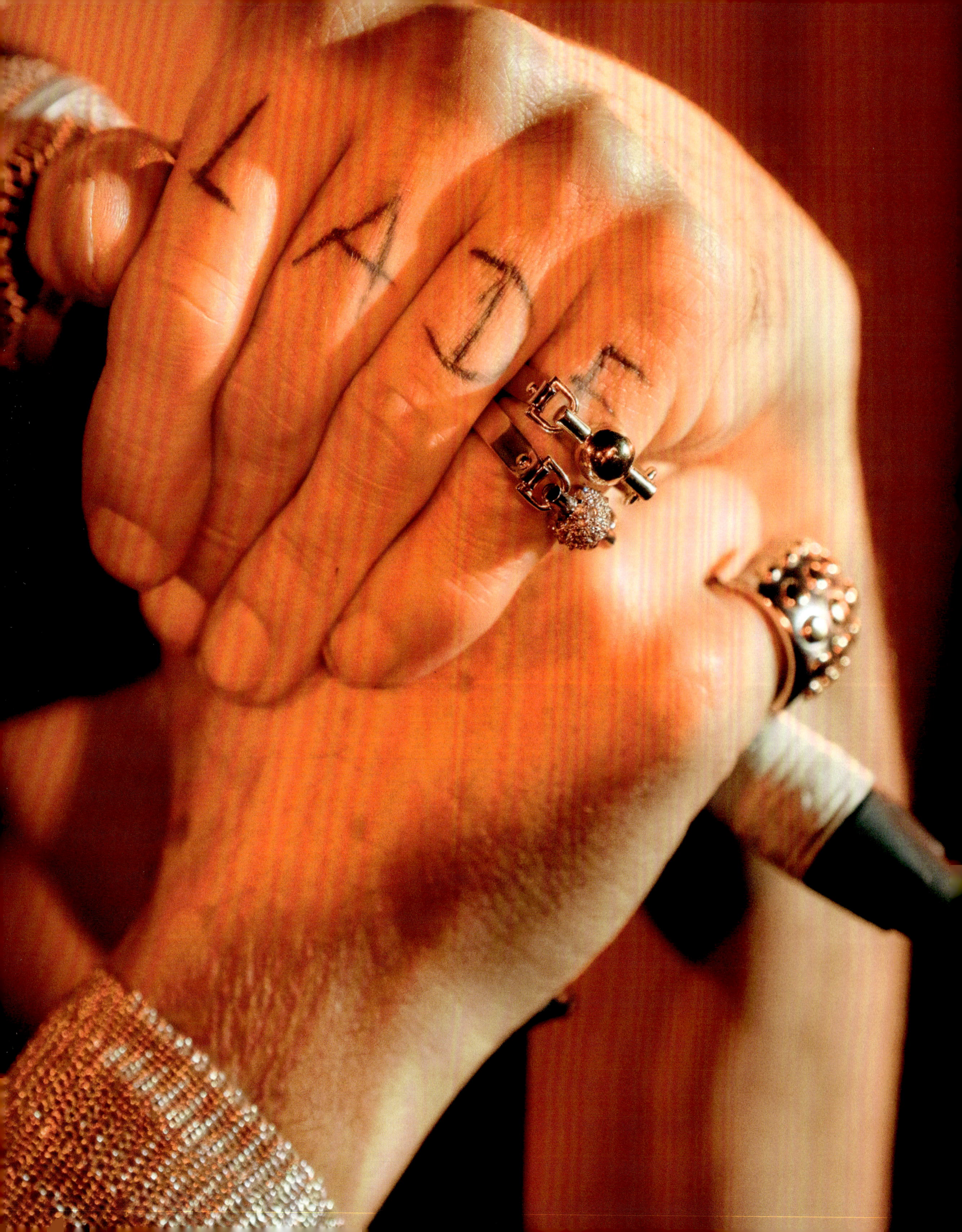
LADE

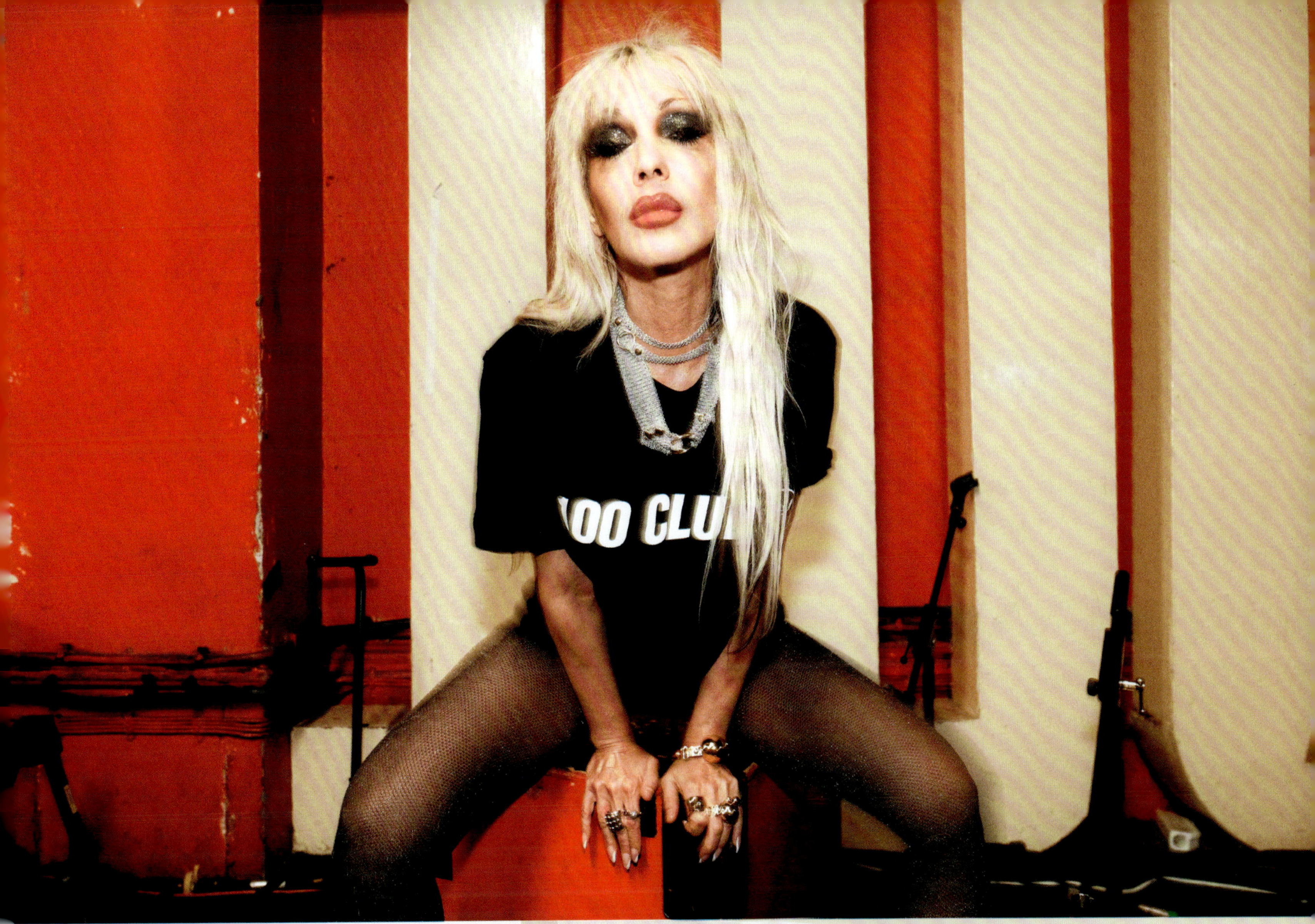
00 CLU

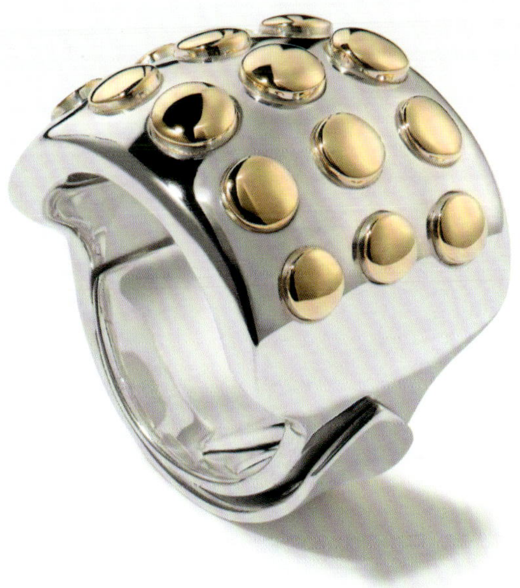

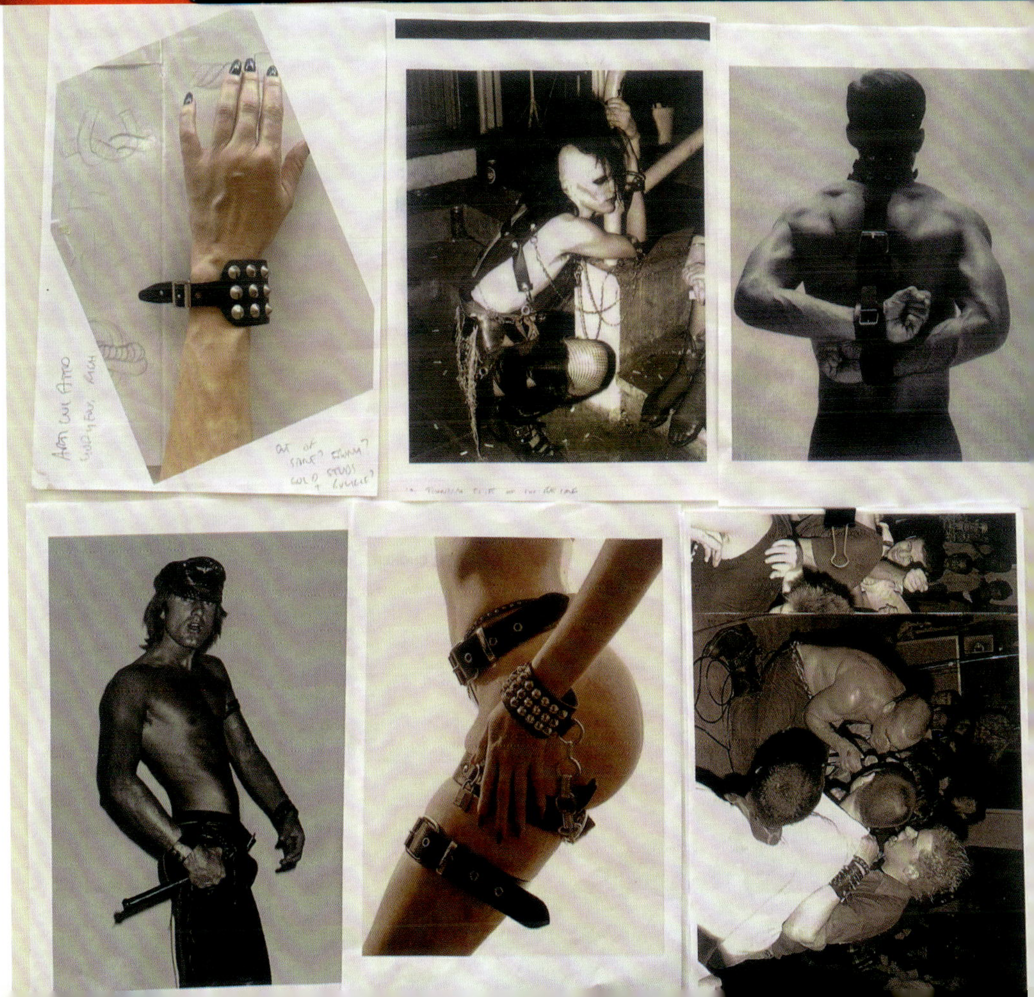

BELTED FLESH.

BUCKLES?

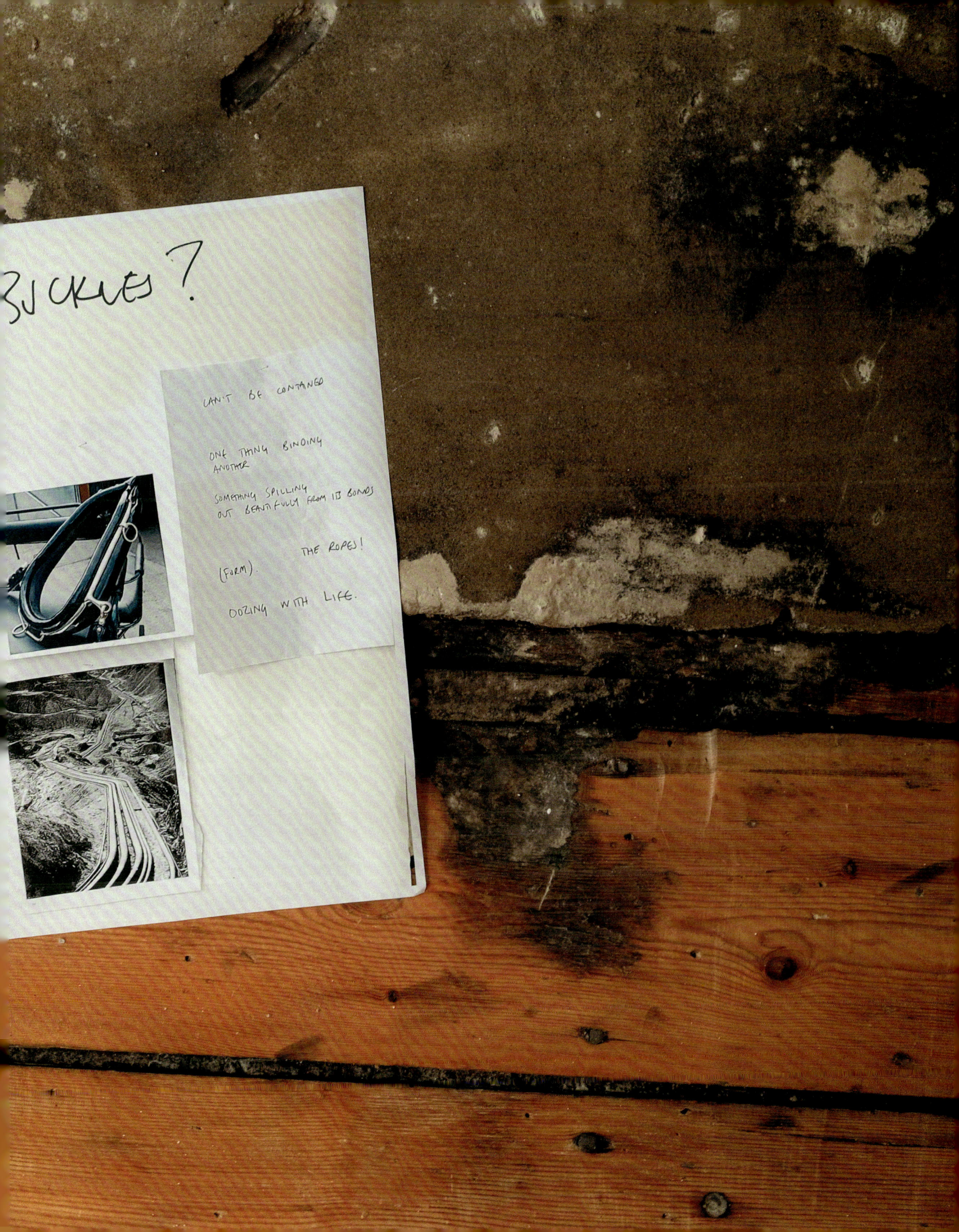

CAN'T BE CONTAINED

ONE THING BINDING ANOTHER

SOMETHING SPILLING OUT BEAUTIFULLY FROM ITS BONDS

(FORM).   THE ROPES!

OOZING WITH LIFE.

DAISY
NOT REQUIRE YOUR
BELIEF IN ORDER
TO FUNCTION
COCKNEY
REJECTS
FREEDOM SOUNDS
THE CROW
STONE CROW
AWAKE
SHROUDED FURNIT
ANAESTHESIA
SUB-REPTILIAN
PN
25.04.19
Criminal Damage
THE SOUTH BANK

'In the end, beyond all the deep thinking and the soul searching, what I really want to do is to make you SMILE. That is my act of rebellion. Because where the fuck would we be without the joy of it all?'

defiant elegance < 211

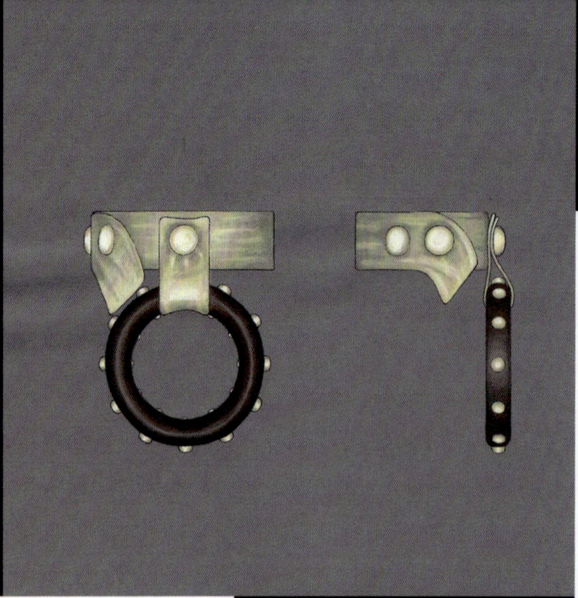
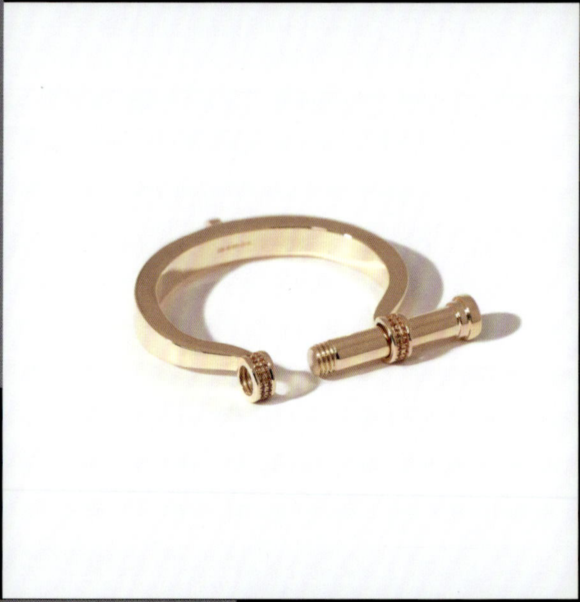
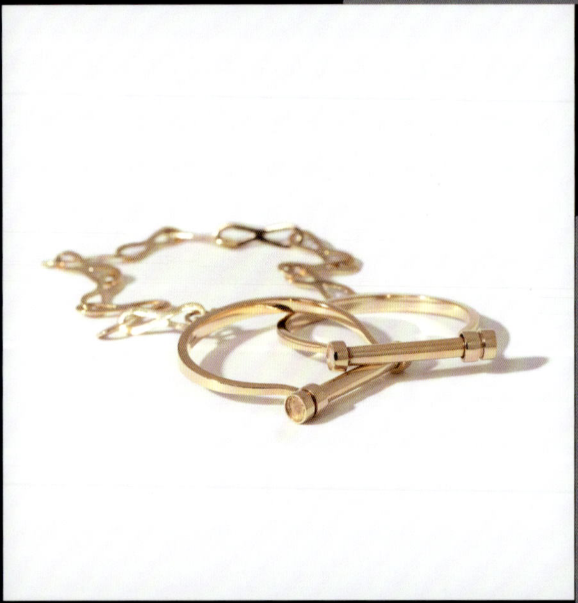
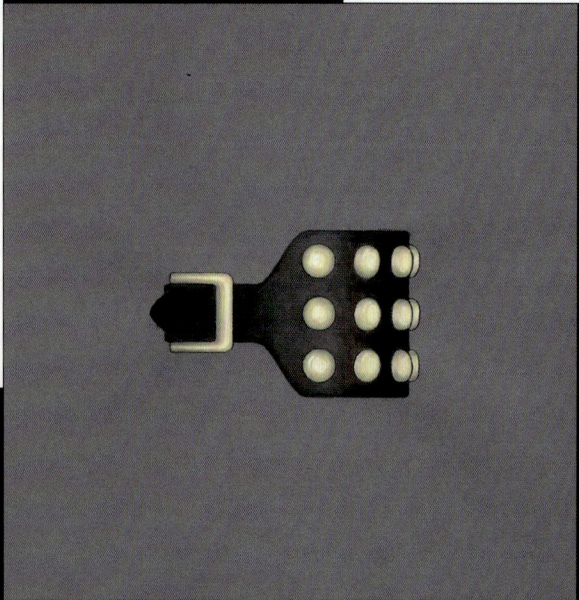

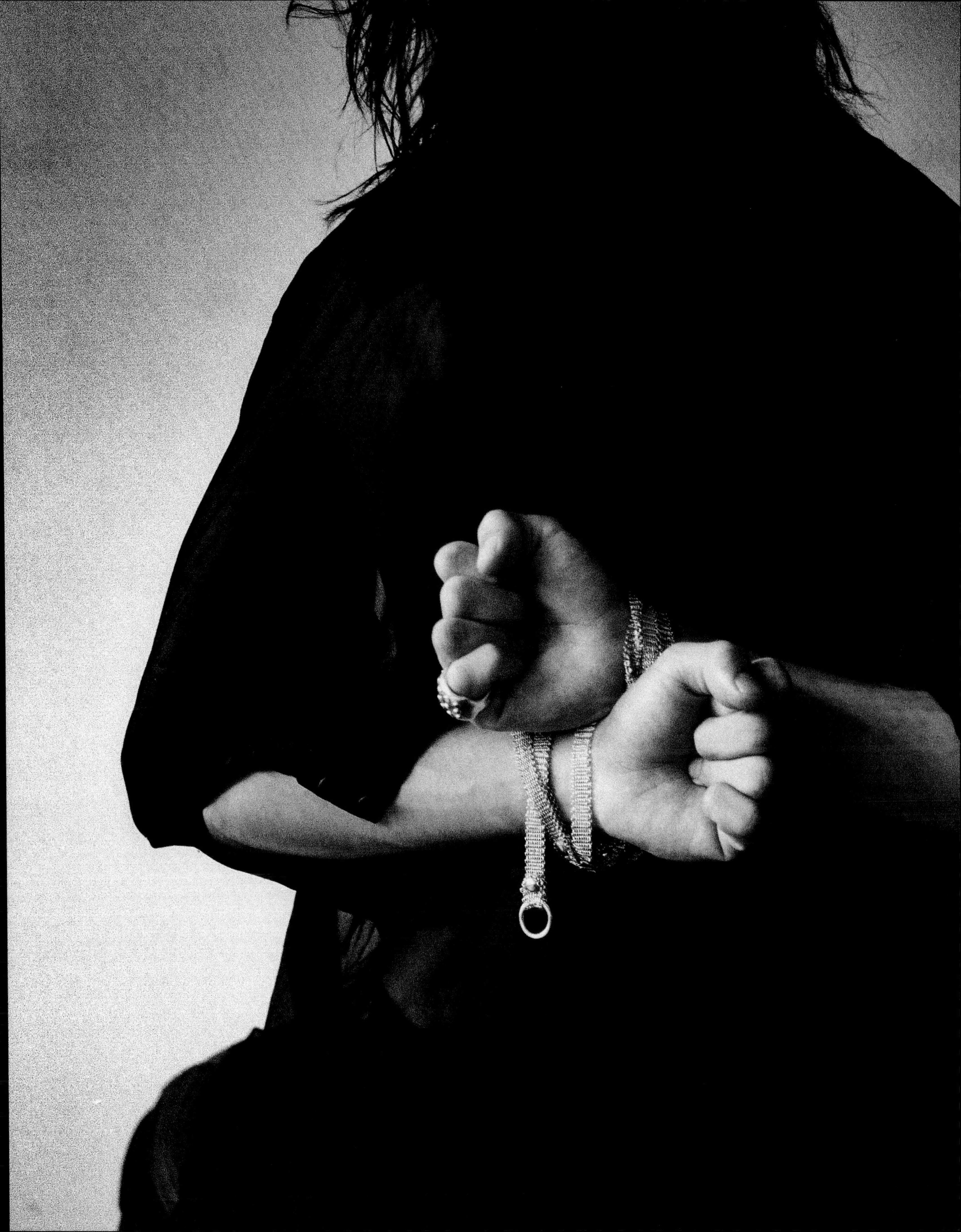

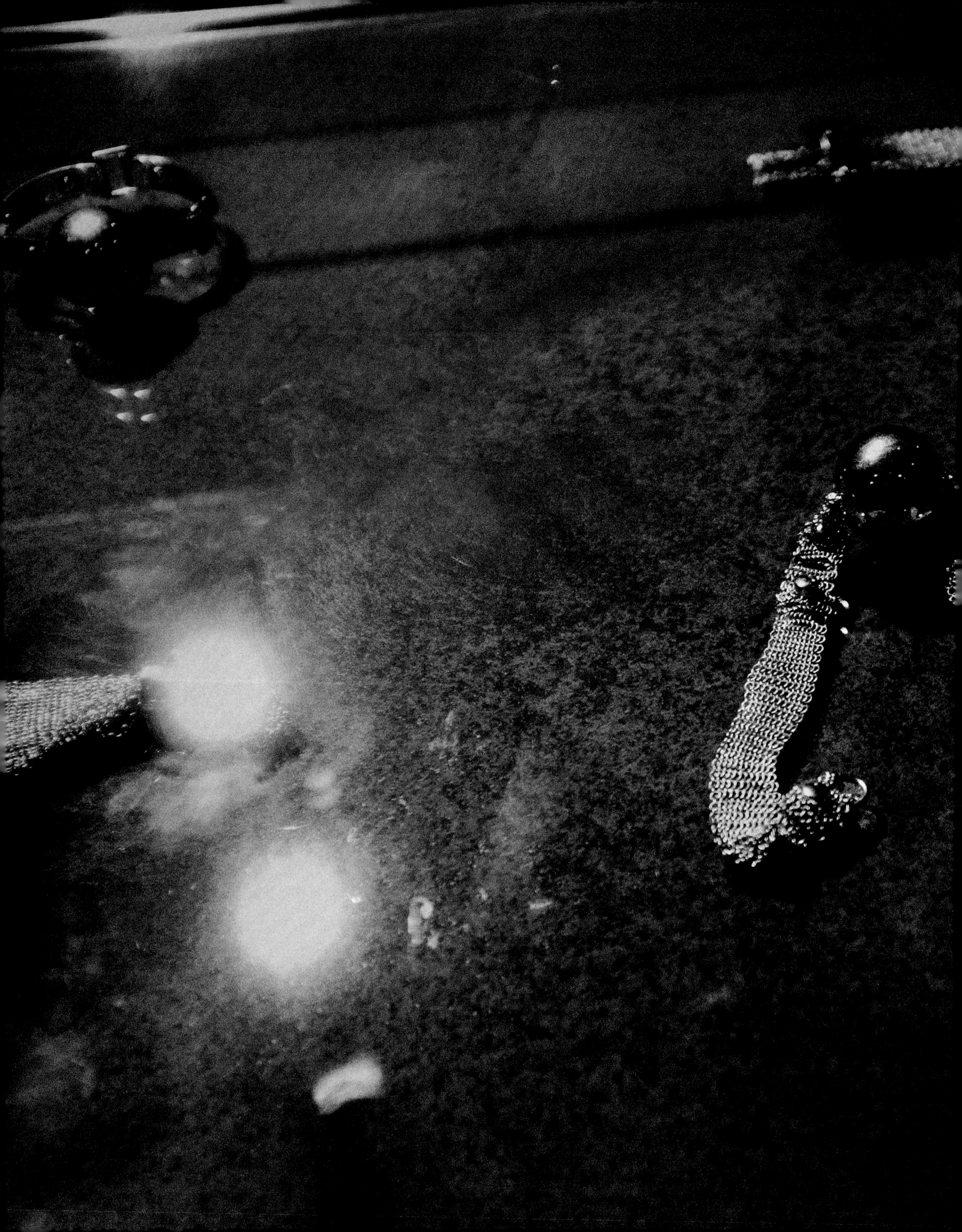

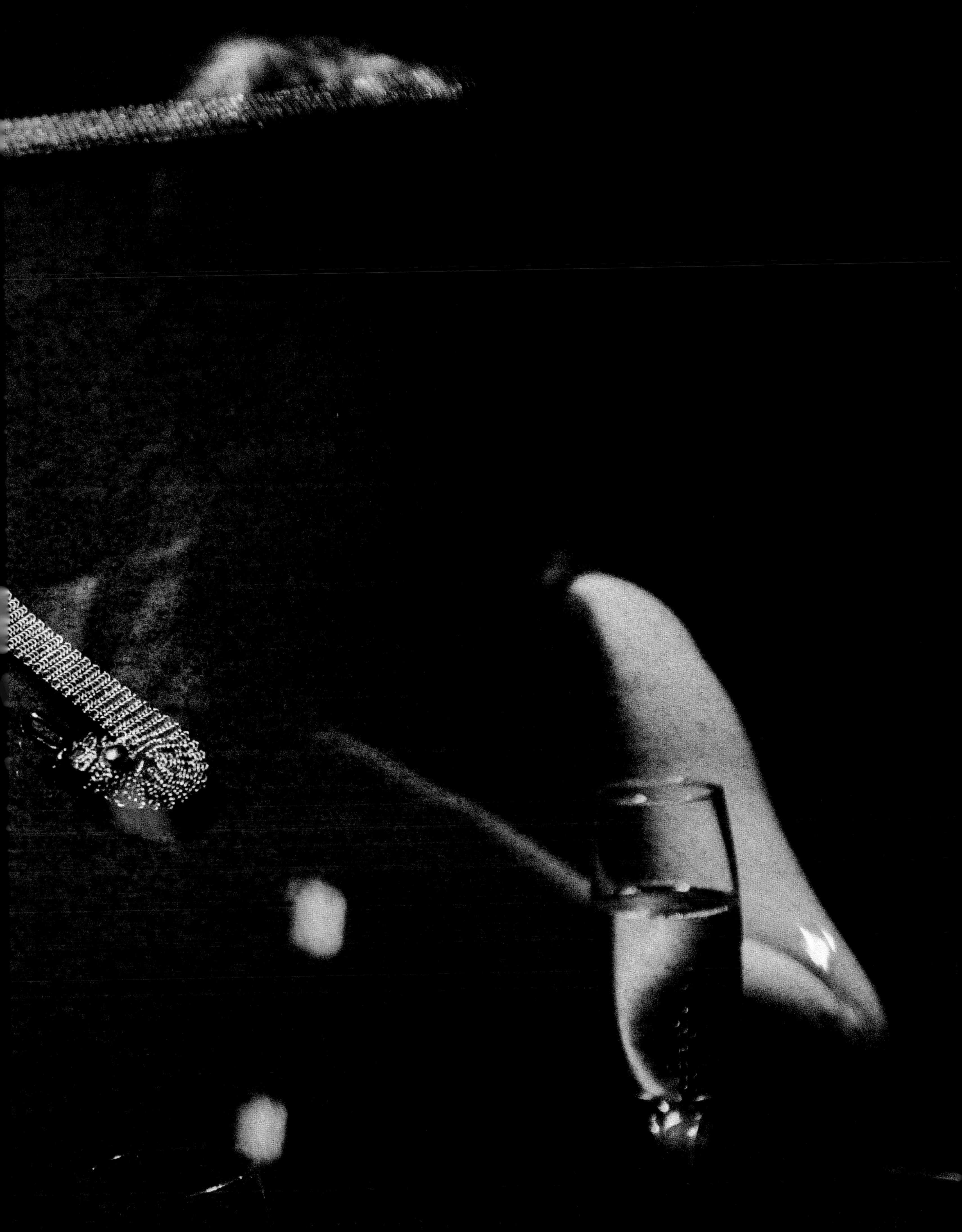

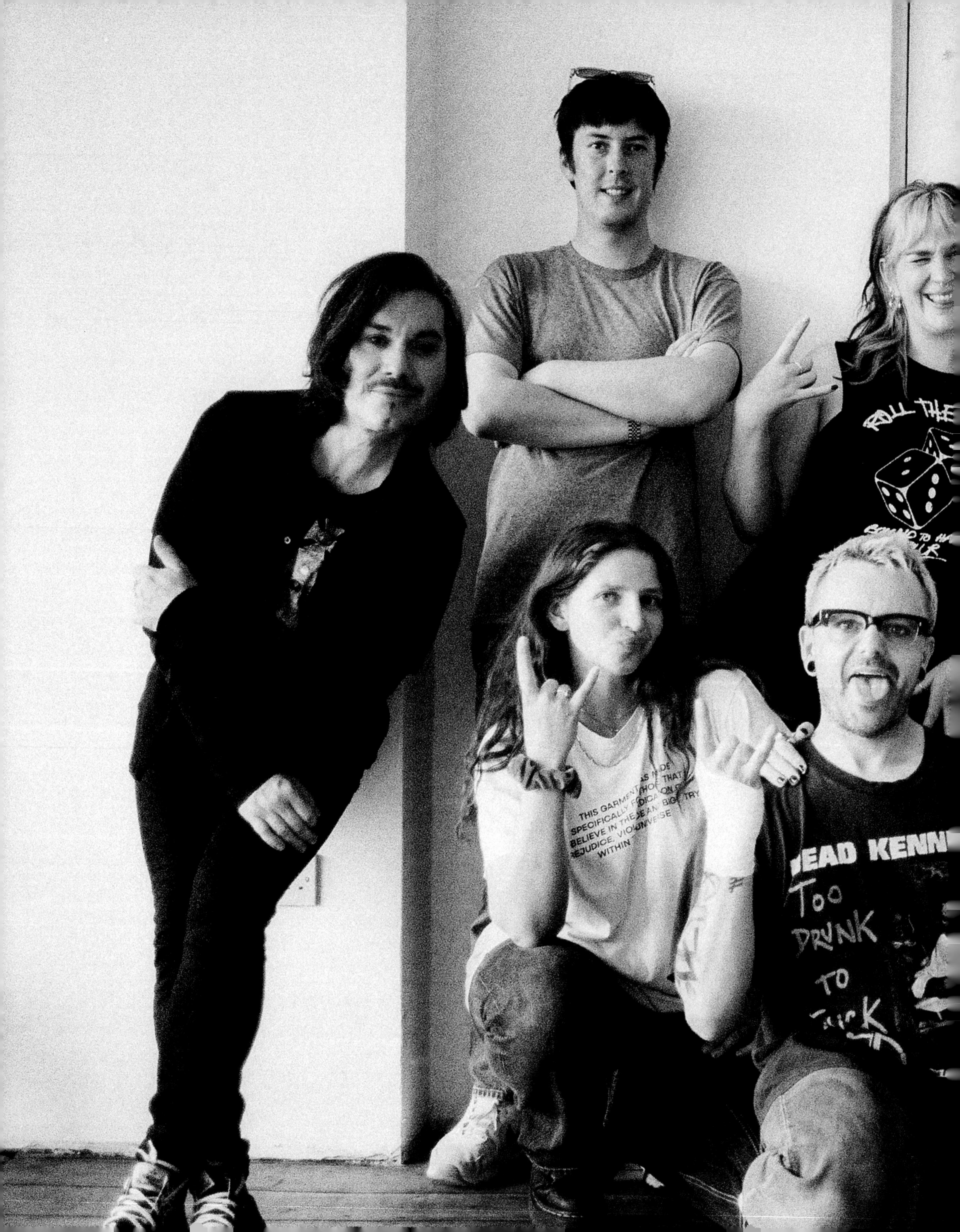
TOO
DRUNK
TO

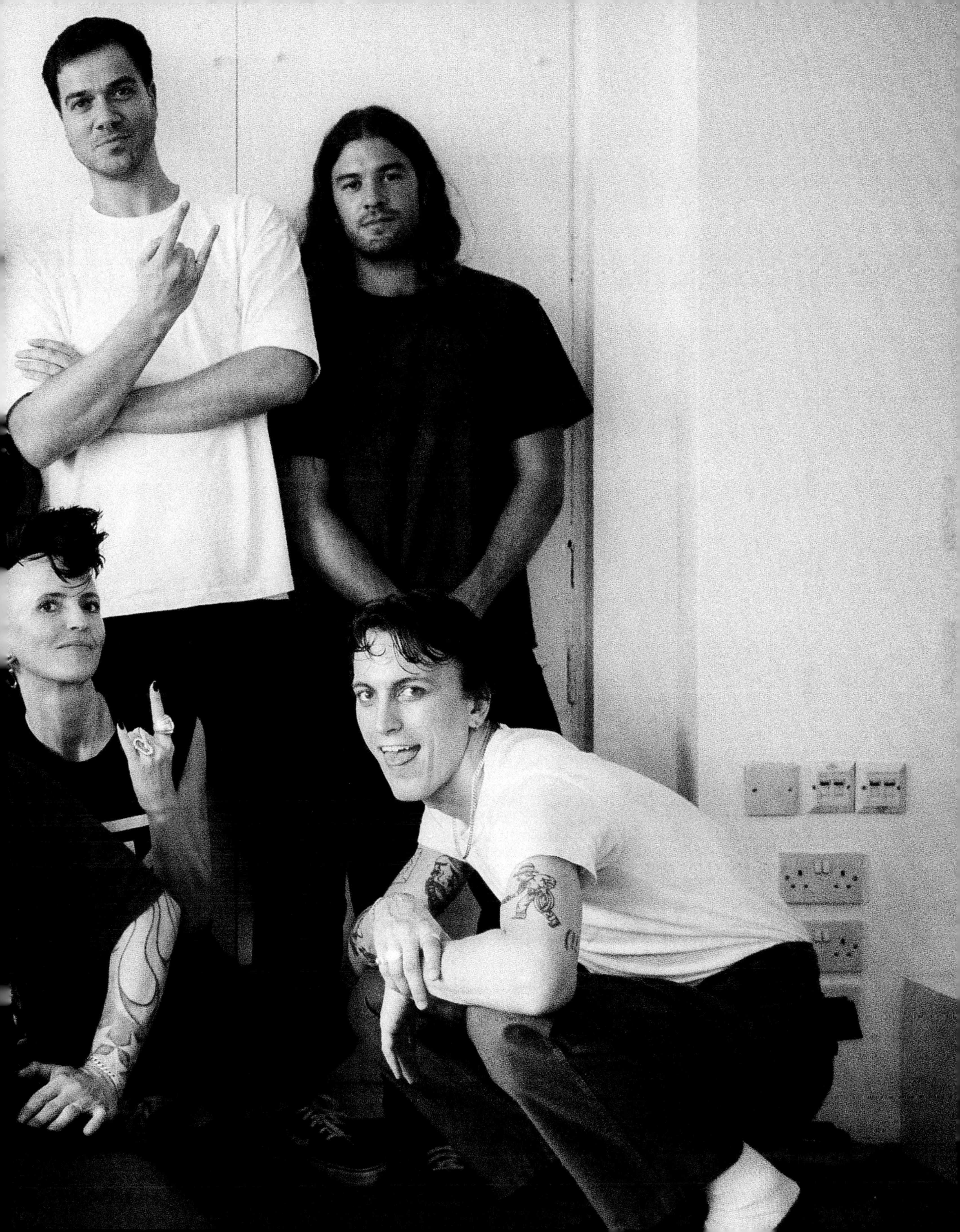

"The biggest rebellion in this world is to feel something real."

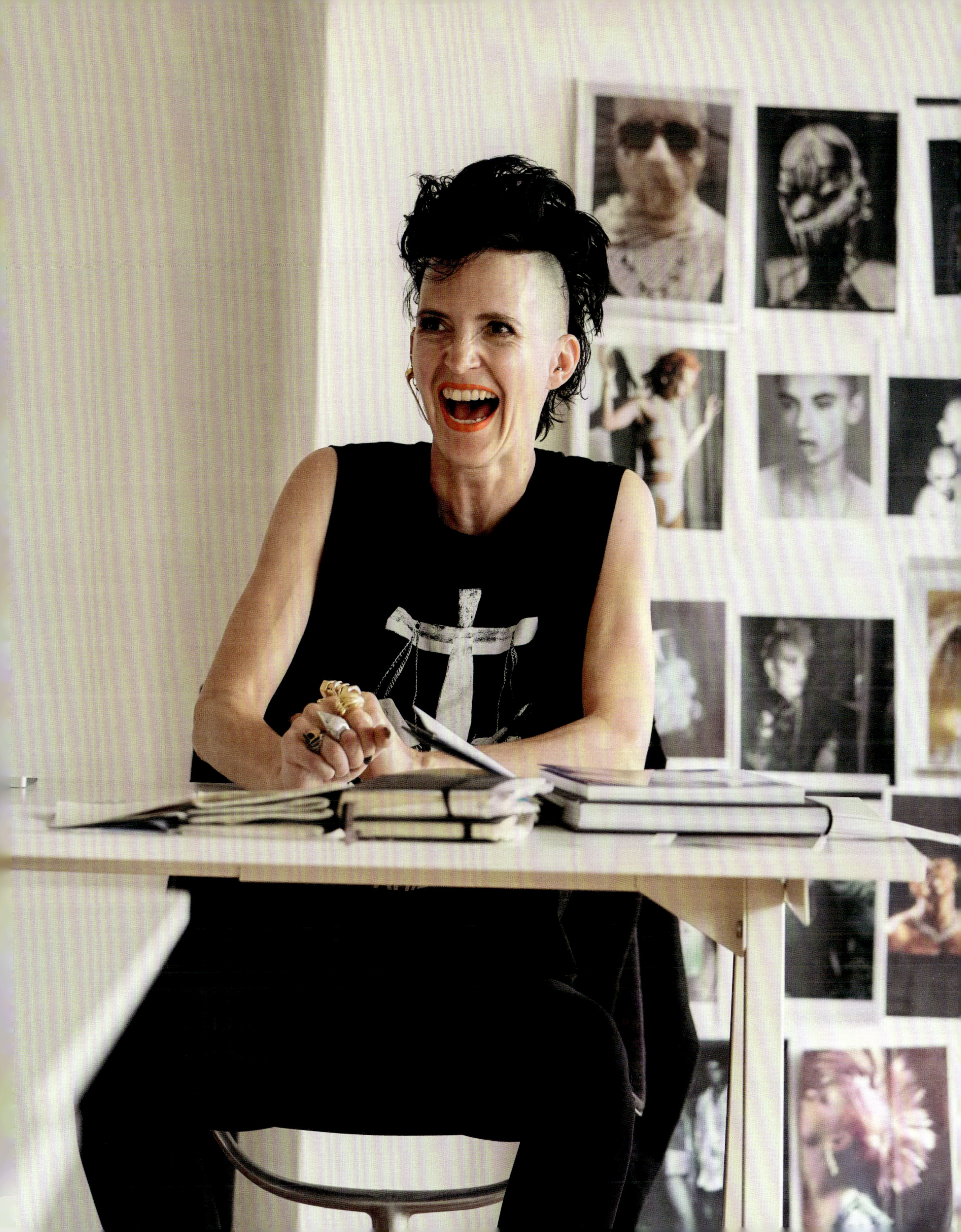

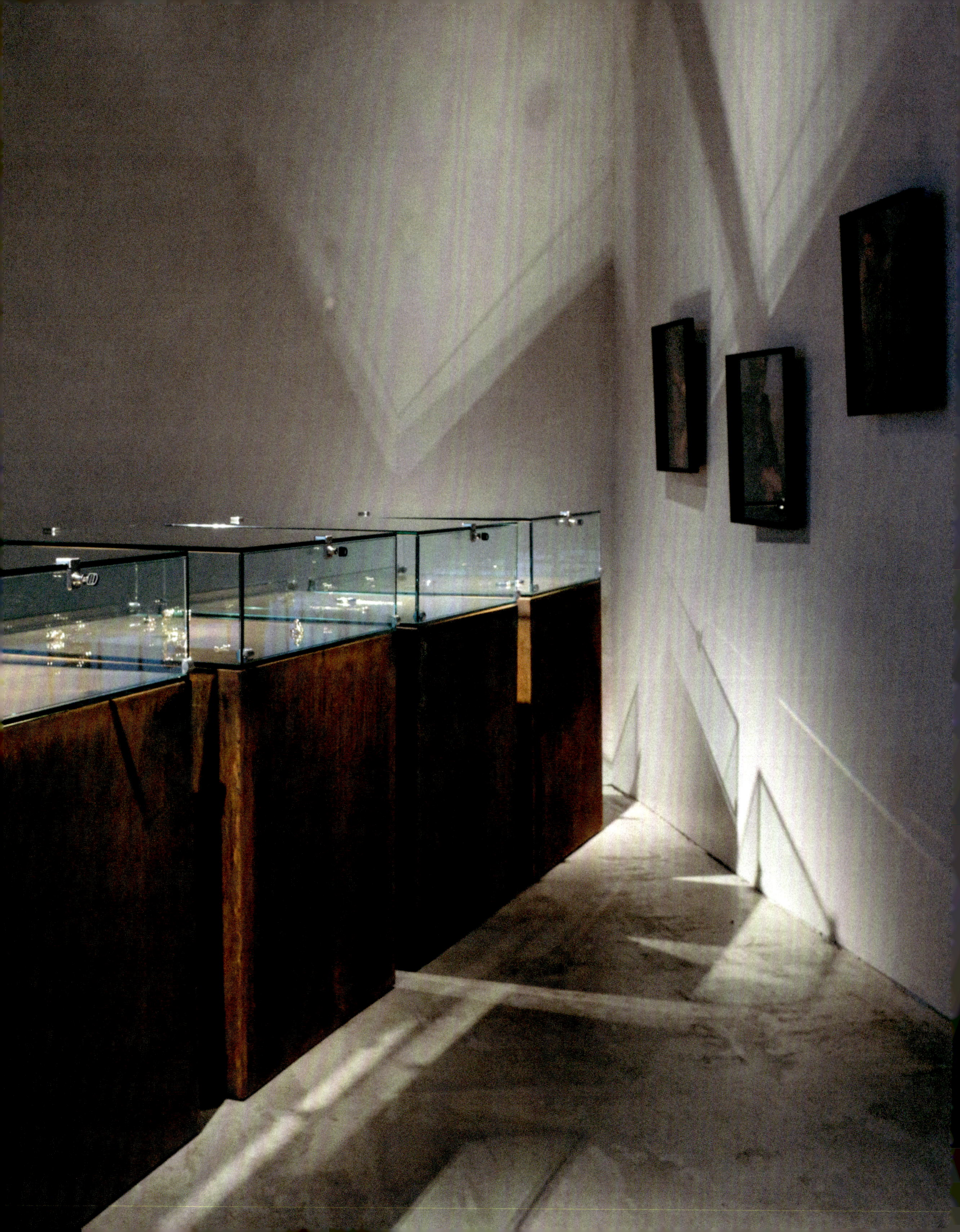

HANNAH MARTIN
LONDON

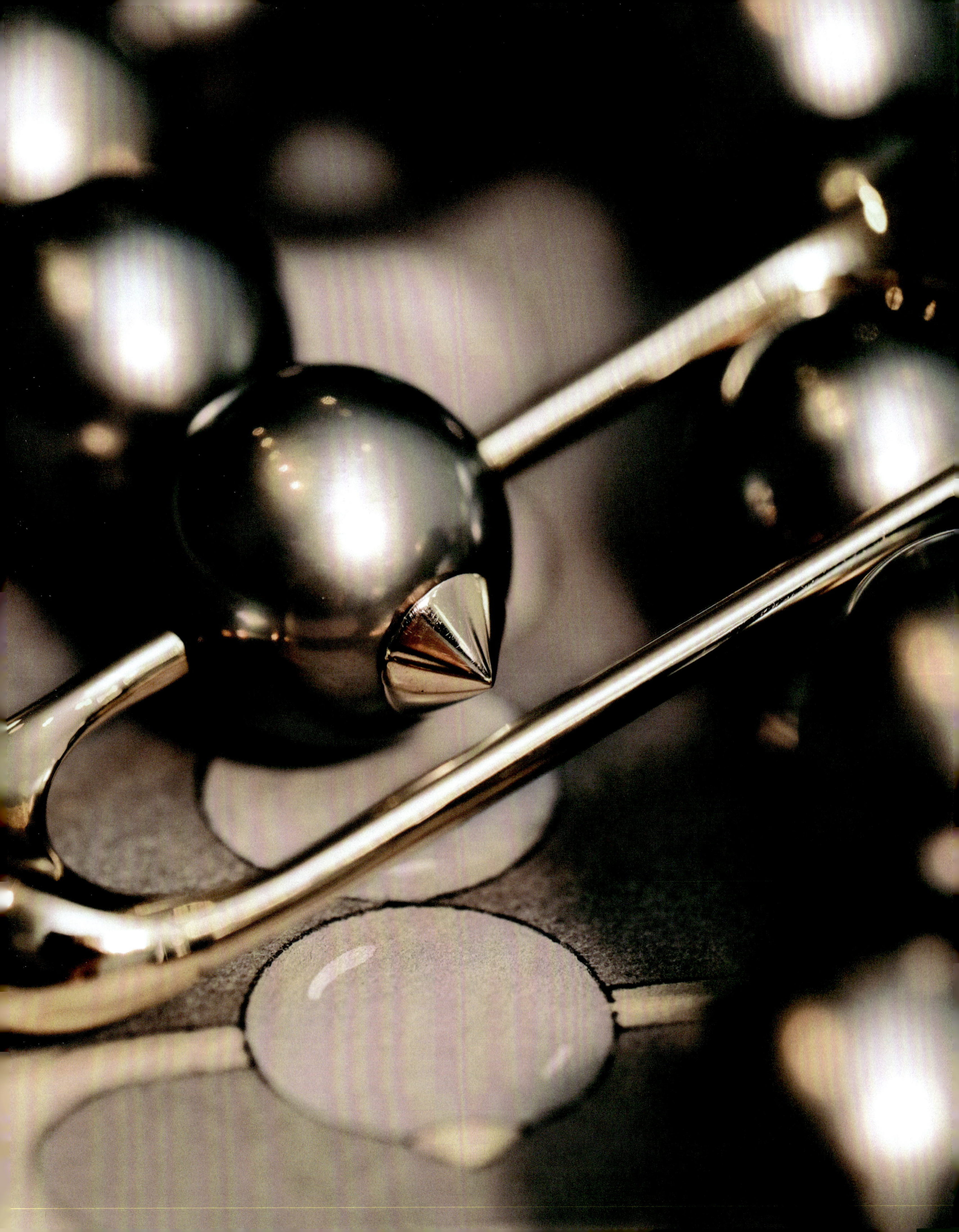

ABOVE FROM LEFT: Delirium Hexagon Earrings, 18ct gold and emeralds, 2014; Night At The Colony Rooms Ring, 18ct gold and diamonds, 2013; Knotted Ring, 18ct gold and cognac diamonds, 2007.

The Art of Transparency

For all its beauty, the jewellery industry remains fraught with ethical complexities, an opacity that Martin finds unsettling.

'Where does this diamond come from?' she asks, lifting a stone at random from her collection. The answer, too often, is obscured, lost in the labyrinthine channels of global supply chains.

Technology offers some solutions – blockchain tracking, for instance, promises a measure of accountability – but true transparency remains elusive. In the meantime, Martin aligns herself with ethical craftsmanship, prioritising materials and methods that honour artistry and dignity.

sourcing < 223

A Legacy of Intimacy

From first sketch to final polish, Hannah Martin's pieces carry an imprint of intent and vulnerability. Over time, these bold, sculptural forms will come to speak for someone else, taking on layers of meaning as they are worn. That, ultimately, is their alchemy.

More than objects, more than finely wrought metals and stones, these jewels are artefacts of an ongoing conversation. They begin as artefacts of the connection between maker and wearer and their significance transforms over time. More than fashion, they are, in the truest sense, a testament to the power of adornment as it has existed for millennia.

They mark, provoke and transform.

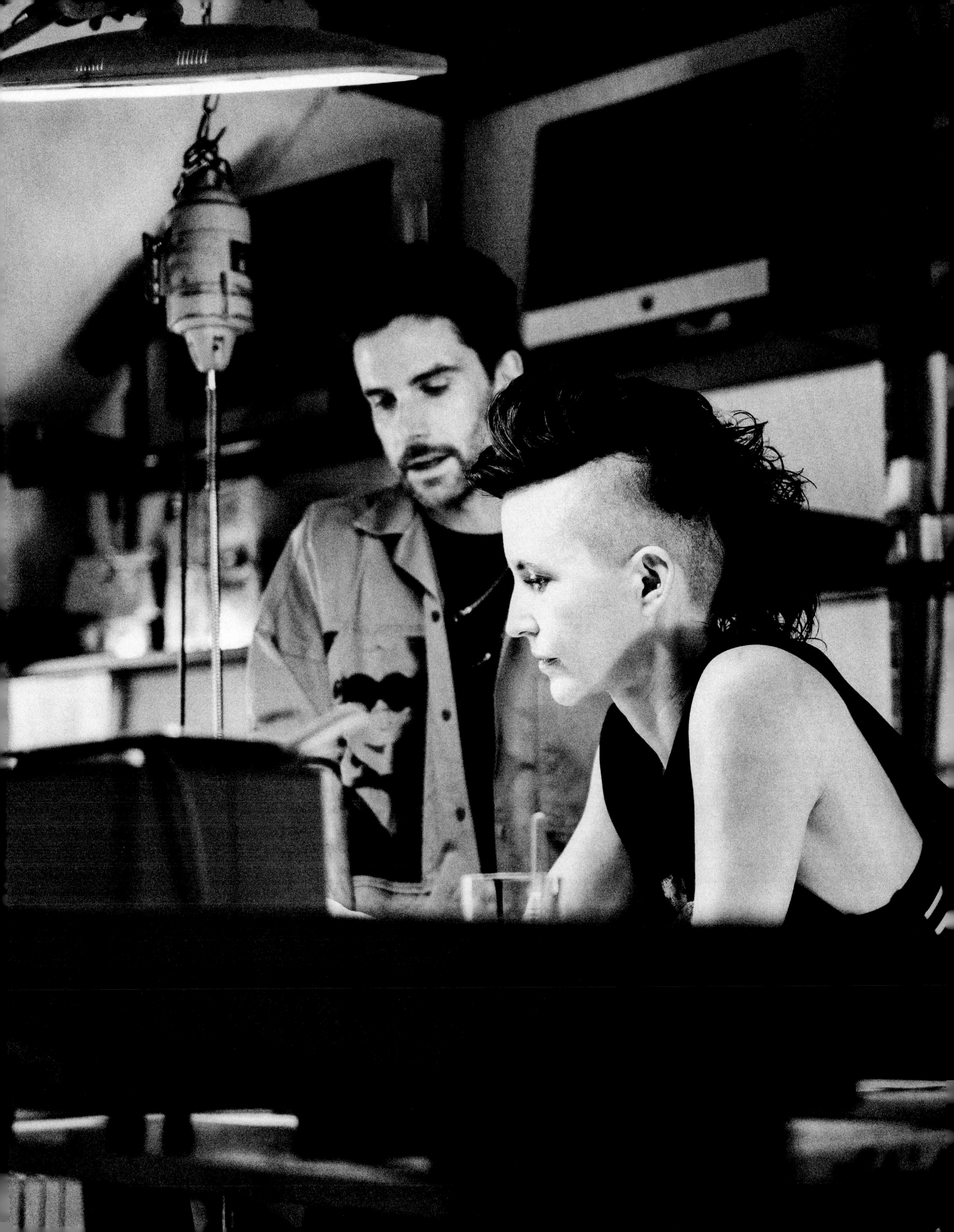

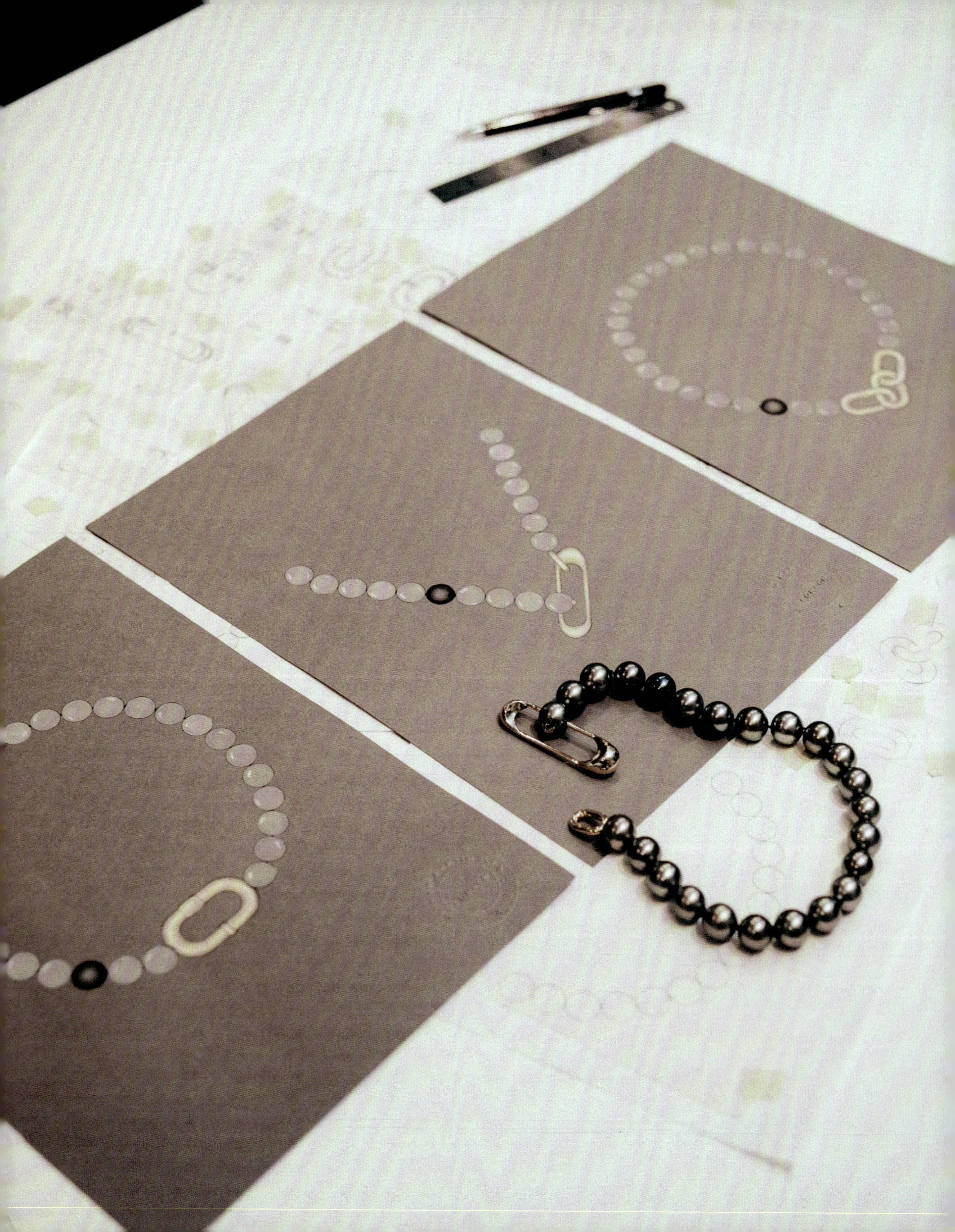

hannah martin bespoke < 227

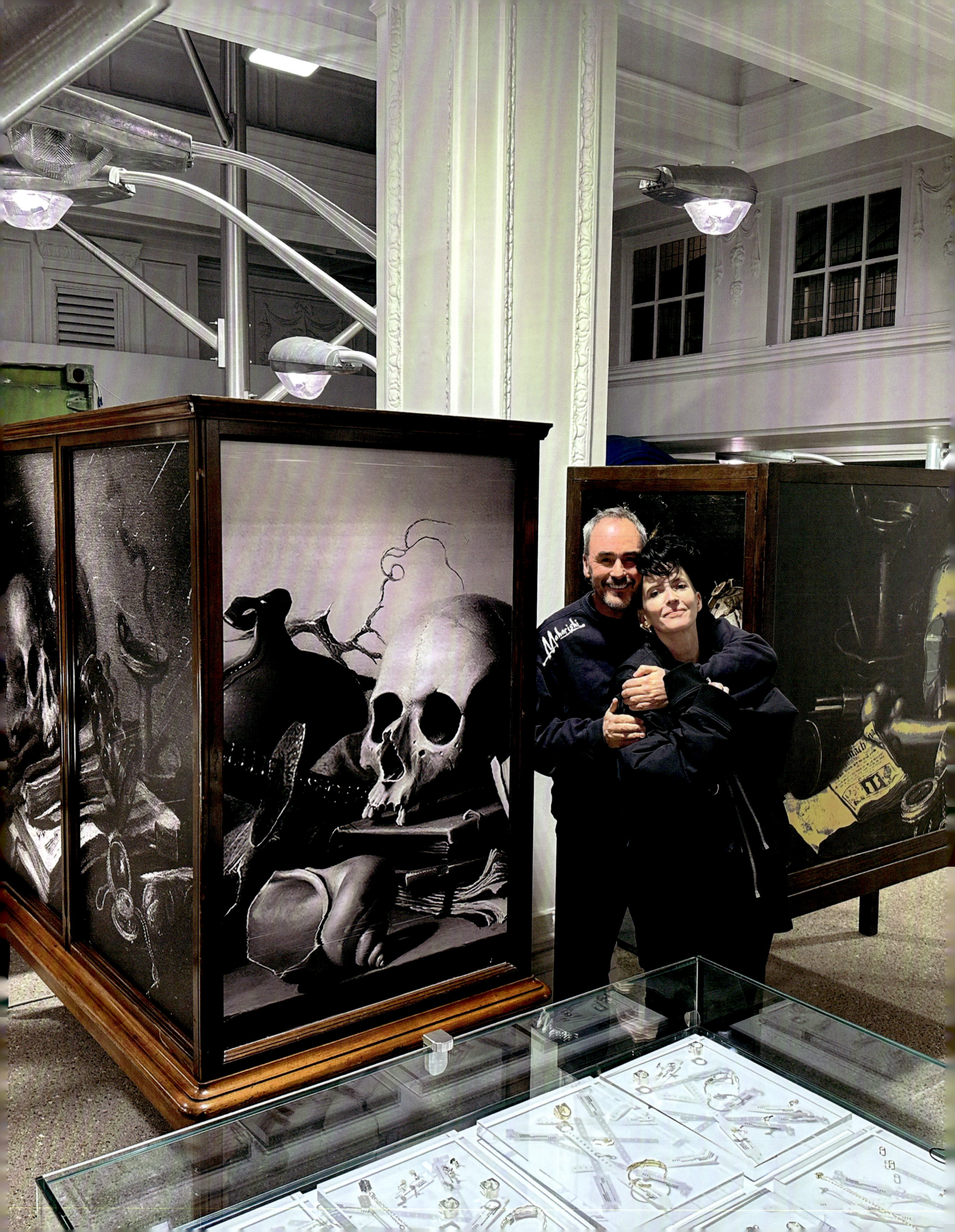

Dover Street Market

❛ The original DSM, on Dover Street in London, had been open about a year when I launched myself out of my Saint Martins bubble and into the real world. It was a mecca of cool, and still is. It is THE place to be, a name mentioned with awed whispers by young designers then and now. I remember how nervous I was going for my first appointment, clutching my bag of jewels and trying to play it cool. It must have gone all right, because Dover Street Market became my first official stockist. Dickon Bowden, Adrian Joffe and the whole DSM team have become like family. Twenty years ago, they saw something in me, and the belief, trust and support over the years has meant the world to me. We have grown up together as businesses and stayed un-grown up together as friends. The risk they took on a scrappy punk jeweller just starting out has evolved into my longest-term relationship to date. ❜

Maxfield

❛ There are speciality stores, and then there is Maxfield. Legendary, iconic, one-of-a-kind – and I do not use those words lightly. There is nothing I love more than hearing stories about the last 50-odd years from Sarah and the OG team. About Tommy's first set up – a small studio next to the infamous Whisky a Go Go nightclub on Sunset Strip in Los Angeles, where the rock 'n' rollers would stop in for a sharp suit or two to wear onstage. From there the family grew, the legends grew – and I am so proud to be a small part of it all. It took a few years and many meetings in that infamous dressing room – if you know, you know – to get rolling, but once we did there was no looking back. Maxfield opened not only their arms but also Los Angeles to me, for which I am forever theirs. ❜

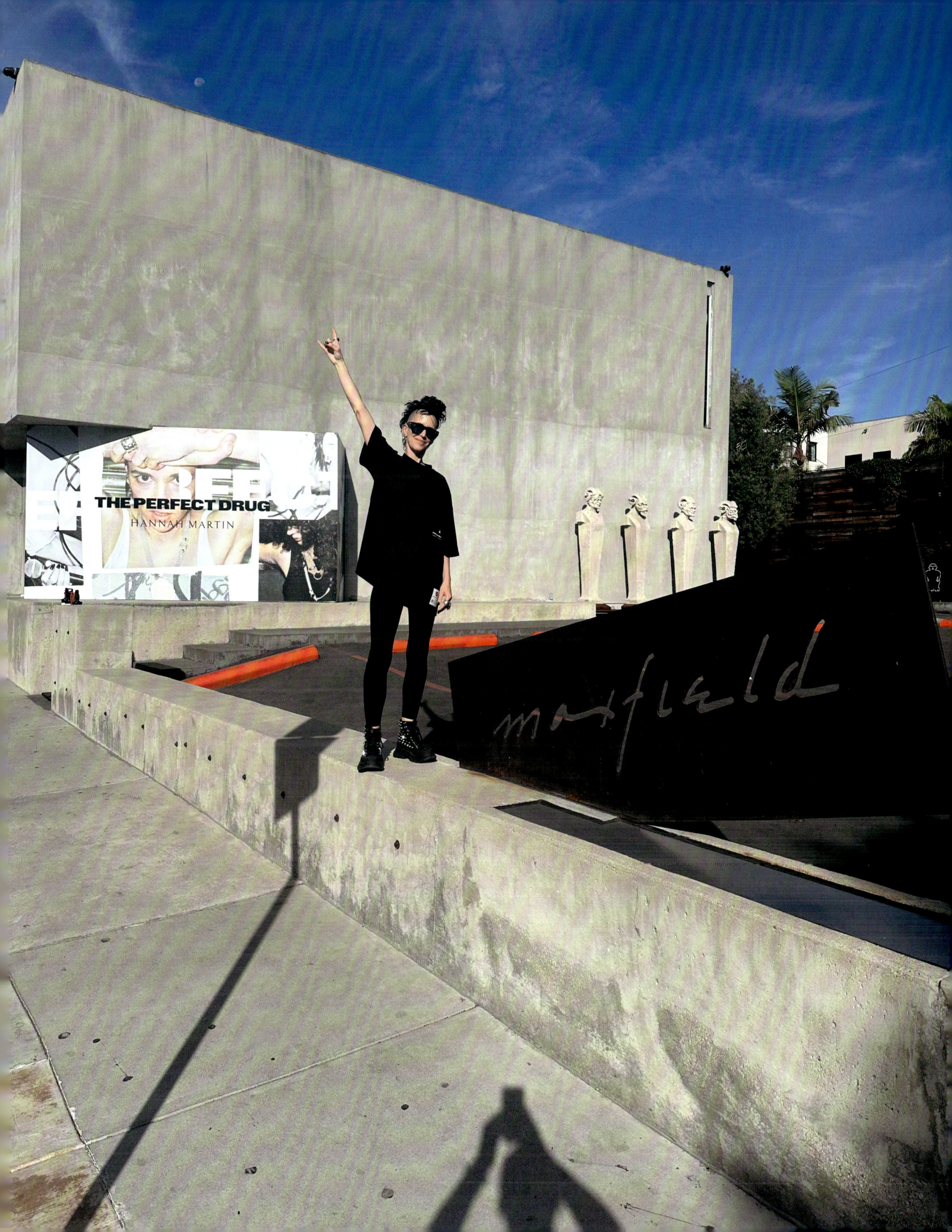
THE PERFECT DRUG
HANNAH MARTIN
maxfield

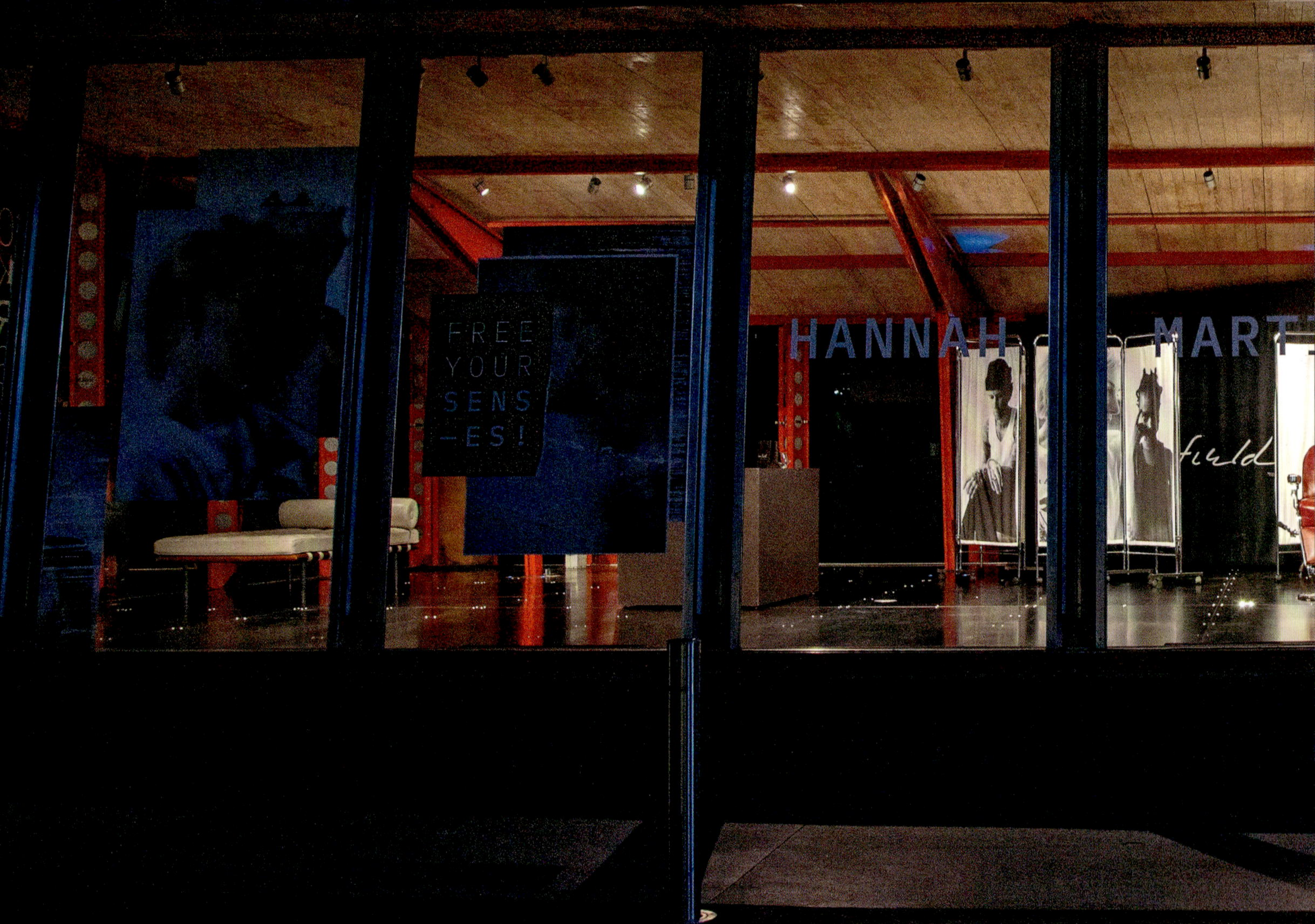
FREE
YOUR
SENS
-ES!
HANNAH
MART

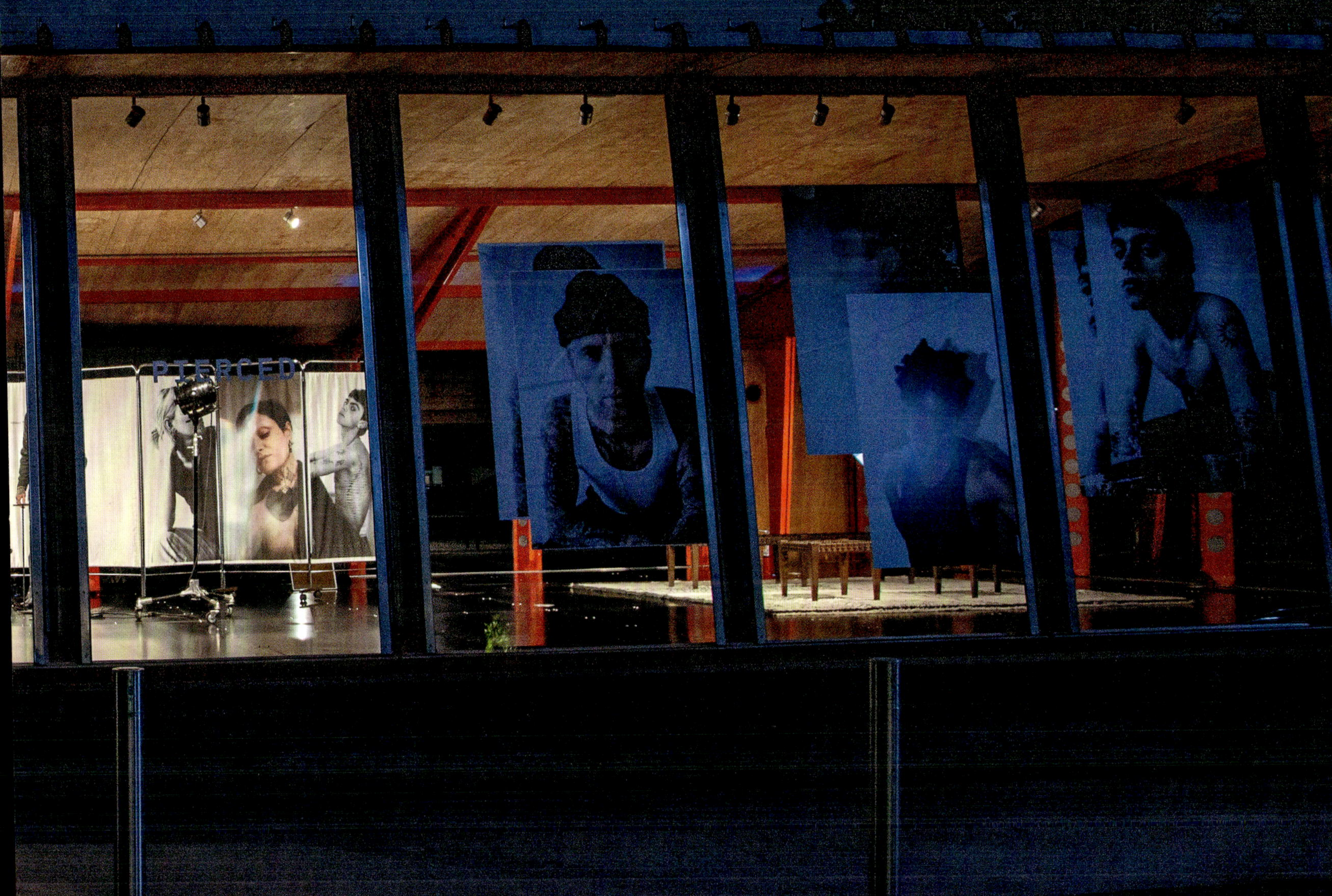
PIERCED

234 > hannah martin collections

2005
Founded Hannah Martin Ltd

IT'S ONLY ROCK 'N' ROLL

Spur Ring – 18ct gold and black diamonds

2007
THE FORGOTTEN TREASURE OF THE INFAMOUS AGUILA DORADA
(affectionately known as 'Aguila Dorada')

Bid For Freedom Shackle Bangle – 18ct gold and sapphires

HM x McKinley & Son

Taxidermy & Gold Sculptures

HM X Coco De Mer: A collection of erotic tools

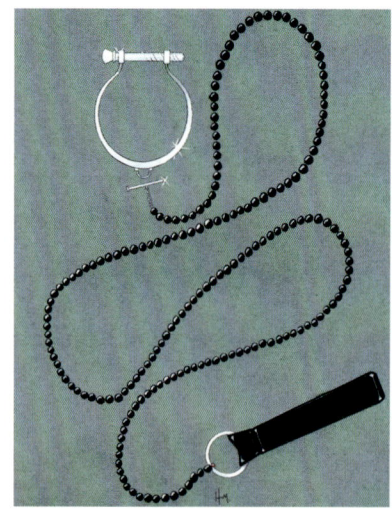

Cock Ring with Black Pearl Leash

2008
THE ONLY PERFORMANCE

Twisted Knife Edge Ring – 18ct gold

HM x Swarovski Runway Rocks

Pearl Fetish

2009
VINCENT

Vincent's Empty Sovereign Ring – 18ct gold and sapphires

HM x Carolyn Massey

AW10 onwards

HM x Hannah Marshall

SS10 onwards

2010
HM x Peter Doherty

Albion Trinketry

2011
THE SHAMAN'S TRIANGLE (Part 1: THE MAN WHO KNOWS EVERYTHING)

The Euphoria of Lights Ring – 18ct gold, rubies and sapphires

HM LEATHER

Key Ring

Every Lyons Howl
(Couture collection in Palladium)

Every Lyons Howl Ring – Palladium, emeralds, black diamonds

HM x The State of Qatar

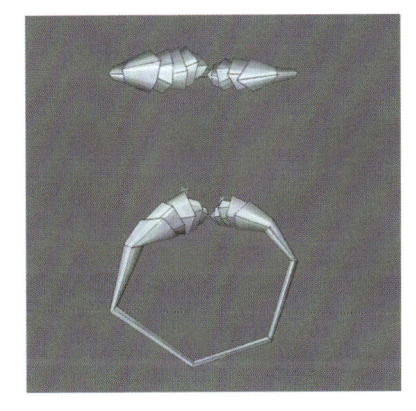

Thai Savigny Bangle – Silver

HM x *Wallpaper Magazine

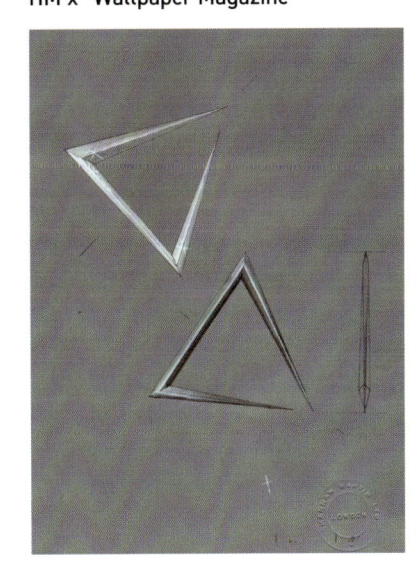

*WallpaperBespoke Letter Opener

2012
SOLARIS (Part 2: THE MAN WHO KNOWS EVERYTHING)

The Orbit Enlightenment Ring – 18ct gold, sapphires, amethysts and diamonds

HM x Hussein Chalayan

HM for The London Design Festival

The London Design Medal
(an annual collaboration to date)

hannah martin collections < 235

236 > hannah martin collections

2013
WHITE HEAT

The Southern Cross Ring – 18ct gold, diamonds

HM x Hendricks Gin

A Hip Flask For Flaneurs

2014
DELIRIUM (Part 3: THE MAN WHO KNOWS EVERYTHING)

Emerald Trance Amulet – 18ct gold, emerald and enamel

HM x The State of Qatar

Limited Edition Vase

2016
SOMEBODY'S SINS

Unknown Pleasures Ring – 18ct gold, sapphires, black jade

HM x Simon Teakle

Aphrodite's Journey – 18ct gold, ancient cameo, diamonds

2018
HM x Motley London

Marvel Cuff – Gold-plated silver

HM x Martine Rose

SS19

2020
A NEW ACT OF REBELLION

Pierced Stone Ring – 18ct gold, malachite

2021
MAD LOVE

The Beat (Pear) Ring – 18ct gold, diamond

I'M WITH THE BAND

Inverted Knife Edge Ring – 18ct gold

HM x Baxter Dury

Album Cover Chains

2022
HANNAH MARTIN PIERCED

Studded Teardrop Barbell XL – 18ct gold, champagne diamonds

HM x The Brits

Brit Award Trophy

2023
A VANITAS

HM with Applied Art Forms
Razor Ring – 18ct gold

2024
THE PERFECT DRUG (DROP 01)

All Access Bracelet – 18ct gold

2025
A VANITAS STONED — SOTHEBY'S

HM with Applied Art Forms
Razor Wristband – 18ct gold, sapphires

THE PERFECT DRUG (DROP 02)

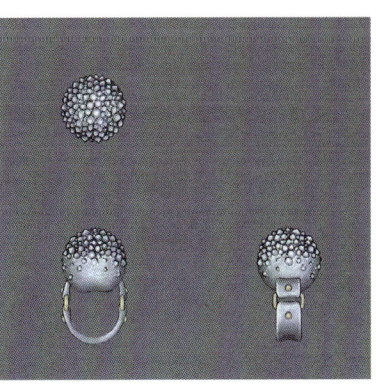

Studded Strapped Orb Ring, gouache – 18ct gold and steel diamonds

hannah martin collections < 237

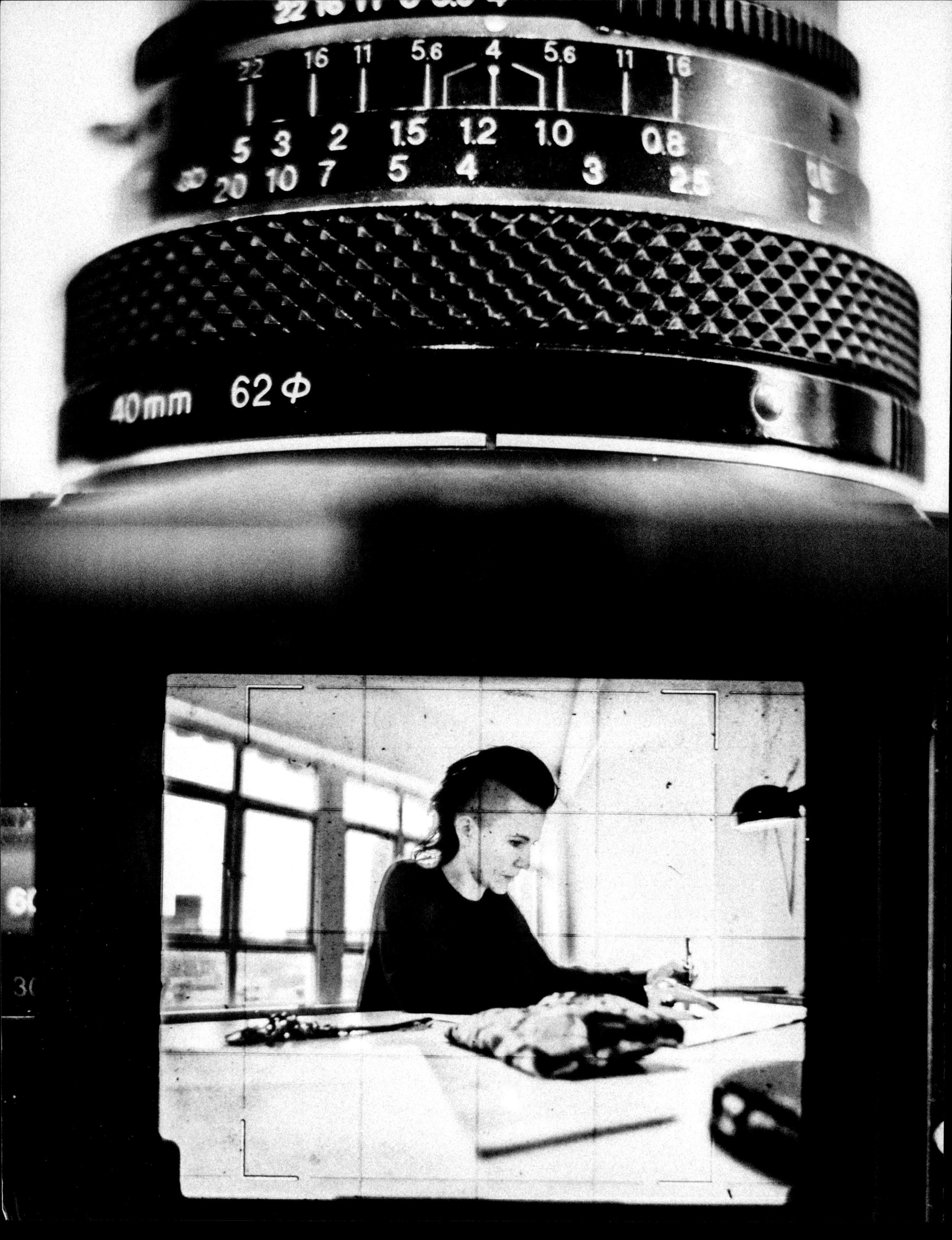
22 16 11 5.6 4 5.6 11 16
5 3 2 1.5 1.2 1.0 0.8
20 10 7 5 4 3 2.5
40mm 62Φ

acknowledgements

Deepest thanks to Hannah Martin for her openness and candour, two of
the most elusive and precious qualities one can hope to find in a subject,
as well as for letting me observe the process behind the scenes in her studio.
Thanks, too, to all those who graciously agreed to speak about Hannah and
her unique worldview and did so with such authentic warmth and respect.
Thanks also to Louise Brody, for her skill and expertise in designing this book.
And, finally, words fail to express my gratitude to Hélène Le Blanc, the
mastermind behind this anniversary project, who not only spotted Hannah's
genius early on but also saw fit to include me in this wonderful adventure.

photo credits

All jewellery photography is the exclusive copyright of Hannah Martin London

Stewart Baxter: 6-7, 12, 17, 18, 21, 26, 29, 34, 36, 41, 44, 47, 49, 52, 58, 62-63, 64, 67, 68, 69, 70, 71, 72, 74, 81, 82, 84, 85, 86, 91, 92, 93, 94, 95, 98, 103, 105, 106-107, 108, 109, 110, 111, 112, 118, 127, 128, 129, 136, 143, 147, 148, 149, 150, 151, 152-153, 154, 155, 156-157, 158, 162, 163, 164, 165, 166, 167, 168, 169, 170-171, 172, 178, 182-183, 184, 185, 187, 188, 189, 190, 191, 195, 206, 207, 210, 211, 213, 214-215, 216-217, 224, 225, 227 (top left, bottom right), 238

Jehnny Beth: 77 (right), 231

Tony Bevilacqua: 76 (right)

Anthony Byrne: 77 (centre), 78, 79, 104, 176 (centre, right), 200-201, 202, 203

Johnny De Domenico: 30, 229 (centre)

Dermot Fowler: 59

Johnny Hostile: 24 (top right)

HM ARCHIVE: 22-23, 24 (top centre, all centre, bottom centre & right), 38, 40, 48, 56, 76 (left, centre), 77 (left), 130, 139, 208-209, 220, 227 (top right, centre, bottom left)

Maxfield: 230, 232-233

Joss McKinley: 39, 61

Andrew Morales: 228, 229 (left, right),

Viktorija Pashuta: 8, 24 (bottom left)

Nicolas Franck Pauly: 2, 50-51, 113, 114, 115, 116-117, 140-141, 222, 226

Mark Read: 176 (left)

Guy Stephens: 97, 99, 100, 101, 120, 125, 126, 142, 144, 145, 146, 159, 160, 161, 174, 197, 205

Jane Stockdale: 4-5, 219

Boris Thuery: 24 (top left)

© 2025 Hannah Martin
World copyright reserved

ISBN 978 1 78884 328 7

The right of Tina Isaac-Goizé to be identified as author of this work has been asserted by her in accordance with the Copyright, Designs and Patents Act 1988

All rights reserved. No part of this publication may be reproduced, stored in a retrieval system, or transmitted in any form or by any means electronic, mechanical, photocopying, recording or otherwise, without the prior permission of the publisher

A CIP catalogue record for this book is available from the British Library

The author and publisher gratefully acknowledge the permission granted to reproduce the copyright material in this book. Every effort has been made to trace copyright holders and to obtain their permission for the use of copyright material. The publisher apologises for any errors or omissions in the text and would be grateful if notified of any corrections that should be incorporated in future reprints or editions of this book.

Project Direction: Hélène Le Blanc
Design: Louise Brody
Editorial Project Management: Andrew Whittaker
Proofread: Hannah Young
Reprographics: Corban Wilkin

Cover photography: Joss McKinley
Sales sheet photography, clockwise from top left: Stewart Baxter, HML, Guy Stephens, HML

EU GPSR Authorised Representative:
Easy Access System Europe Oü, 16879218
Address: Mustamäe tee 50, 10621 Tallinn, Estonia
Email: gpsr@easproject.com Tel: +358 40 500 3575

Printed in China by C&C Offset Printing Co. Ltd.
for ACC Art Books Ltd., Woodbridge, Suffolk, UK

www.accartbooks.com

ACC ART BOOKS